P9-BZH-830

References for the Rest of Us

COMPUTER BOOK SERIES FROM IDG

Are you intimidated and confused by computers? Do you find that traditional manuals are overloaded with technical details you'll never use? Do your friends and family always call you to fix simple problems on their PCs? Then the ... *For Dummies™* computer book series from IDG is for you.

... *For Dummies* books are written for those frustrated computer users who know they aren't really dumb but find that PC hardware, software, and indeed the unique vocabulary of computing make them feel helpless. ... *For Dummies* books use a lighthearted approach, a down-to-earth style, and even cartoons and humorous icons to diffuse computer novices' fears and build their confidence. Lighthearted but not lightweight, these books are a perfect survival guide to anyone forced to use a computer.

Already, hundreds of thousands of satisfied readers agree. They have made ... *For Dummies* books the #1 introductory level computer book series and have written asking for more. So if you're looking for the most fun and easy way to learn about computers, look to ... *For Dummies* books to give you a helping hand.

IDG BOOKS

LOTUS
NOTES
FOR
DUMMIES™

LOTUS NOTES FOR DUMMIES™

by Stephen Londergan and Pat Freeland

IDG BOOKS

IDG Books Worldwide, Inc.
An International Data Group Company

Foster City, CA ♦ Chicago, IL ♦ Indianapolis, IN ♦ Braintree, MA ♦ Dallas, TX

Lotus Notes For Dummies™

Published by
IDG Books Worldwide, Inc.
An International Data Group Company
919 E. Hillsdale Blvd.
Suite 400
Foster City, CA 94404

Library of Congress Catalog Card No.: 93-080872

ISBN: 1-56884-212-0

Printed in the United States of America

10 9 8 7 6 5 4 3 2

1D/QU/QR/ZV

Distributed in the United States by IDG Books Worldwide, Inc.

Distributed by Macmillan Canada for Canada; by Computer and Technical Books for the Caribbean Basin; by Contemporanea de Ediciones for Venezuela; by Distribuidora Cuspide for Argentina; by CITEC for Brazil; by Ediciones ZETA S.C.R. Ltda. for Peru; by Editorial Limusa SA for Mexico; by Transworld Publishers Limited in the United Kingdom and Europe; by Al-Maiman Publishers & Distributors for Saudi Arabia; by Simron Pty. Ltd. for South Africa; by IDG Communications (HK) Ltd. for Hong Kong; by Toppan Company Ltd. for Japan; by Addison Wesley Publishing Company for Korea; by Longman Singapore Publishers Ltd. for Singapore, Malaysia, Thailand and Indonesia; by Unalis Corporation for Taiwan; by WS Computer Publishing Company, Inc. for the Philippines; by WoodsLane Pty. Ltd. for Australia; by WoodsLane Enterprises Ltd. for New Zealand.

For general information on IDG Books in the U.S., including information on discounts and premiums, contact IDG Books at 800-434-3422 or 415-655-3000.

For information on where to purchase IDG Books outside the U.S., contact IDG Books International at 415-655-3021 or fax 415-655-3295.

For information on translations, contact Marc Jeffrey Mikulich, Director, Foreign & Subsidiary Rights, at IDG Books Worldwide, 415-655-3018 or fax 415-655-3295.

For sales inquiries and special prices for bulk quantities, write to the address above or call IDG Books Worldwide at 415-655-3000.

For information on using IDG Books in the classroom, or ordering examination copies, contact Jim Kelly at 800-434-2086.

is a registered trademark of IDG Books Worldwide, Inc.

About the Authors

Stephen Londergan

Stephen Londergan has been explaining how computers work for over ten years — and the funny part is that sometimes people listen. Once when he was a student in the sixth grade, his teacher (a.k.a. co-author Pat Freeland) saved him from the clutches of death when an errant garter snake ran amok during a science experiment. Steve works with Pat for Lotus Development, where he helps people figure out how to use Notes.

Steve lives in lovely Dorchester, Massachusetts with his wife Robyn and his two sons, who are named Michael and Richard. The Londergan family does *not* own any animals, and they do not plan to own any in the future.

Pat Freeland

Pat Freeland has taught public school, owned his own home repair business, taught the use of computer software, and done QA at Lotus Development Corporation. Currently he is the editor of the technote database for Lotus Notes. His greatest claim to fame, however, is having been a teacher in the same school where cute little Stephen Londergan was a student. Pat taught Steve everything he knew. During the other 179 days of the school year, each pursued other interests that eventually led to the writing of *Lotus Notes For Dummies*.

Pat lives in Hingham, Massachusetts with his wife Vicki, his children Michael and Catherine, two dogs, a cat, a gerbil, and a hermit crab.

ABOUT IDG BOOKS WORLDWIDE

Welcome to the world of IDG Books Worldwide.

IDG Books Worldwide, Inc. is a subsidiary of International Data Group, the world's largest publisher of computer-related information and the leading global provider of information services on information technology. IDG was founded more than 25 years ago and now employs more than 7,000 people worldwide. IDG publishes more than 220 computer publications in 65 countries (see listing below). More than fifty million people read one or more IDG publications each month.

Launched in 1990, IDG Books Worldwide is today the #1 publisher of best-selling computer books in the United States. We are proud to have received 3 awards from the Computer Press Association in recognition of editorial excellence, and our best-selling ...For Dummies™ series has more than 12 million copies in print with translations in 25 languages. IDG Books, through a recent joint venture with IDG's Hi-Tech Beijing, became the first U.S. publisher to publish a computer book in the People's Republic of China. In record time, IDG Books has become the first choice for millions of readers around the world who want to learn how to better manage their businesses.

Our mission is simple: Every IDG book is designed to bring extra value and skill-building instructions to the reader. Our books are written by experts who understand and care about our readers. The knowledge base of our editorial staff comes from years of experience in publishing, education, and journalism — experience which we use to produce books for the '90s. In short, we care about books, so we attract the best people. We devote special attention to details such as audience, interior design, use of icons, and illustrations. And because we use an efficient process of authoring, editing, and desktop publishing our books electronically, we can spend more time ensuring superior content and spend less time on the technicalities of making books.

You can count on our commitment to deliver high-quality books at competitive prices on topics consumers want to read about. At IDG, we value quality, and we have been delivering quality for more than 25 years. You'll find no better book on a subject than an IDG book.

John Kilcullen
President and CEO
IDG Books Worldwide, Inc.

Dedications

Stephen Londergan

My work here is dedicated to my parents, Elaine and Richard; my brother Andrew; my lovely wife, Robyn; my sons, Michael and Richard; Paula Dowd, and anyone else who would be offended if I left them out.

Pat Freeland

To Michael, Catherine, and Vicki — I love you. Thanks for your support, understanding, and love.

Acknowledgments

We'd like to both acknowledge and thank:

IDG's own Janna Custer, our Acquisitions Editor, for her foresight;
the great Raphael Savir, our Technical Editor, for his insight;
the alliterative Angie Allen, our Copy Editor, for her hindsight;
and the one-and-only Kristin Cocks, our Project Editor, for her oversight.

(The publisher would like to give special thanks to Patrick J. McGovern, without whom this book would not have been possible.)

Credits

**Executive Vice President,
Strategic Product Planning
and Research**
David Solomon

Editorial Director
Diane Graves Steele

Acquisitions Editor
Megg Bonar

Brand Manager
Judith A. Taylor

Editorial Managers
Tracy L. Barr
Sandra Blackthorn

Editorial Assistants
Tamara S. Castleman
Suki Gear
Stacey Holden Prince
Beth Reynolds
Laura Schaible
Kevin Spencer

Acquisitions Assistant
Suki Gear

Production Director
Beth Jenkins

Project Coordinator
Cindy L. Phipps

Pre-Press Coordinators
Tony Augsburger
Steve Peake

Project Editor
Kristin A. Cocks

Editor
Angela Allen

Technical Reviewer
Raphael Savir

Production Staff
Paul Belcastro
Chris Collins
Sherry Dickinson Gomoll
Barry C. Jorden
Carla Radzikinas
Dwight Ramsey
Patricia R. Reynolds
Kathie Schnorr
Gina Scott

Proofreader
Jennifer Kaufeld

Indexer
Nancy Anderman Guenther

Book Design
University Graphics

Cover Design
Kavish + Kavish

Contents at a Glance

Foreword .... *xxiv*

Introduction 1

Part I: The Basics **7**

Chapter 1: What Is Groupware, Anyway? 9

Chapter 2: How You Begin to Use Notes 19

Part II: Using Electronic Mail (No Stamps Required) **35**

Chapter 3: The E-Mail's Here! 37

Chapter 4: Sending a Message 45

Chapter 5: After the Reading — Managing Your Messages 63

Chapter 6: Power Memos 73

Part III: Entering the Brave New World of Notes Databases **87**

Chapter 7: Database Basics 89

Chapter 8: Once You're in the Database 101

Chapter 9: Using Documents 111

Chapter 10: This Old Database 131

Part IV: Fine-Tuning the Way Notes Works **149**

Chapter 11: Adding a Personal Touch 151

Chapter 12: Doctoring Your Documents 169

Chapter 13: Have It Your Way 191

Chapter 14: Notes on the Road 211

Chapter 15: Working Together: Notes and Computer Programs 239

Chapter 16: Full Text Search: Important Stuff that Got Shoved
to the End of the Book 253

Part V: The Part of Tens 267

Chapter 17: Ten SmartIcons You're Sure to Use a Lot 269

Chapter 18: Ten Cool Tricks You Can Use to Impress Your Friends 273

Chapter 19: Ten Time Savers 281

Chapter 20: Ten Things You Should Never Do 291

Chapter 21: Ten Neat Things You Can Buy for Notes 295

Chapter 22: The Ten Most Common Problems 299

Part VI: Appendixes 303

Appendix A: Installing Notes as a Workstation 305

Appendix B: The Lotus Notes SmartIcons 311

Appendix C: Menus, Hot Keys, and Function Keys 319

Appendix D: The Lotus Notes Database Templates 327

Appendix E: Remote Setup 331

Appendix F: Macintosh Tips 337

Appendix G: Glossary 341

Index 349
Reader Response Card .... Back of Book

Cartoons at a Glance

By Rich Tennant

Page 87

Page 7

Page 298

Page 35

Page 148

Page 267

Page 44

Page 149

Page 210

Page 303

Table of Contents

Foreword .... *xxiv*

Introduction *1*

About This Book 2
Foolish Assumptions 2
How to Use This Book 2
How this Book is Organized 3
    Part I: The Basics 3
    Part II: Using Electronic Mail (No Stamps Required) 3
    Part III: Entering the Brave New World of Notes Databases 4
    Part IV: Fine-Tuning the Way Notes Works 4
    Part V: The Part of Tens 4
    Part VI: The Appendixes 4
What You Don't Need to Read 5
Icons Used in This Book 5
And Finally, a Few Verses about Versions 5
So Off You Go 6

Part I: The Basics *7*

Chapter 1: What Is Groupware, Anyway? 9

OK, What the Heck Is Groupware? 10
My Mail, Your Mail, E-Mail 10
Databasically 12
    What Notes isn't 13
    What Notes is 14
Compound Documents — Feel the Power 15
Service with a Smile: Notes Servers 16
Down by the Workstation 16
Your User ID: The Key to Notes 17
Replication: An Explanation 18

Chapter 2: How You Begin to Use Notes 19

Before You Start Notes for the First Time: Stuff You Need to Ask Someone
    About 19
Starting the Program 21
Setting Up Notes 22
When It's Time to Say Good-Bye... 26
I Must Multi-Task! 26
Understanding the Desktop 27
    The menus 27
    The SmartIcons 29
    Dealing with the desktop and database icons 31
    The Status Bar 33

Part II: Using Electronic Mail (No Stamps Required) 35

Chapter 3: The E-Mail's Here! 37
May I Have the Envelope, Please 37
The Views from Here — Viewing the List of Incoming E-Mail 39

Chapter 4: Sending A Message 45
Good Manners — Memo-wise 45
I'm Gonna Sit Right Down and Write — Composing a Memo 46
   Make me a memo 48
   Get me the manager 54
   It's for you 55
   How shall I answer thee? 56
   Hey y'all — Reply to all 56
   Forward, memo! 56
The Little Black Book — Company-Wide 57
Save Me, Send Me 60

Chapter 5: After the Reading — Managing Your Messages 63
The Scrap Heap of History 63
A Place for Everything — Using Categories 67
Oh Where, Oh Where? 69
All the News That's Fit to Print 71

Chapter 6: Power Memos 73
Enclosed Please Find 73
   I'm gonna paste you 73
   Attaching attachments 74
   I got an attachment — now what? 76
   Importing files 78
Can You Keep a Secret? 80
Sign Here 81
Mail Is More Than Just Memos 82
Reading Your E-Mail on a Friend's Computer 82
   May I see some identification, please? 82
   Now the icon, please 84
Making a List, Checking It Twice 85
   Join the group! 85
   Ooh, my aching wrists! 86

Part III: Entering the Brave New World of Notes Databases .. 87

Chapter 7: Database Basics 89
Words You'd Better Know by Now 89
Opening a Notes Database — Nothing Could Be Simpler 90

I Haven't Got the Icon: Finding a New Notes Database 90
    Servers, servers, everywhere 92
    Digging into directories 92
    I hear you knocking — certification problems 94
    To open or to add, that is the question 94
What Am I Going to See When I Open the Database? 95
    Welcome to my database 96
    Out of sight, out of mind: How do I find the Policy Document later? ... 97
When You Need Help 97
    Using the Notes help system 97
    Using a database's help 98
    Notes documentation 99
    Using this book 100
    Your friends 100
    Last, but not least, using the documentation databases 100

Chapter 8: Once You're in the Database **101**
I Was Just Thinking of View 101
What's in a View, Anyway? 102
Changing Views 104
Categories 104
Expanding and Collapsing Categories 105
So What Can You Do with the Documents in a View? 106
    Selecting documents 106
    Reading documents 108
    Printing from a view 108
    Deleting documents 109

Chapter 9: Using Documents **111**
The Makings of a Document 111
    Static text 112
    Fields 112
    All the myriad fields 113
    Buttons 117
    Popups 119
    Doclinks 119
    Objects 120
    Icons 121
Come on in and Join the Party! 122
    Using the Compose menu 123
    Moving around in your new document 124
    Saving your new document 124
    Abandoning your new document 125
    Play by the rules 125

A Document Catches Your Eye 126
      Print it 126
      Edit it, maybe 127
      Delete it, maybe 127
      Hey Bob, did you see this?! 128
   And When Things Get Sensitive 128
      Using encryption to make fields private 128
      Hiding a document altogether 130

Chapter 10: This Old Database **131**
   Why Reinvent the Wheel? 131
   Creating the New File 132
   Customizing Your New Database 133
   Peeking Under the Hood: Changing the Forms and Fields 133
      Adding some static text to the form 135
      Changing a field's color 135
      Adding options to a Keyword field 136
      Changing the form color 138
      Adding a new field 138
      Saving the new and improved form 140
   Views You Can Use 140
      Creating a new view 141
      Changing a column's definition 142
      Changing a column's width 142
      I'll have a new column, please 143
      Checking your progress 144
      Giving the view a name 144
      Saving it 144
   The Icon 144
   Deciding Who Can Do What in Your Database 145
   Put It on the Server 147

Part IV: Fine-Tuning the Way Notes Works **149**

Chapter 11: Adding a Personal Touch **151**
   Changing Characters 151
      You're it! 152
      Now that I have your attention 153
      Putting it all together 157
      Can it be bold if it doesn't exist? 159
   Paragraphs with Character 160
      All margins great and small 162
      One paragraph, indivisible 162
      Keeping tabs on your paragraph 164
      The incredible disappearing paragraph 164
      Get in align 165
      Give me some space 166
      Puttin' on the style 167

Chapter 12: Doctoring Your Documents **169**
  Break It Up!.. 170
  Let's Put Our Cards in a Table 170
      Put 'er there, pardner 170
      The tables they are a changin' 173
      Open table, insert row 176
      No more row four 177
  Trying to Get a Header 178
      One doc — one header 178
      A header for all docs 180
  Set 'Em Up, Boys 182
  Search and Rescue 183
  If You're a Bad Spellar 184
  Whistles and Bells 186
      Doclinks 186
      Hey, get your popups 187

Chapter 13: Have It Your Way **191**
  Mail That Says, "ME" 192
      A form with fashion 192
      A form is born 195
      A custom view, designed by you 196
      Icons customized while u wait 200
  Certify Me, Quick 201
  Honey, Where Are My Encryption Keys? 202
  Hammering on Notes with Some Tools 205
      Some ID ideas 205
      Tools that set up the user 208

Chapter 14: Notes on the Road **211**
  Replicating Is Where It's At 211
  Getting Your Computer Ready to Go 212
      Taking a computer on a trip 213
      Telling Notes about your modem 213
      Setting up your Personal N&A Book 217
      Making a copy of the database to bring with you 219
  Using Your Computer Away from the Office 224
      Location setup 225
      Sending mail from afar 226
      Reading documents while on the road 227
      Reading your e-mail from afar 227
      Composing documents from afar 228
      OK! Enough talk! Let's call the server and replicate! 228
      Scheduling 232
  Saving on Phone Bills 234
      Selective replication 234
      Truncate and remove 236
  Dialing in to a Server "Live" 236
  Shooting Troubles 237

Chapter 15: Working Together: Notes and Computer Programs **239**

Scissors 'n Glue 239
Got a Paper Clip? 240
Importing a File into a Document 241
Converting a Document to Something Else Altogether 243
View-Level Imports 244
    What to do first 244
    What to do second 245
Converting a View into a Spreadsheet 247
DDE 248
OLÉ 251

**Chapter 16: Full Text Search: Important Stuff that Got Shoved to
the End of the Book** **253**

Just What Is Full Text Search, Anyway? 254
Performing a Search 254
    Not all databases are created equal 254
    Show me the Search Bar 255
    Using the Search Bar 255
    The results of a search 256
    Reading the resulting documents 257
    Make it easy for me: using the Query Builder 257
    How about a Query by Form? 259
    Searching more than one database at a time 260
Creating Your Own Index 262
    Maybe not 262
    Creating the index 263
    Add this to your daily chores: maintaining the index 264
No More Searches — Not Today, Not Tomorrow, Not Ever 266

Part V: The Part of Tens *268*

Chapter 17: Ten SmartIcons You're Sure to Use a Lot **269**

Print 269
Spell Check 269
Cut 270
Attachment 270
Copy 270
Paste 270
Navigate Next Unread 270
Categorize 271
Mail Address 271
Forward 271

Chapter 18: Ten Cool Tricks You Can Use to Impress Your Friends 273
  Double-Click the Right Mouse Button 273
  Press Tab to Check for New Documents 273
  Press F9 to Update Databases 274
  Hold Down Control while Changing Views 274
  Make a Document Private 274
  Change the Music That You Hear When You Get New E-Mail 275
  Automatically Reply to Incoming Messages while You're on Vacation 276
  Automatically Categorize Your Incoming E-Mail 278
  Press the Right Mouse Button to Preview What a SmartIcon Does 279
  Turn Off New E-Mail Notifications 279

Chapter 19: Ten Time Savers 281
  Using the Status Bar to Check for E-Mail 281
  Deliver de Letter — de Sooner, de Better 282
    Grappling with groups 282
    Managing mammoth monikers 284
  Replication for Those on the Run 285
  Eclectic Replication 286
  Those Who Ignore History 287
  Replicating and Chewing Gum at the Same Time 288
  Replicating and Sleeping at the Same Time 288

Chapter 20: Ten Things You Should Never Do 291
  Don't Change Your Notes Name 291
  Don't Delete Your E-Mail Database 292
  Don't Save or Send a Message without Spell-Checking It First 292
  Don't Remove Your Password 292
  Don't Forget to Press F5 When You Go to Lunch 293
  Don't Let Temp Files Pile Up 293
  Don't Forget to Consult the Manuals 294
  Don't Forget to Save Early and Often 294
  Don't Forget to Turn on Server-Based Mail When You Get Back
    to the Office 294
  Don't Talk to Strangers 294

Chapter 21: Ten Neat Things You Can Buy for Notes 295
  InFax 295
  OutFax 295
  Beeper Gateway 296
  CompuServe 296
  WorldCom 296
  A Mail Gateway 297

Carthage Today 297
Memory 297
PhoneNotes 297
More Copies of This Book 297

Chapter 22: The Ten Most Common Problems **299**

Your Laptop Won't Connect to Your Server 299
You Can't Edit a Field 300
You Can't Use a Doclink 300
Your Server Isn't Responding 300
You Don't Have the Right Certificate 300
You Can't Open a Database 301
You Can't Use Full Text Search 301
You Can't Delete a Document You Composed 301
You Can't Launch an Object 302
You Don't Know Who Your Administrator Is 302

Part VI: Appendixes *303*

Appendix A: Installing Notes as a Workstation **305**

So How Do I Do It? 305

Appendix B: The Lotus Notes SmartIcons **311**

Appendix C: Menus, Accelerator Keys, and Function Keys **319**

The Menu and Accelerator Keys 319
  File 319
  Edit 321
  View 322
  Mail 322
  Compose 322
  Text 323
  Tools 323
  Design 325
  Window 325

Appendix D: The Lotus Notes Database Templates **327**

Putting the Templates to Work 327
  Correspondence 328
  Customer Tracking and Response 328
  Discussion 328
  Document Library 329
  Mail 329

Meeting Tracking 329
News and Custom View 329
Reservation Scheduler and Setup 330
Service Request Tracking 330
Status Reports 330
Things To Do 330

Appendix E: Remote Setup **331**

Before You Start 331
Setting Up a Remote Workstation 332
Setting Up a Stand-Alone Workstation 334

Appendix F: Macintosh Tips **337**

No Right Mouse Button 337
Command Instead of Ctrl 337
Command Key Combinations 338
Dialog Boxes 338
No Background Program 338
No Local Full Text Indexes 338
Notes Data Folder 338
NOTES.INI 339
No Underlined Menu Options 339
Balloon Help 339

Appendix G: Glossary **341**

Index *349*
Reader Response Card .... *Back of Book*

Foreword

. . . .

*W*ho reads the Foreword anyway? When Steve and Pat asked me to write the Foreword for their book, I was flattered and a bit perplexed about what to write. My experience with Notes is both as a user and as the person in charge of all of those wizards who support Notes customers and answer their technical questions at Lotus every day.

Lotus Notes truly transforms the way people work together. That officially said, let me tell you how I really feel. With Lotus Notes, you can do things you could never do before, including things you never even thought of — like participate in a "live" discussion, work on a project with lots of people in different places in different time zones, make sense of piles of information, or even (more boring but infinitely useful) send and receive electronic mail to and from anyone, anytime, anywhere in the world.

Doing things you never thought of doing before is always a little bit intimidating, especially when you involve scary things like computers, networks, and databases (and those are the kinder, gentler words). *Lotus Notes For Dummies* demystifies Lotus Notes, helps you start doing exciting things quickly, and can transform you into an expert (assuming you'd like to be an expert, or at least sound like one).

Mary Kuppens
Lotus Customer Support Director
Lotus Development

Introduction

Your company has bought Lotus Notes. Suddenly you face the prospect of communicating with your fellow human beings using a computer keyboard instead of pieces of paper. The prospect is as frightening as having a root canal — terms like *database* and *e-mail* are as threatening as *anesthesia* and *scalpel*.

Who needs Notes anyway? For as long as you can remember, you have been sending memos on little pieces of paper to your fellow workers, calling people in distant offices and jotting notes as you chat, and then filing these shreds of papers in the things-to-do basket on your desk. Company policies, sales projections, meeting agendas, and lists of miscellaneous stuff are right where you need them, in ever-growing piles at your fingertips. Although they sometimes fall, get rearranged by the cleaning service, blow off your desk when the window is open, or disappear entirely, this is a wonderful and time-honored system that doesn't need to be changed.

Of course, there are times when things grind to a halt while you look for a report. Sending the same memo to 25 people requires a lot of time copying, addressing, and making sure that all copies get where they're going. Ensuring that the same up-to-date information is available to everyone who needs it can be a bit difficult when you have to collate 250 copies of the latest figures. Getting it all organized would be great.

Notes, huh? Maybe it's an idea whose time has come.

Notes is the product to use when you begin to realize that you and your fellow employees are not working as efficiently as you should. It helps you streamline communication, organize large bodies of information, get that information into the hands of those who need it, and keep it out of the hands of those who don't need it. And that's not all — Notes works in Windows, in OS/2, on the Macintosh, and on Unix platforms, too.

Yeah, but that means learning a whole bunch of new skills, and on a computer! Who has the time?

This book is the one to read if you want to learn the power of Notes and then put it to work quickly, but you have little or no working knowledge of Notes.

The book is for anyone planning to use Notes or Notes Express who feels a need to get acquainted with either product before diving into it. Just remember, you Notes Express users, that your e-mail forms are slightly different from those pictured in this book, and that you can only use certain databases. Also, if you're a Notes Express user, you can't create your own databases, so don't waste any of your valuable time reading Chapter 10!

About This Book

We know that you are busy and you hate to read manuals. So we designed this book to help you learn what you need to know as quickly and painlessly as possible. The parts of the book and the individual chapters provide information about the different types of tasks that Notes will help you accomplish.

You will learn, among many other things, the following:

- ✔ How to send a memo to individuals, to several people, and to members of a group without leaving your desk, using a copier, or stuffing mailboxes

- ✔ How to read your incoming mail and then print, delete, forward, or save it without nearing a filing cabinet or getting a paper cut

- ✔ How to use Notes databases to create and store data on any subject you choose without having to worry about whether the information is up to date and available to everyone

- ✔ How to protect sensitive information from being seen by the wrong people without investing in locks, vaults, or shredders

- ✔ How to create attractive documents that catch the reader's eye without reaching for markers, rulers, or the kids' crayons

- ✔ How to communicate with the home office when you're away without having to wait until business hours

Foolish Assumptions

We are making the following assumptions about you, the reader. First, we assume that you want to know the *what*, but not the *why*. This book will get you up and running as quickly as possible, with a minimum of delving into the reasons why a certain action is the one to perform. Second, we assume that you have a computer and an installed version of Notes on it. Check Appendix A if you need to know how to install Notes on your computer.

How to Use This Book

You have a choice. You can either read from start to finish or pick the individual topics that you want to learn about and read them in the order that you want to learn them. In general, the concepts are straightforward and we carefully avoid technobabble, so you won't have any trouble jumping around from chapter to chapter. If a term is unfamiliar to you as you read a chapter, check the glossary, index, or table of contents to clarify any confusion.

If you need to type something, it will be in this format: **TYPE THIS**. Then press Enter when you're done typing.

Sometimes we refer to text that you see on your screen. If we refer to the exact wording as it appears on the screen, it will be *monospaced* and will appear `like this` or like this:

```
This is how exact on-screen text or computer code will look.
```

Most of the time you will be making menu selections or clicking SmartIcons. There will be a picture of the SmartIcon you should use. Menu items are presented like this: Choose <u>F</u>ile⇨<u>D</u>atabase⇨<u>O</u>pen.

Click the menu item or press the underlined letter if you're not using a mouse. (Go ahead and live a little — get a mouse if you don't already have one.)

If a dialog box appears as you use a command, we show it to you and tell you what choices to make in it.

How this Book is Organized

The arrangement of chapters in this book generally mirrors the way most people learn Notes.

Part I: The Basics

Here we get the inevitable definitions out of the way and then tackle getting Notes running on your computer. It's sort of like learning where everything is on the dashboard and then starting your car.

Part II: Using Electronic Mail (No Stamps Required)

This part deals with the most frequent use of Notes: sending, receiving, and reading e-mail and memos.

Part III: Entering the Brave New World of Notes Databases

The chapters in this part show you how to gain access to existing Notes databases, how to read and create documents, how to create your own databases, and how to expand your already dazzling command of the program.

Part IV: Have It Your Way: Fine-Tuning the Way Notes Works

Eventually you'll need to create characters not found on the keyboard, like © (copyright symbol); to modify the style of individual paragraphs; to customize the way Notes works on your computer; to use Notes with other programs; or to use Notes when you're far away from home, lonely and alone.

Part V: The Part of Tens

A part of every ...*For Dummies* book, this is where we present an assortment of tidbits that are useful in many circumstances. We have stuff here like the ten SmartIcons you're most likely to use, ten tricks you'll find handy, ten ways to save your valuable time, ten things not even a dummy should ever try with Notes, ten things you can buy to make Notes more useful, ten small toes to wiggle in the sand, and ten of the most common problems users encounter when they use Notes.

Part VI: The Appendixes

Appendix A deals with the installation of a Notes workstation on your computer and Appendix B lists and explains the SmartIcons. Appendix C "explodes" the menus, touches on the hot keys, and explores the functions of the function keys. Check out Appendix D for information about the database templates that are supplied with Notes. If you frequently work away from your office, don't skip Appendix E; it unlocks the mysteries of remote setup — setting up your Notes workstation so you can use it even when you're not attached to the network at the office. Appendix F offers you some tips for using Notes on a Macintosh. We've also included a glossary — a handy dictionary of common Notes terms. Although we do not give the pronunciation and language history, we do give you a definition for Notes-related words that you may read or hear about that confuse you.

What You Don't Need to Read

We'd like to think that every word in this book is a pearl of wisdom, but we admit that there are times when many users would like to skip sections because they're sleepy, in a hurry, or simply don't need to know whatever it is that we are explaining. Usually this information is clearly marked with special tech icons so that you know you can skip it without leaving a gaping hole in your knowledge.

Icons Used in This Book

In this book, you'll see little pictures (we like to call them *icons*) that signify different types of information you find in this book. Read on to find out what kind of information each icon symbolizes.

This is information for those who are well, um . . . computer nerds — the types of people who make classes and meetings last longer because they always have a couple of questions at the end when everyone wants to leave.

Some little shard of knowledge is coming that will make using Notes just a little bit easier to use. The information marked by this icon is well worth reading.

As you stumble down the pathway of life, these little commandments are things that you should never forget. A good example is . . . well, it's something about . . . um, we'll get back to this.

The Surgeon General has determined that the following keystrokes can be injurious to your database. Ignore this icon at your own peril.

And Finally, a Few Verses about Versions

When Lotus Notes was first released to the public it was called (no surprise here) version 1.0. Then came version 2.0; a couple of years later came the most recent major release — version 3.0. Since then, some minor changes have been made to Notes, and each group of changes is called an *upgrade*. The most recent upgrade to Notes is version 3.2. The point is that there have been a few upgrades since Lotus began selling version 3.0, and you may find that you're using a version of Notes that looks slightly different from what you see depicted throughout this book.

The good news is that the differences between each version are so minor that you don't have to worry about them. In fact, because the changes between version 3.1 and 3.2 are all related to how the server functions, and because you'll be using a workstation (not a server), you needn't worry about the changes; just rest assured that something at the other end of the network is working better than ever. You may notice as you read this tome that some of the pictures look a little different than what you have. For example, when we took a screenshot of a mail message for one of the figures in the book, we were using version 3.1. Maybe your company uses 3.2, so on your mail memo the buttons are at the top of the screen, and the picture you see in our pictures has the buttons at the bottom of the screen. No big deal, we promise. Same buttons, same functions, just in a different place.

So Off You Go

This book is a good foundation in Notes. You only need to experiment to increase your command of Notes. On this foundation alone you can build a towering structure of knowledge — designing customized forms, creating new databases, straining metaphors, and impressing those lucky enough to work with a genius like you. Don't be afraid to try new things, and check the Help feature when questions arise.

Part I
The Basics

The 5th Wave — By Rich Tennant

"IT'S A SOFTWARE PROGRAM THAT MORE FULLY RE-FLECTS AN ACTUAL OFFICE ENVIRONMENT. IT MULTI-TASKS WITH OTHER USERS, INTEGRATES SHARED DATA, AND THEN USES THAT INFORMATION TO NETWORK VICIOUS RUMORS THROUGH AN INTER-OFFICE LINK-UP."

In this part...

You can't follow the game if you don't know the players, and you can't go driving if you can't start the car. The players in this case are the terms used with programs like Notes, and you'll be driving Notes, so learning how to start it is pretty important.

As much as we try to avoid it, we have to use some jargon, so we soften the shock by giving you in Chapter 1, free of charge and without any obligation whatsoever, a few definitions. Anyway, it never hurts when you're standing around the coffee pot to let fly with a couple of high-tech terms so that everyone thinks you're a sophisticated computer user. Watch the eyebrows raise when you say "Yep, sure is easy replicating my mail database to my remote workstation, especially with my new 14.4 baud modem."

The second chapter gives you the information that you need to start Notes. It's more than just clicking an icon, and you never will be able to "replicate your mail database" if you can't get Notes running.

Chapter 1

So What Is Groupware, Anyway?

• •

In This Chapter

▶ Grasping groupware

▶ Deciphering databases

▶ Exploring e-mail

▶ Conquering compound documents

▶ Surveying servers

▶ Working at workstations

▶ Understanding the User ID

▶ Regarding replication

▶ Mastering miscellaneous terms you ought to know

• •

*L*otus Notes is a program designed to make working with other people easy. This doesn't mean to imply that you find working with others difficult; it's just that suddenly you'll find it a lot easier than it used to be. If you're a hermit and never plan to share information with others, save your money. Use a database, word-processing, or spreadsheet program. If, however, you need to get information to lots of people, even over long distances, then the most popular groupware program, Lotus Notes, is for you.

What is especially nice about using Notes is that you don't need to know a thing about *how* the information gets from your computer to other people's computers. Leave the worry about the network to someone else and concentrate on firing off memos and creating documents, serene in the knowledge that a few keystrokes are all it takes to keep in touch with everyone and anyone you want.

OK, What the Heck Is Groupware?

Groupware is software that allows you to be part of a group. That was easy, wasn't it? It won't make you a better golfer or help you win friends and influence people (use Dale Carnegie for that), but it can help you do the following:

- ✔ Send messages to individuals and groups
- ✔ Create databases and put information into them that you, everyone, or only people you choose can have access to
- ✔ Be sure that the same information on any particular subject is available to everyone who is supposed to see it, regardless of where they are
- ✔ Allow everyone in the organization to communicate with each other as quickly as possible, whether the communication is gossip, news, or vital corporate data; it's up to the individual to tell the difference
- ✔ Be sure that forms and documents used in your organization are standard so that you all seem organized, even if you're not
- ✔ Keep information in a safe and readily available place, rather than in piles on everyone's desk
- ✔ Prevent prying, nosy, unauthorized busybodies from rummaging around in places where they have no business looking
- ✔ Collect information from widely scattered sources
- ✔ Eliminate the need to buy reams of paper, thus threatening our forests; instead, electronically store mountains of documents in a space smaller than a bread box
- ✔ Combine data, graphics, text, and tables from many different software packages
- ✔ Share information easily among people who are using Macintosh, Windows, OS/2, and Unix without expensive conversion utilities
- ✔ Hold information and e-mail for the user who is only occasionally connected

My Mail, Your Mail, E-Mail

E is for Electronic. Take off the *E* and you have mail, and that's what e-mail is all about. E-mail is messages that you send using electricity rather than paper, which makes e-mail faster — so much faster that we "tech types" refer to paper messages as "snailmail." It's also cheaper; instead of buying a stamp for every message you want to send, all you have to do is put someone's name at the top of a memo and click the Send button. Put several names at the top of the memo and the memo goes to everyone. Of course, there is the little matter of someone buying a computer for everyone, connecting them all together, and then buying Notes, but that's beside the point.

E-mail is also faster because you don't have to wait for the postal service to move a piece of mail from place to place. In many cases, the delivery of a message can be almost instantaneous — making the message's travel time a few seconds, rather than a few days.

In Notes, the e-mail you send goes to everyone you address it to and *only* to those people. If you write a nasty note about the boss and send it to a friend two floors down, you don't have to worry that the boss will see it (unless the friend forwards it to the boss or prints it and puts it on the bulletin board).

In Notes e-mail, you can add text enhancements like boldface, italics, or underlining; you can change colors and fonts; you can add tables, doclinks, and graphics. Instead of sending messages that make people yawn, you can make people sit up and take notice.

Barring the rare system breakdown, you can be confident that the message will be delivered. Contrast this assurance with a memo slipped into a company mailer and left to languish in the slow quagmire of interoffice mail. Figure 1-1 shows a memo addressed to Steve Londergan, with a courtesy copy (cc) to a group called the Planning Department. Everyone in the Planning Department will receive the memo in time for them to be able to act on the schedule changes.

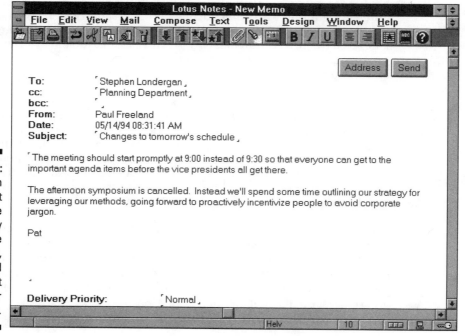

Figure 1-1:
You can
send short
memos like
this to many
people
quickly,
easily, and
without
leaving your
desk.

If you place paper copies of memos in mailboxes, you can't be certain that the recipients will get them. Of course, to receive the electronic memo, recipients have to turn their computers on and start Notes, but that's more likely to happen than everyone checking their little mail cubby frequently. If Notes is already running, a friendly beep instantly notifies recipients when they receive e-mail.

Notes memos can be as long and complex as you need, from a quick "Meet me for coffee at 10:00" to long involved letters that include information from other programs.

Databasically

The most important concept in Notes is the *database*. In fact, the entire program is organized around databases. A *database* is a bunch of information organized so that you can retrieve selected data. A phone book is a database — it's organized in alphabetic order, with the name, address, and phone number for each individual entry all kept together. The only way to select data in a phone book is to turn the pages and let your fingers do the walking, but electronic databases are much more useful.

When you use Notes, you create *documents:* memos, company policy statements, sales records, or listings of baseball statistics. These documents are stored in databases with other documents of the same type. You can select information from that database without ever turning pages or scanning long lists. Ask it to show you all sales contacts in Alabama, for instance, and as quick as the electrons can arrange themselves, the list of Alabama sales contacts appears on-screen.

A good example of a Notes database is a discussion database, which is the electronic equivalent of the backyard fence. You can express your opinion on a particular subject by composing a main document. Then someone in the Singapore office may compose a reply to your statement telling you that you're all wet. Someone in Stockholm can compose a response to that response, telling the Singapore person to lay off you. And so on. Others may sound off about their own opinions by writing entries to the discussion database. People anywhere and everywhere in your organization can respond to these opinions.

You may write your opinion using Notes working in Windows, while the response is created on a Macintosh, and others may be using Unix or OS/2. All the documents are readable by everyone regardless of what kind of computer the documents were composed on. All of you can share not only your highly-sought-after opinions, but also drawings, enhanced text, and data from other programs in which you are writing.

In Notes, databases contain *views*. Views contain *documents*. Documents contain *fields*, and fields contain individual pieces of data. See, the whole concept is based on data, and that's why it's called a database. We explain all these terms more fully in future chapters; we just want to give you the big picture now. You can also refer to the glossary if you forget what a term means.

What Notes isn't

For all its power and glory, there are some things that Notes isn't. It is a database program for sure, but it isn't a true *relational database*.

Unless you're the designer of a database, you probably don't give two toots about whether a database is relational or not. *Relational databases* allow you to enter data in a field in one database and then use that data in another database. The bad news, in case you're curious, is that fields in other databases or forms can't use rich text fields. Other fields (those which aren't rich text fields) can be used relationally, so there are some relational qualities about Notes.

That fact means some good news and some bad news. The good news is that Notes is not rigid. Unlike other databases, Notes doesn't require you to set the size of a field and then limit entries in that field to your specified maximum size. You can enter any amount of data in a Notes database field without having to redesign your database. For example, in other programs, you would have to decide how many characters a Last Name field would accept. Suppose you allow 20 characters, and then you hire John-Jacob Jingleheimerschmidt. You would either have to be satisfied with "J J Jingleheimerschm," or you would have to go through the nail-breaking procedure of redesigning the database — and risk losing some data. With Notes, you just type away, secure in the knowledge that Notes will accept every character you type.

Because it isn't rigid, Notes allows you to create *rich text fields*. A rich text field is one in which you can add such fancy stuff as character formats (boldface and italics, for instance), linked or embedded objects, or video clips.

Not only is Notes not a relational database, it also isn't the program to use for *transaction-based systems*. An example of what that mouthful means is airline ticketing. Imagine lots of offices selling tickets for a particular flight and recording the data on their local copy of the reservations database. Later, at flight time, a huge crowd appears, everyone with tickets for the same flight. When you need *immediate* sharing of information everywhere, you should use terminals connected to a single gigantic computer somewhere. Notes allows periodic, but not immediate, sharing of updates to databases.

What Notes is

Notes is a truly useful and powerful program because of its ability to send e-mail *and* create databases of all sorts that every person in the organization can share, add to, and use. This pair of abilities makes Notes able to leap tall buildings in a single bound, more powerful than . . . well, more powerful than programs that allow you only to send e-mail or only to create databases.

Rich text fields and other Notes fields have an advantage over those in regular databases: they don't have a field size limit. In other database programs, changing the size of a field in a large database can be a heck of a lot of work and, if not done correctly, can corrupt your database. Whether you put one word or a whole book in a Notes field makes no difference to Notes.

Fields in other databases are dull fellows to be sure — no boldface, no variety in fonts, and no possibility for attachments or embedded objects. Not so with rich text fields, because they contain more than just information. Rich text fields can contain anything your heart desires to put there in order to set them apart from the mundane, to educate and excite the readers, and to allow you to express yourself as the creative genius that you are.

Using Notes, you can create databases for any of the following uses:

- ✔ *Reference:* Members of your organization seeking knowledge can find what they need to know, contributed by those who have knowledge to share — from each according to his or her ability, to each according to his or her need. Kind of brings a tear to your eye.

- ✔ *Workflow:* Those charged with a broad task can record the individual assignments and proclaim the completion of each, documenting progress toward a job well done.

- ✔ *E-mail:* Anyone in the organization can communicate privately or publicly with anyone they choose.

- ✔ *Fax:* One of the means by which valuable data stored in your organization's databases can be distributed to a needy and grateful public.

This, then, is Notes. More than just a program, more than just a database, more than just an e-mail facility — Notes is a dynamic tool allowing the sharing of knowledge throughout the organization. Because, when all is said and done, knowledge is power.

Compound Documents — Feel the Power

You've heard of compound fractures, right? Well, compound documents are nothing like them. Does that help? No? Well, they're not like the compound eye on an insect either. Getting clearer? Well, let's try this.

Normally, when you are busy using Notes, you are typing a memo or filling in a form or writing some text to be included with other similar entries in a database. Sometimes, however, you need to put more than just text in your document.

To emphasize a point you're making about sales figures, you may want to include a spreadsheet that you created in Lotus 1-2-3. A graph that you made in Freelance would help — and maybe a couple of paragraphs in Microsoft Word that the company president wrote in praise of the sales force. So, you copy and paste them all into your document.

The result? Guess. Take your time now. Right, it's a *compound document*, containing data, graphics, or other features from other programs. Figure 1-2 is a simple example of a compound document containing a small spreadsheet and a graph.

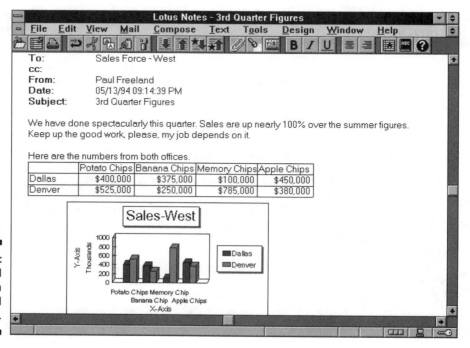

Figure 1-2: This e-mail memo is a compound document.

Service with a Smile: Notes Servers

Notes uses computers all hooked together in a *network*. In some ways, a network is like a department in a corporation, because it has individual workers and someone in charge. The individual computers need to be connected to a "boss" computer in order to be able to work together. No doubt your boss serves the same vital role in your department. It is a curious twist of fate that the computer in charge of a Notes network is called the *server*.

The server acts as a central shared computer for the others, storing the mail databases for all the people whose computers are hooked to it and regulating the flow of information. It may also store other databases created by users who want the information for others to share. It usually is a more powerful computer with more storage than the ones connected to it, and it is kept in a physically secure and remote location. Is this beginning to sound like your boss — powerful, having the best equipment, remote, and in charge? Maybe it's also like your boss in that it's not where the regular work in Notes is done. The actual work is done on the individual computers connected to the server.

In large organizations, many servers, each with their own cluster of attached computers, are connected together over the company-wide network.

Down by the Workstation

Your computer is a *workstation*. This is where the real work is done by the individual users. Workstations usually contain the Notes program files for each individual user, as well as any databases that the users create for their own personal use.

Not all workstations are always connected to a server. If you go on a business trip and take your laptop computer, you would need a long network cable to connect directly to the office, unless your business trip only takes you to the parking lot. When you use your computer to connect to the server by phone line and modem, your computer is called a *remote workstation*. Some workstations are both LAN and remote. If you have a laptop, you can hook it to the LAN when you are at the office and then use its modem for a remote hookup when you are on the road.

No matter how fast your modem is, you'll find that using it is much slower than using Notes on the LAN. So plan on taking extra time with the modem and be sure your teenager won't need the phone for a while.

Your User ID: The Key to Notes

Don't expect to get a copy of Notes, install it on your computer, and then be able to tap into the nerve center of your company. Even if you're the company president and have a fist full of Notes disks, even if you do lunch rather than eat it, even if you may have the fanciest car in the lot, until a Notes administrator *certifies* you, you don't even exist as far as Notes servers are concerned.

Once you get your Notes ID and tell Notes where to find it, then and only then have you arrived. You now have the key that gets you access to your own mail database and the other databases in the company. Figure 1-3 shows one author's User ID. To you it may only look like a series of numbers and letters, but to the servers it is what makes him a legitimate user of Notes in his organization.

Examine ID File
Type: Non-Hierarchical ID   [Done] [Issued By...]
ID File: D:\NOTES\PFREELAN.ID
ID Number: 3B60 DBBD CD05 0A04 DBD5 29DF 53F8 7C49
License: North American
Name: Paul Freeland
[Certificates...]   [Encryption Keys...]
[Copy Public Key]   [Create Safe Copy...]

Figure 1-3:
This is the Notes User ID for one of the authors.

Those last three words are very important, by the way. Your User ID makes you a member of *your* organization. You can't sneak into your competitors' offices down the street and use your User ID in their Notes network because the User ID is created by and recognized only by your own organization.

Keep a copy of your Notes User ID on a floppy disk so that you'll be able to copy it back to your hard disk if you accidentally delete your Notes program files, or if you experience the heartbreak of computer failure. It also enables you to use another person's computer as if it were your own.

Keep your Notes User ID in a secure place (under lock and key). If others get it, they can read your mail and they can send memos using your name. Next April Fool's Day, they may send an insulting memo to the president of the company under your name. Next April 2 you may be looking for a new job.

Replication: An Explanation

Replication is what makes Notes the great program that it is. Oh sure, other programs allow you to send e-mail, but they don't replicate. We'll explain replication a few paragraphs down the road. You've already heard that your mail database is only one kind of database that can exist in Notes. It is likely that other databases have been created throughout your organization. *Replicas*, copies of that database, may be on many servers in your organization around the world.

One example is a database listing all employees, including name, employee number, location, shoe size, and other important data. At each location, these replicas are updated as people are hired, fired, or change their shoe size. Obviously each replica of the database will contain different information. How does Notes arrange to have all the databases contain the same information? Your User ID? Pay attention — this section is about replication.

Replication is the process by which Notes guarantees that two or more copies of a database are the same. When the process is finished, all replicas have the same information. Up-to-date information is available everywhere.

Replication is also the process by which remote workstations update their own local databases, including your mail database. The frequency of replication is a decision that the owner of the remote workstation makes. In a database that has a rapid turnover of information, replicating several times a day might be necessary. Another database that doesn't change often, such as one listing corporate policies, it may be necessary to replicate only about once a month.

Platforms and WANs and LANs, oh my!

Here we briefly mention some confusing, technical computer terms. We don't want you nodding off when there's work to do and all those other chapters you've got to read.

Platforms and *operating systems* refer to the type of computer that you are using and the software that runs your computer and network. Notes can run on Macintosh, Windows, OS/2, and Suns with Unix.

LANs are local area networks. They are the computers connected together with network cable.

WANs are wide area networks. They are too big to allow the use of network cables, so connection of all the computers is usually done over phone lines, leased communication lines, or special link such as a satellite. A WAN connects your office in Boston with your office in New York City.

Protocols are the means by which data travels along the network cables among workstations and servers. Now that you've seen the term you can forget it. It's the concern of your administrator.

Gateways are the means by which information is transferred into and out of Notes, and into other environments such as fax or on-line data services like CompuServe.

That wasn't too bad, was it?

Chapter 2
How You Begin to Use Notes

In This Chapter
▶ Setting up Notes
▶ Starting and stopping the program
▶ Facing the Notes interface
▶ Getting smart about SmartIcons

*W*ow, your company finally got Lotus Notes, and you're thrilled at the idea that you'll be using this powerful, state-of-the-art program that you've heard so much about. Alternately, maybe you aren't so thrilled. Your boss told you that you had to start using Notes, and you're not exactly overjoyed at the prospect of installing and learning yet another software program. In either case, the good news is that learning how to set up, start, and stop the program isn't all that difficult.

This is the one and only chapter in this whole book where you have to be careful to follow the steps exactly as they're outlined. (Sometimes you just gotta play by the rules...).

Before You Start Notes for the First Time: Stuff You Need to Ask Someone About

You may be used to programs that let you just install them, start them, and get to work. Not Notes. When you start Notes for the very first time, you need to be prepared to answer a few questions, and the best way to get the answers is to ask someone. Your Notes administrator will be able to provide you with the information that you need for your first "date." Don't even bother trying to use the program until you've got the answers.

Get on the phone, call your administrator, and ask for the answers to the following questions. And don't worry if you don't understand the answers (or the questions)!

Table 2-1 Stuff to Ask Your Friendly Notes Administrator

The Question	*The Answer*
How will I be connecting to my Notes server?	Pick one:
( ) By the network	( ) By a modem
( ) Both ways	( ) Neither way
How will I get my User ID?	Pick one:
( ) From the Name and Address Book	( ) On a disk
User ID filename: ( )	
What is my password?	( )
What is my exact User Name?	( )
What is the name of my home server?	( )
What is my network type?	( )
Some time info:	
What is my time zone?	( )
Do we follow Daylight Savings Time?	( ) Yes ( ) No

Notes administrators are important people because they can make your life with Notes nothing but smooth sailing, or they can make your life with Notes an absolute nightmare. So, we advise being very nice to them. Be polite and be courteous to them on the phone — and don't rule out a small cash gift from time to time, just to keep them cheerful. You'll thank yourself for this fore-thought when you need them to dig you out of a problem.

When you start Notes for the first time, there's a little bit of work the program has to do — like find your mail database, set up your desktop, and so on. How Notes proceeds with this process depends on how you'll be connecting to your Notes server, and the steps are quite different if you're using Notes on a network, at home, in a hotel room, or in any other place that's not connected to a network. If you need to set up Notes for the first time "remotely," you need to check out Appendix A.

Starting the Program

First things first: you need to start the program. To do this, double-click the Notes program icon. Where is this mysterious Notes icon and what does it look like? Well, that all depends. *Where* it is depends on where you put it when you installed the program. (Refer to Appendix A for more information on how to install the program.) *What* it is depends on which version of Notes you're using. Look for something like the cute little pictures in Figure 2-1. (The exact appearance of your Notes Program icon depends both on your operating system and on which version of Notes you'll be using. But it will definitely, positively look like one of the icons pictured here. Really!)

Figure 2-1:
Your Notes
program
icon looks
like one of
these icons.

Lotus Notes

Lotus Notes

Now that you've finally found the icon, double-click it to start the program. Notes starts, and you see what's called the splash screen, as shown in Figure 2-2. (Don't worry if the splash screen you see is a little different than the one you see pictured here!)

WARNING!

Don't double-click unless you have answers to all the questions in Table 2-1.

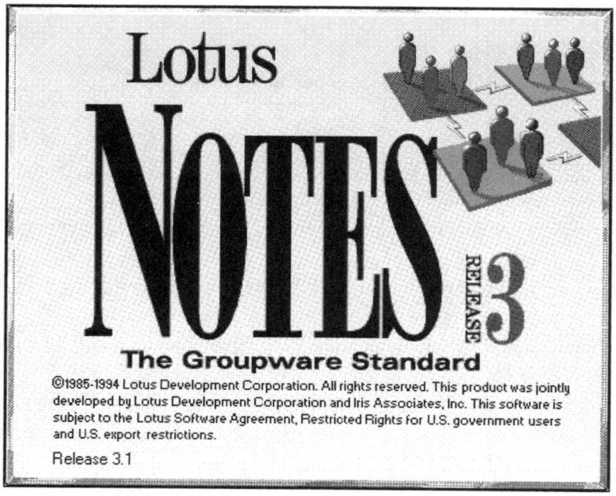

Figure 2-2:
This splash
screen is
what you
see when
you start
Notes.

Lotus

NOTES

RELEASE 3

The Groupware Standard

©1985-1994 Lotus Development Corporation. All rights reserved. This product was jointly developed by Lotus Development Corporation and Iris Associates, Inc. This software is subject to the Lotus Software Agreement, Restricted Rights for U.S. government users and U.S. export restrictions.

Release 3.1

ation...

Setting Up Notes

You will not be able to set up Notes without first consulting with your Notes administrator. Read the beginning of this chapter if you haven't done so yet.

Now that you've seen the splash screen, Notes is smart enough to figure out that it is your first time using the program. Here comes the tricky part: the setup questions. To answer them, make sure you have the worksheet in Table 2-1 handy.

The first time you start Notes, the program leads you through the dreaded Setup. Notes is going create your desktop, build a Personal Name and Address Book for you, and much, much more. The good news is that this laborious process only has to happen once the very first time you start Notes. Next time, Notes won't have to ask you all these questions. That's a promise!

The very first thing you see after the splash screen is a dialog box that looks like Figure 2-3. Here you tell Notes how you'll be connecting to your Notes server and where your User ID is coming from.

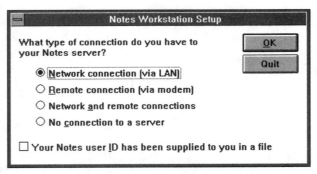

Figure 2-3: Use this dialog box to tell Notes how you connect to your Notes server and where your User ID is.

Your User ID is a file that was created for you by your administrator, and you need it to run the program — this time and every time. If you don't know what a User ID is (never mind where it's coming from!), refer to the Introduction.

Using the worksheet in Table 2-1, you will be able to figure out the answers.

What you see after you click OK in Figure 2-3 depends on whether you clicked the box that says Your User ID has been supplied to you in a file. If you didn't click that box, you'll see the dialog box shown in Figure 2-4. If you did click that box, you'll see dialog box that's shown in Figure 2-5. Of course, you knew what to do, because you kept that worksheet handy, right?

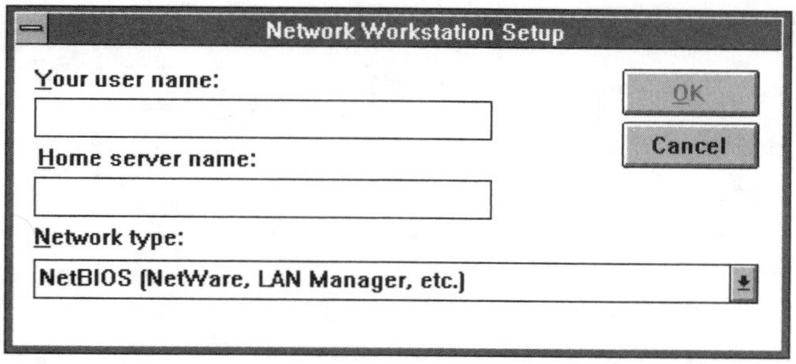

Figure 2-4:
Telling
Notes your
name, your
home
server's
name, and
your
network
type.

Figure 2-4:
Telling
Notes your
name, your
home
server's
name, and
your
network
type.

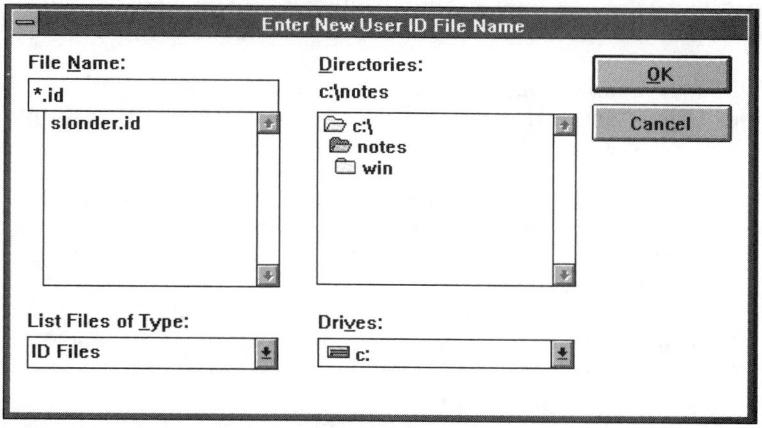

Figure 2-5:
This dialog
box lets you
tell Notes
the filename
and location
of your
User ID.

If your User ID was supplied to you in a file (in other words, your administrator gave you a disk), Notes will ask you if you want to Copy your User ID to your data directory. If you choose Yes, your User ID is copied to your hard disk, and Notes will look there every time you run the program. If you choose No, you'll have to insert the floppy disk that you got from your administrator each and every time you want to use the program. (More secure, but less convenient.) Most people choose Yes.

After you've told Notes where your User ID is and what your home server's name is, you have to prove to Notes that you are who you say you are by entering your password in the dialog box shown in Figure 2-6.

Figure 2-6:
Notes
displays a
bunch of *X*s
as you enter
your
password.

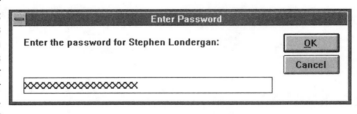

Get used to entering your password, because Notes will ask you for it every time you use the program, day in and day out. Later on you should change your password to something that your administrator won't know, but for now you can enter the one that your administrator assigned to you.

When you change your password, make it something easy to remember but not too obvious. Forgetting your password or using an easily guess-able password is a Bad Thing.

Don't be surprised to see a bunch of *X*s as you type your password; Notes displays them so that someone who might be looking over your shoulder can't figure out what your password is. (Consequently, we do not recommend making your password a bunch of *X*s.)

After you've entered your name, User ID, and home server name, Notes has a little work to do. Be patient; the work shouldn't take more than five minutes.

Don't be surprised if your administrator tells you that your User Name has a bunch of slashes in it. Notes names are things like "Robert Donnelly/Sales/NTS Associates," or maybe "John Noonan/IDG." His mother might call him Jack, but to Notes he's "John Noonan/IDG."

The last dialog box you'll have to deal with during Setup asks you about your time zone. Pick the appropriate time zone, tell Notes whether or not you observe DST, and click OK. Hey, congratulations — Notes Setup is complete! Remember, starting the program next time won't be so arduous — it was only painful because this was your first time. Your reward for completing this long, drawn-out, painful process is the dialog box you see in Figure 2-7.

After setup has completed, you'll notice (pay attention!) that Notes has automatically added three database icons to your desktop, as shown in Figure 2-8. These three icons represent your own personal mail database, your own

Personal Name and Address Book, and your company's Public Name and
Address Book. (We discuss how you actually use each of these databases later
in Chapters 4 and 5.)

In a few cases, your new Notes desktop will have more or fewer icons than the
standard three. As usual, it depends on how your administrator has set up
Notes at your company, so don't be alarmed if what you see on your computer
is a little different than what you see in Figure 2-8.

Figure 2-7:
Notes tells
you when
you're done
setting up.

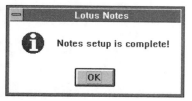

Figure 2-8:
When
you're
finished
setting up
Notes, you'll
have three
databases
on your
desktop.

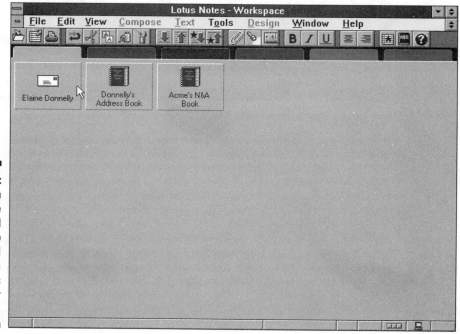

When It's Time to Say Good-Bye...

When you're finished using Notes (is it time to go home already?), exit the program the way you exit any other. The easiest way to tell Notes you're done is to choose File➪Exit. There may be other ways to end the program, but that depends on your operating system. For example, if you use Windows, you can use Program Manager to end the Notes task. There's a similar process in OS/2. So, if you're a techno-jock and you know some other fancy way to shut down Notes, we say go for it. But when you're done showing off, the easiest way to stop Notes will always be to choose File➪Exit.

I Must Multi-Task!

One of the advantages to using Windows, OS/2, Macintosh, or Unix is that these operating systems can *multi-task*. Multi-task is a $10 computer word that means these operating systems can run more than one program at the same time.

What does that mean to you? Let's say that you're using Notes to read e-mail. After you've finished reading your e-mail, you have to do some work in your spreadsheet program. Sure, you could exit Notes and then start Excel, but what happens when you want to check your e-mail again in a half-hour? Are you going to shut down Excel, start Notes, and then, after you've read your new e-mail, shut down Notes to start Excel again? Of course not! You're going to multi-task. (Sounds exciting, doesn't it?)

If you want to temporarily leave your Notes session to start a different program, don't exit Notes. Use your operating system command to leave Notes "up and running" while you go do your other work. (As always, the way you do this depends on the operating system.) If you leave Notes running while you're in that other program, you'll be able to switch back and forth between the programs much more quickly and easily.

The really cool thing about leaving Notes running is that it is able to notify you when you've received new mail, even when you're using another program. You'll occasionally hear a sort of "beep beep beep" message, which is Notes' way of telling you that you have new mail.

If you want to get the "beep beep beep — New Mail has Been Delivered to You" messages while you're using some other program, you have to leave Notes running while using other programs. You will not get this notification if you shut down Notes the instant you're finished with it. In fact, most people leave Notes up and running all day long.

The way you switch from one active program to another depends on the operating system you use.

- ✔ *In Windows:* Press Ctrl+Esc to get the task list dialog box, choose the program you want to switch to, and click OK. If the program you want isn't on the list, select Program Manager from the list, click OK, and then start the other program as you would normally.

- ✔ *On a Macintosh:* From the Application menu, choose the program you want to switch to. To start a new program, choose Finder from the Application menu and then start the program as you would normally.

- ✔ *In OS/2:* Press Ctrl+Esc to get the task list and then choose the program you want to switch to. To start a new program, choose Main from the dialog box and then start the other program as you would normally.

Understanding the Desktop

Now that you have Notes running, how do you get started? At the starting gun, you should see something that looks pretty much like Figure 2-9 — it's the desktop. You need to know the five main elements of the Notes desktop:

- ✔ The menus
- ✔ The SmartIcons
- ✔ The workpage tabs
- ✔ The database icons
- ✔ The Status Bar

The menus

More good news: the menus work exactly the way you'd expect them to, and you're already familiar with a lot of the options in them, because a lot of the options in Notes work the same way as they do in other programs you may use. For example, you save a document in Notes the same way you save a spreadsheet in Lotus 1-2-3, which is the same way you save a document in Microsoft Word.

If you are a mouse user, you can open any one of the items on the menu by clicking it. If you don't like to (and don't want to) use the mouse, you can press Alt and then use the right- and left-arrow keys to select the menu you want.

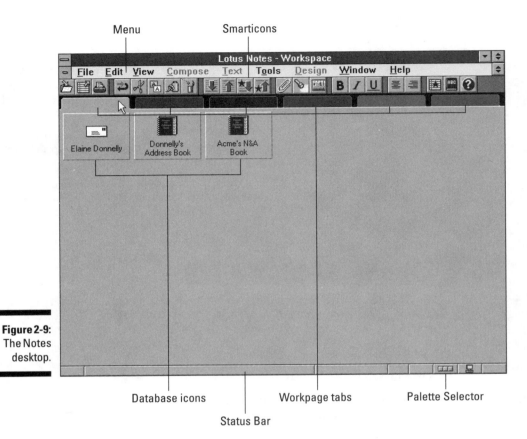

Figure 2-9:
The Notes
desktop.

Menu   Smarticons

Database icons   Workpage tabs   Palette Selector

Status Bar

(Press Enter when you've got it selected.) You can use the same strategy to actually pick any of the items in a menu; use the arrow keys to select the item you want to choose and then press Enter, *or* just click it.

You'll notice that some of the words in the menus are gray, and others are black. You can only choose the black ones, because when a menu option is *grayed out*, that means that the choice isn't appropriate right now. For example, if you were in the middle of editing a document and took a look at the Edit menu, you'll see that the Select by Date... option is gray. That just means that Selecting by Date (whatever that means!) is not an option while you are editing a document.

You'll also notice that some of the items in the menus have a little triangle after them. (Check out the Tools menu for an example.) Whenever you see an item in a menu followed by one of these little triangle things, you know that menu item leads to *another* menu item, as you see in Figure 2-10.

In addition to seeing triangles all over the place, have you noticed that some of the options in the menus are followed by an ellipses (that's three dots to you and me)? Those three dots tell you that *that* item leads not to another menu, but to a dialog box. (Like the Call item in Figure 2-10.)

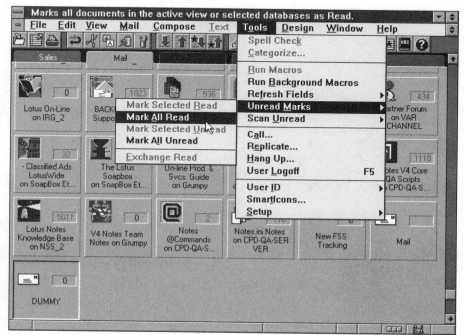

Figure 2-10:
Menu items followed by ellipses signal a dialog box.

The SmartIcons

If you've ever used any of the Lotus SmartSuite applications before, you should recognize the row of small pictures that's stretched across the top of the screen; these pictures are what Lotus calls *SmartIcons*. SmartIcons are just a way for you to execute certain commands very quickly — without having to use the menus. For example, if you want to print the document that's on the screen, you can choose File⇨Print, but it's easier and faster to click the Print SmartIcon, which is shown in Figure 2-11. (Lotus probably wouldn't like to admit it, but their SmartIcons are an awful lot like the buttons found on Microsoft's Button Bar. Or maybe Microsoft's buttons are an awful lot like Lotus' SmartIcons....)

Figure 2-11:
Very often,
the quickest
and easiest
way to do
something
in Notes is
to use a
SmartIcon.

Some of the SmartIcons are obvious — or relatively obvious, anyway. For example, you can probably guess that the one that looks like a small jar of library paste is the one you use to paste from the Clipboard. Some of the SmartIcons aren't so obvious, though. What about the fourth one in from the left — the one with two arrows? That's the one that you use to do an Undo. Fear not, though, you don't have to be an Egyptologist to use the SmartIcons.

If you can't guess what a SmartIcon is going to do for you, point to it with the mouse and click the right mouse button. You'll see a little hint in the upper-left corner of the screen. (OK, so even some of the hints don't make sense, but a lousy hint is better than no hint, right?) If you use Macintosh, stop looking for your right mouse button, because you don't have one. If you want to see the SmartIcon hints on your Mac, you'll have to choose Balloon Help⇨Show Balloons (that's the little question mark in the upper-right corner of the screen).

If you want to know even more about what any particular SmartIcon is going to do for you, take a look at the Tools⇨SmartIcons dialog box. (Choose Cancel when you're done looking.)

More SmartIcons exist than would first appear; in fact, probably more than you'll ever use. (There's probably a SmartIcon for just about every item in the menus.) Because so many SmartIcons are available, Lotus has collected them into *palettes*. The idea here is that the SmartIcons you'll use when you read a message are probably not the best ones to have around when you compose a message. So, before starting to compose a new message, you might first switch to the Editing SmartIcon palette.

To change to another SmartIcon palette, you click the SmartIcon Palette Selector down in the lower-right corner of the screen. Presto — you have a whole bunch of new SmartIcons.

Even though there are tons of SmartIcons available, you'll probably use the Default set most often, because it contains shortcuts to the most-used commands.

Dealing with the desktop and database icons

The *desktop* is the part of the screen that you use more than any other part. It is made up of a series of six *pages*, each of which can hold many *database icons*. We'll discuss exactly what these pages are all about a little later in this chapter, but for now, think of each page as being a place to hold a bunch of database icons.

"So," you ask, "just what is a database icon, anyway?" Each of the little blocks on the screen is called a database icon and represents a Notes database. The icon usually has a little picture (your mail database has a picture of an envelope) and a title (your mail database's title is probably "Stephen Londergan's Mail," assuming your name is Stephen Londergan).

Opening a database

When you want to open a database to read the documents that are inside it, just double-click the icon for that database. If you are mouse-phobic, use the arrow keys instead to select the icon you're after and then press Enter.

Closing a database

Closing a database is one of the simplest things in the world. If you're in a database and you want to close it and return to the desktop, choose File⇨Close Window.

You can also close a database by pressing Esc. Alternatively, you can close it by double-clicking the right mouse button — unless you're a Mac user, in which case you don't have an alternative. (Sorry.)

Making the icons more informative

You have a couple of ways to change the way icons look.

If you choose View⇨Refresh Unread, the icons expand to show you the number of new, unread documents in each database, as you can see in Figure 2-12.

Figure 2-12: Show the number of new, unread documents in each database by choosing View⇨ Refresh Unread.

Whenever you want Notes to update the number of unread documents that appear in the icons, you can press F9 or choose <u>V</u>iew⇨Refres<u>h</u> Unread. Notes then checks each database to see if any new documents have been added to the databases since you started the program (or since the last time you did a <u>V</u>iew⇨Refres<u>h</u> Unread).

If you choose <u>V</u>iew⇨Show <u>S</u>erver Names, the icon titles usually change to include the location of the database. We say usually because if the database icon doesn't change after you choose <u>V</u>iew⇨Show <u>S</u>erver Names, the database is not on any server but is instead on your own computer's hard disk.

Confused? This is easier to see than to read. Try <u>V</u>iew⇨Show <u>S</u>erver Names and then look at your icons for the Name and Address Books. (If you're not sitting in front of your computer, just take a look at Figure 2-13.) In our example, one of the databases is named Lotus N&A Book on BERYLLIUM, and the other is just named Freeland's Address Book. Because the first database's title includes the words on BERYLLIUM, you know that it is on a Notes server named Beryllium. Because the other database is just named Freeland's Address Book, and because its name does not include the words "on *some servername*," you know that this database is on your computer.

Figure 2-13:
When you choose <u>V</u>iew⇨Show <u>S</u>erver Names, the database icons show you where each database is located.

Moving, arranging, and deleting database icons

Besides opening a database, you can do two other things with the database icons: move 'em and delete 'em.

To move a database icon to another part of the page or to another page altogether, do the following:

1. **Point to it with the mouse.**

2. **Press and hold down the left mouse button.**

3. **Drag the icon to its new home. (Welcome to the neighborhood!)**

   (If you want to drag the icon to a new page altogether, drop it on the page's Tab.)

You can also choose View⇨Arrange Icons to have Notes make all the icons on the current workpage nice and neat.

To delete a database icon, follow these steps:

1. **Select the database icon that you want to delete by clicking it once or by using the cursor keys to select it.**

2. **Press Delete (or choose Edit⇨Clear).**

Deleting an icon just means that you don't want that database on your screen every day; it does *not* delete the database from the server.

If you blow it and end up deleting an icon that you shouldn't have deleted, just use File⇨Open Database to get it right back again.

The pages

As you can see in Figure 2-14, the Notes desktop has six *pages*. Each of the pages is used to store and organize database icons. You might decide to put all the database icons from your marketing project on one page, all your icons related to mail on another page, and so on.

If you want to see the icons that are on a different page than the one you're on, click that page's tab. The screen then changes to show you the icons on that page.

You can also give each of the pages a name by double-clicking the page's tab. You'll get a dialog box like the one in Figure 2-15; here you can enter the (relatively short) name you'd like for the page and choose the tab's color.

Notes "comes with" six pages, and you can't have any more because there's no way to add a new page. Fear not — you will never run out of space, because you can put as many icons on a page as you want. In fact, if you're a slob, you might have all the icons you use piled onto one page and be none the worse for it.

The Status Bar

The last element of the screen is the *Status Bar*. (If you use any other Lotus products, you will already recognize it, because all of Lotus' SmartSuite products have it.) The Status Bar is a band that runs along the bottom of the screen and is another shortcut of sorts. It displays information for you (that's where you'll see the "New mail has been delivered to you" messages), and it is also used to change fonts and type sizes. Refer to Chapter 11 for more information about the Status Bar.

The tabs

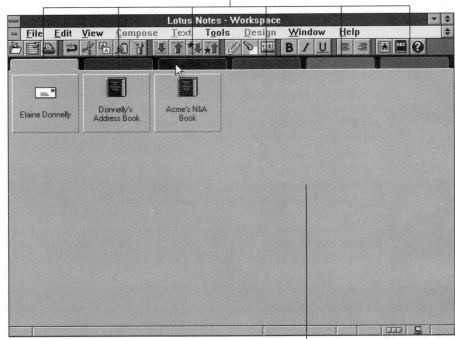

The work page

Workspace Page Name

Name:

OK

Cancel

Color:

K W R G B M Y C 1 2 3 4 5 6 7

Part II
Using Electronic Mail (No Stamps Required)

In this part...

Notes running? Seat belt fastened? Mouse handy? If you can answer yes at least to the first question, you are ready to explore the use and the power of Notes. First of all, you had better check your e-mail, and then you can go on to the other tasks you will accomplish. If you haven't been able to start Notes, take the time to read Chapter 2 in the previous section, because there are a few things you need to do before you click the Notes icon.

The chapters in this section teach you what you need to know to read e-mail, send e-mail, keep your e-mail database organized, get fancy about addressing e-mail, and then get fancy about the types of e-mail you send.

It is logical to deal with your e-mail first, because it is the most active database you use and because the information in it is usually more immediately important that the stuff in the other Notes databases that we talk about in future chapters. As you are reading this, for instance, you may be missing an important meeting or a lunch date that you've been trying to arrange. Quick — read the next chapter.

Chapter 3
The E-Mail's Here!

In This Chapter

▶ Reading your e-mail

▶ Views you can choose and use to list your e-mail

*Y*our regular mail probably arrives in a mailbox or gets slipped through a slot in your front door. Your mailbox for e-mail, on the other hand, is shaped remarkably like a computer. Actually, your e-mail database is on your Home Server, not your own computer. To get at your e-mail, you need to have an icon in your desktop for your e-mail database. If it's not there, consult Chapter 2 for the information that you'll need to be able to add the icon.

May I Have the Envelope, Please

To open your e-mail database, double-click your e-mail database icon, or select it and press Enter. There, in a list, is your e-mail, which looks very much like Figure 3-1. Each line in the list corresponds to a single document (you could as easily call the documents *memos* or *messages.*)

Of course, no envelope is involved, but you do have to *open* each document to read it. To open a memo, select the document using the arrow keys and press Enter, or double-click anywhere in the line of the memo you want. At last, you're reading your e-mail. Each e-mail document is called a *memo* or a *message*—the terms are interchangeable.

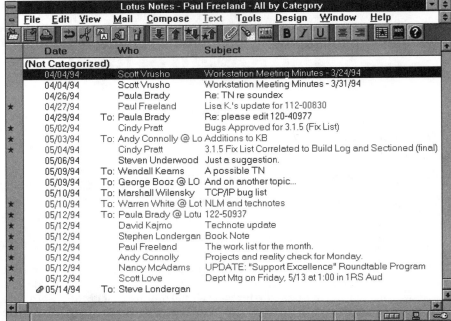

Figure 3-1:
The list of
e-mail in Pat
Freeland's
e-mail
database.

For the time being, let's assume that you just want to read your e-mail. (In Chapter 5 we tell you what else you can do with your e-mail — politely, of course.) After you read a memo, you can dismiss it from the screen, unless it brings you such pleasure that you can't bear to remove it. When you're done reading a memo, you can clear it off the screen with any of these steps:

- ✔ Press Esc. The memo disappears, and the list of all e-mail reappears.

- ✔ Choose File⇨Close Window. The memo disappears, and the list of all e-mail reappears.

- ✔ Double-click anywhere in the memo with the right mouse button. Same results.

- ✔ Double-click the smaller minus sign in the menu line. Same results.

- ✔ Press Enter. The next message in the list (if there is one) appears otherwise, the keystroke is ignored.

- ✔ Press Backspace. The previous message in the list if there is one appears.

- ✔ Press Tab to move to the next unread message or press Shift+Tab to move to the previous unread message, if any.

> 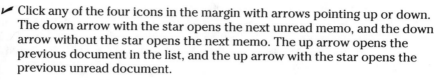 Click any of the four icons in the margin with arrows pointing up or down. The down arrow with the star opens the next unread memo, and the down arrow without the star opens the next memo. The up arrow opens the previous document in the list, and the up arrow with the star opens the previous unread document.
>
> 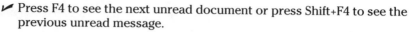 Press F4 to see the next unread document or press Shift+F4 to see the previous unread message.

If you're getting cold feet trying to figure out how you'll remember all those options, don't bother trying. Pick the one that works best for you and forget the others.

The Views from Here — Viewing the List of Incoming E-Mail

Take another look at Figure 3-1. What you see is a list, but if you really want to speak the language of Notes, you should call it a *view*, which is a way of looking at a list of documents. Later we show you how to create your own view (Chapter 10). This view of your database shows your documents by category. You may be wondering, "So why are all my messages listed as Not Categorized?" *You* have to create categories and put the documents in those categories (see Chapter 5), and until you do, your e-mail won't be categorized.

If you're lucky enough to have a color monitor, you'll notice that the data for each document is in red type, and a star sits to the left of the documents. Both the color and the star (useful if your monitor isn't color) are telling you that you haven't read that document. After you read it, the text in the line becomes black and the star is gone. That means you *have* read it.

To the left of the documents, you may occasionally see some other little symbols in addition to the star, such as the paper clip next to the last document in Figure 3-1. A few simple keystrokes allow someone to send you an attachment to their Notes memo: a letter created in Ami Pro or Microsoft Word, or a spreadsheet created in Lotus 1-2-3, for example. Each memo that has an attached file has a paper clip symbol. You can learn about attaching and detaching files in Chapter 6.

Other symbols that you may see are a check mark (indicating that you have selected the document for further action) or a little trash can (showing that you have marked the document for deletion).

Although you have probably already figured out what the columns in the view mean (especially because they're labeled), a bit of explanation may be helpful. The first column, *Date*, is the date the memo was e-mailed to you. If someone started it on Monday but didn't actually send it until Friday, Friday's date appears in this column and on the memo.

The second column, *Who*, names the sender if the memo was e-mailed to you, or the first addressee if you sent it. You may have e-mailed it to lots of people, but only the first person's name will show in the view. The *Subject* column lists whatever the sender wrote in the Subject: section of the memo.

There are times when you need to find a memo written by or to a particular person. Naturally, you can scroll up and down the list of memos in the current view and look for the memo that you want, but there is an easier way. Change views. You can not only list your memos by the category, but you can also choose View from the main menu to select other ways of listing and viewing the documents. Figure 3-2 shows the views available in your e-mail database.

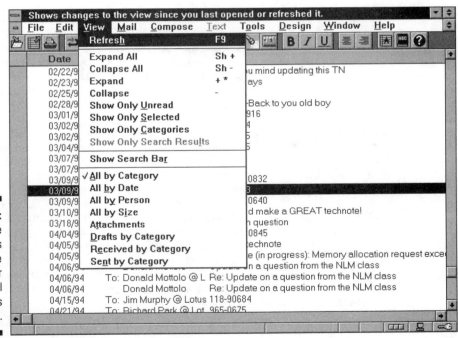

Figure 3-2:
These are
the views
available
when your
e-mail
database is
on screen.

To find a memo sent by a particular person, choose View➪All by Person. Press the first letter of the first name of the sender and a list of people appears, through which you can scroll and choose that special person. If only one name matches that letter, the person's name will appear on the screen with all the memos that are to or from him or her.

If you sent the memo to lots of people and the person you're looking for was not the first addressee, you will not find that person's name in the All by Person view. You will only be able to find the name of the first addressee in the All by Person view.

Use Edit➪Find to search for documents which contain the names of other addresses than the first one.

But wait, that's not all. No, for the same low, low price, you also get other views. Now what would you pay? But don't answer yet — first take a look at the other dazzling and useful views.

The All by Date view, visible in Figure 3-3, is useful if you want to delete the older, moldier memos. The list is arranged (*sorted*) with the oldest memos at the top of the list so that you can get started right away deleting the least current ones.

Lotus Notes - Paul Freeland - All by Date
File Edit View Mail Compose Text Tools Design Window Help

Date	Who	Subject
★ 05/12/94	Andy Connolly	Projects and reality check for Monday.
★ 05/12/94	To: Carl Hero @ Lotus	Ignore previous messages about this TN
★ 05/12/94	Carl Hero	Re: 103-40685
★ 05/12/94	Nancy McAdams	UPDATE: "Support Excellence" Roundtable Program
★ 05/12/94	Steve Graham	Congratulations to David Kajmo
★ 05/12/94	Barry Smith	Out of the Office
★ 05/12/94	Kevin Bergquist	Out of the Office 5/13 - 5/20
★ 05/12/94	Dwight Morse	New default frame type with OS/2 2.1 Netware Requester
★ 05/12/94	Paula Brady	122-50937
★ 05/12/94	Pat Doherty	On vacation
★ 05/12/94	Scott Love	Dept Mtg on Friday, 5/13 at 1:00 in 1RS Aud
05/13/94	To: Sales Force - West	3rd Quarter Figures
05/14/94	To: Stephen Londergan	Changes to tomorrow's schedule

Figure 3-3:
The All by Date view of an e-mail database. Older messages are on top.

Use the All by Size view if you get an angry message from your administrator saying that your e-mail database is too darn big and you have to delete some messages. It's not the number of memos you delete, it's the size. The Size column in Figure 3-4 shows, for all to see, that this irresponsible user has been harboring a memo that is over 800,000 bytes. If the user has any sense, he'll delete the behemoth before the server collapses under its own weight or he gets his wrists slapped. The largest memos (measured in bytes) are at the top of the list. Delete the biggest ones first if you want the Good Citizenship award.

The Attachments view lists all the documents that have attachments. This is another way to pick memos to delete if you need to reduce the size of your e-mail database. In Figure 3-5 you can see that the memos are arranged by date (oldest at the top), with the number of attachments shown in the second column from the right. The most important column is the right-most one, because it shows the filename and file size of each attachment in the user's e-mail database.

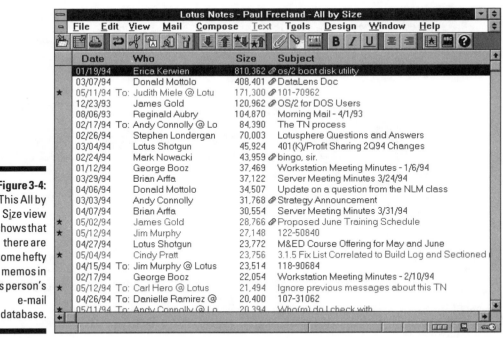

Figure 3-4:
This All by Size view shows that there are some hefty memos in this person's e-mail database.

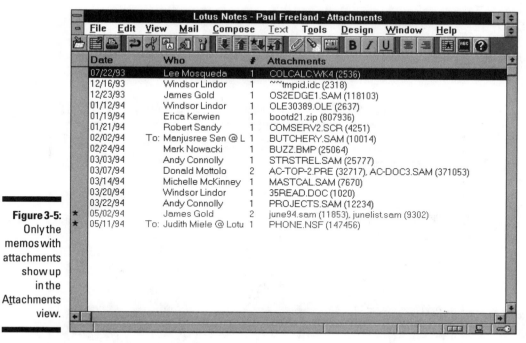

Figure 3-5:
Only the
memos with
attachments
show up
in the
Attachments
view.

Do you ever start to write a memo and then save it and forget to ever finish and
e-mail it? If so, check the Drafts by Category view. All the memos there are ones
that you left on the back burner. Naturally, you won't see any categories for the
memos to fit in until you create some and assign the memos to them.

The last two views, Received by Category and Sent by Category, list all the
memos you have received or sent, arranged in the category to which you
assigned them.

The 5th Wave — By Rich Tennant

"UNFORTUNATELY, THE ADMINISTRATOR'S NOT VERY FAULT-TOLERANT."

Chapter 4
Sending A Message

In This Chapter

▶ Memo writing etiquette

▶ Writing the memo

▶ Using the Company Name and Address Book

▶ Replying to a message you have received

So you've read your e-mail. You had your lunch date (but you had to call to confirm because you didn't know how to answer an e-mail using Notes), and you didn't miss the meeting. Still, there must be a couple of messages in your recent e-mail that deserve an answer. And maybe you need to write a few of your own.

This chapter deals with an activity you'll spend a lot of time doing when you're using Notes — writing memos. The purpose here is not to turn you into a Shakespeare or a Hemingway. What you say in your memos is up to you. We just want to give you some pointers so that the message gets to where it's going.

Good Manners — Memo-wise

This will probably come as no surprise, but you shouldn't use Notes memos for some things:

- ✔ Vicki and I are giving a little wedding for our daughter next week. Can you make it? Bring your own champagne.

- ✔ I'm sorry your parakeet died; hope it wasn't anything serious — or catching.

- ✔ Hey, J. B., here are a few suggestions about how to get this company turned around. Fire all your vice presidents.

- Smedley, you're fired. Be out of your office in five minutes. We've already hired a replacement.
- Fire! Everyone leave the building as quickly as possible!
- Don't you think the president is a jerk? I sure do. What a moron! I could do the job better than that idiot.
- I just found out that Rogers is making $90,000.

Each of those points may have their place in some form of communication, but not in e-mailed memos. Before you put fingers to keyboard, pause to ponder the following points:

- There are times when more formal styles of communication are desirable.
- There are also times when talking face to face is preferable.
- Don't go over your boss's head in writing if you wouldn't consider it under other circumstances.
- Resist the temptation to include the whole world in your cc: list.
- A message may be *delivered* almost instantly, but that doesn't mean everyone is going to *read* it instantly.
- Although Notes is a secure e-mail system (a message only goes to the people you address it to), there's nothing to stop them from sending it on to other people.
- If you have composed a nasty-gram, sleep on it before sending it.
- Rogers is only getting $70,000.

I'm Gonna Sit Right Down and Write — Composing a Memo

Having dispensed with the indispensable lesson in memo manners, you are ready to compose an actual real-life memo. Before you let your thoughts flow out through your fingers, make sure that your mail database is the current database. It doesn't have to be open: it's OK just to click once on the icon for your mail database.

You'll have to check with your administrator to find out to whom you can send messages. You may be able to send messages to your chums on CompuServe. You may even be able to send faxes. Then again, you may only be able to send mail to folks in your own organization. The point is that having Notes doesn't automatically guarantee you the right to send e-mail to just anyone.

When you choose Compose, you can choose any of the options from the drop-down menu shown in Figure 4-1.

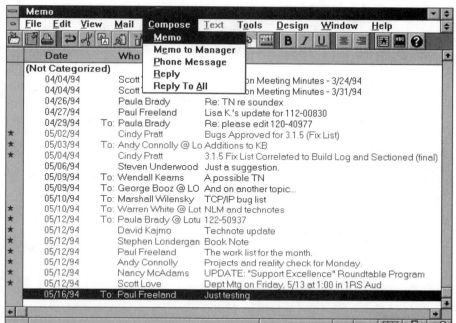

Figure 4-1:
Items you
can
compose.

Actually, you have a choice of menu items for composing a memo. You may use Compose⇨Memo or Mail⇨Compose⇨Memo. The difference is that by using Mail⇨Compose⇨Memo, you can compose your memo while you are using a database other than your regular mail database.

Most of the time you will be composing memos, but once in a while you'll need these other options:

✔ Memo To Manager — sends a memo to the manager of the current database (in this case, your e-mail database). You are not the manager; the manager is the person in charge of all e-mail databases on that server. You normally wouldn't choose this option in your mail database, but you might do it in a different database. Choosing Memo to Manager in another database automatically sends the memo to all people who have manager access to that database. Use this form for suggestions, comments, criticisms or complaints, help, or requests for a change in your database privileges.

✔ Phone Message — a way of filling in the on-line version of one of those little pink While-You-Were-Out-the-Phone-Rang-and-It-Was-for-You forms.

✔ <u>R</u>eply — a standard memo form automatically addressed to the person who sent you the message that you are reading.

✔ Reply to <u>A</u>ll — a standard memo automatically addressed not only to the author of a memo but also to everyone else in the original's To: list.

Note: To use the Reply to <u>A</u>ll form or the regular <u>R</u>eply form you must open your e-mail database and, in one of the views, at least highlight the memo to which you want to reply. Of course you can open the original memo. How else would Notes know whom you were replying to if you didn't somehow specify a particular memo?

You may also send a memo from other products. For instance, in Lotus 1-2-3 for Windows, you would choose <u>F</u>ile⇨Send <u>M</u>ail to send a memo.

Make me a memo

To compose a memo, choose <u>C</u>ompose⇨<u>M</u>emo or <u>M</u>ail⇨<u>C</u>ompose⇨<u>M</u>emo. The blank memo form in Figure 4-2 appears. If you are one of those people who has trouble writing, think of writing a memo as filling in the fields in a record in a database. Does that help? Well, it was worth a try anyway.

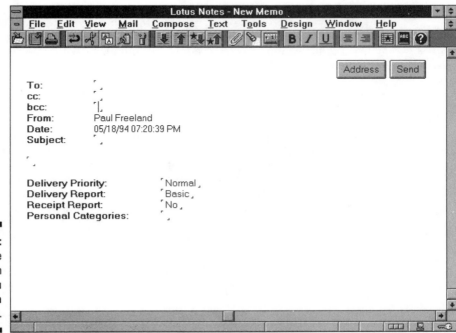

Figure 4-2:
This is the blank form in which you compose a memo.

The memo form consists of labels (like To:), most of which are followed by little corners, which are the end markers for each field. In the upper-right corner of the form are two *buttons* labeled Address and Send. We tell you what they do later in the chapter. Associated with each of these buttons is a *macro*, a set of recorded actions that play back when you click the button. You can push a button by pointing to it with the mouse arrow and clicking or by using the arrow keys to navigate to the button and then pressing the Spacebar. Shoving your thumb tip against the screen will only put a smudge on your monitor.

At this point we think it's a good idea to tell you that what you're reading here may not be true. Or, this section may be true, but later in the book you may notice that what we describe is not what you see on your screen. If there is a discrepancy between what you are reading and what you are seeing, one of the following excuses may apply:

- ✔ We don't know what we're writing about.
- ✔ You can't always believe everything you read.
- ✔ This book is actually about a different Lotus product.
- ✔ Lotus Notes is a very flexible program, and your Notes administrator may have changed something about the way your organization uses Notes. Some examples? Someone may have changed the memo form. Addressing may be done a bit differently in your organization. Your organization may have opted to use a different e-mail program. (It is possible to use Notes for its database capabilities but use a separate program to send e-mail among members of the organization.)

If the e-mail menu looks different from the one in Figure 4-3 or if the e-mail menu is grayed out, then you're using a different e-mail program. You can skip this whole part of the book and go on to Part 3 — you're not using Notes for your e-mail. When all else fails, check with your administrator.

The only field that you *must* fill in is the To: field. In other words, you may send an absolutely blank memo to someone as long as you supply at least one recipient. That recipient may be an individual or a group that you or some other member of your organization defined. You'll learn how to create a group in Chapter 6.

Don't worry if you can't spell the exact name of the recipient. You may be wondering, for instance, whether to use Tom Smith, Tommy Smith, or Thomas Smith; maybe he spells his name Smythe, or maybe you can't spell Smith. Then again, maybe you're not even sending your message to Tom Smith. There are two ways to handle this little bit of confusion:

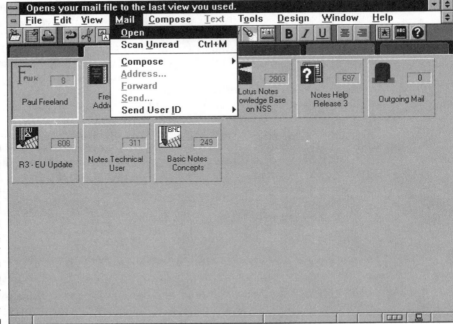

Opens your mail file to the last view you used.

Figure 4-3:
The Mail
menu. If
your mail
menu looks
different,
then your
organization
doesn't use
Notes for
e-mail.

✔ Do your best to spell the name of the recipient. When the time comes to send the message, Notes will check each recipient's name. If you got someone's name wrong, Notes will correct it automatically. If it's Thomas Smith and you typed Tom Smith, in other words, Notes will change it automatically to Thomas Smith. If there are lots of Smiths and a couple of Smythes, Notes will present you with a list of all of them and you'll have to pick the one to whom you want to send the memo.

✔ Choose Mail⇨Address (located in the upper-right corner of your memo) or use the Address button. Either of these will call the Company Name and Address Book into view so you can search for the name of the person who will be the lucky recipient of your first memo. Double-click a name to enter it in the To: field of your memo. Now you can be sure you got it right. See the next section for information about the Company Name and Address Book.

One way to get the address right the first time is to have the person you want to send a memo to send one to you first; then you just compose a reply. The proper address will appear automatically in the To: field. (We explain replies later in the chapter.)

Enter as many names and group names as you like into the To: field.

If you plan to use a Notes *gateway*, which is a way of transferring Notes mail to other networks or services such as CompuServe or fax, you may need to create an address that turns a simple name into something that looks more like a computer program. For example:

```
Susan Brown @Apex @abcd.com @Wirenet.
```

or

```
721143,617 @ compuserv.com
```

So you see, addressing a memo may sometimes be a tiny bit more complicated than simply typing someone's name. Your Notes administrator should give you the information you need to address memos properly. Chin up, though — in Chapter 6 we show you how to use your Personal Name and Address Book to write these addresses only once and then make Notes associate a simple name with a handful of keystrokes.

The *cc:* field actually stands for *courtesy copy*, because the term *carbon copy* is a bit too low-tech for us computer types — don't you agree? Otherwise, the field is used the way it has always been used: the people or groups listed here are people who may be interested in the memo but are not directly involved.

Use the *bcc:* field (blind courtesy copy) to send the memo to someone without the rest of the recipients knowing about it. Imagine, for instance, that you send a memo to a co-worker asking to have a certain job done. You want your manager to know you have made the request, but you don't want the co-worker to know that your manager is aware of what's going on. Send the memo To: the co-worker with a bcc: to your manager. When your co-worker receives the message, the bcc: field won't be visible, so your secret is safe.

Notes automatically fills in the *From:* and *Date:* fields. Your name is taken from your Notes ID file and placed in the From: field, so you can be sure that no one is sending e-mail with your name. The Date: field is the date and time you started the memo, unless you save it and then retrieve it later to continue working on it. If you save it and then open it later and add to it, the date and time reflects the most recent edits that you make.

The *Subject:* field tells the recipients what they're about to read. That sounds like it's a bit unnecessary, doesn't it? Only people with tiny brains need a line that says "You're about to read about the office party" when they're about to read details of the office party. However, Subject: is one of the fields that shows in a view of all your memos. It's rather important, because it gives the first hint of what's in the memo before you even open it and reminds you of its contents when you are hunting for a particular memo.

Below the Subject: field is a field that doesn't have a name on the screen but is the most important field in the whole memo: the *Body* field. Use this area to write the actual text of the memo. You may wonder how you are going to fit all that you have to say between those two end markers. Rest assured that the field expands (just like all the other fields in the memo), so you can fill this field with as much information as you want.

Speaking of those little corner markers, notice that they are red, even though all the other fields have black end markers. If you have a monochrome monitor, both markers look just the same. The red corners mean that the Body field is an encryptable field. More on that subject in Chapter 6, but we'll tell you here that the body field is the only field in the memo form that you can scramble so that it is absolutely unreadable until the recipient opens the memo.

Below the Body field are four more fields, the first three of which affect the actual mailing of your memo:

- ✔ Delivery Priority
- ✔ Delivery Report
- ✔ Receipt Report
- ✔ Personal Categories

Delivery Priority tells the Notes e-mail system how quickly you want the memo to be delivered. If the memo is intended for someone on another LAN, your mail server may elect to store your memo for future delivery depending upon the priority you choose. The default is Normal, but you may choose High or Low as well. Choose High if you want the memo to be delivered as soon as possible, regardless of the cost. Choose Low if you want to save the company some money. You may want to use low priority if you are sending a particularly large attachment, because your message will take longer to send. These priority settings affect the delivery of e-mail across long distances, where phone charges may be high. Low priority messages are sent when the costs are lowest, normal priority messages are held until several can be sent at once, and high priority messages are sent immediately.

Don't bother to set the priority if you are sending the message to people who are all on the same LAN as you are. On your own LAN, the memo is delivered as quickly as possible, regardless of the setting.

Delivery Report has Notes inform you when your message is delivered. The default, *Basic*, only lets you know if a message is not delivered. Generally, no news is good news — if you don't get a delivery failure report, you can assume that your message got to the recipient's mail database. The other two choices for this field, besides Basic, are *No Report* and *Confirmed.* Use No Report if you sent your memo to a huge crowd of people and you don't care if the message doesn't get to them all. Use Confirmed if you absolutely insist that Notes inform you when it delivers the message to each recipient's e-mail database. Figure 4-4 shows you a delivery confirmation report.

A delivery report doesn't mean that the message has been read — it only means that the message has been placed in the recipient's mail database.

If you want to know when (if ever) the recipients read your memo, use the *Receipt Report* field. You have a bewildering array of choices here: No (the default) or Yes. No means that there will not be any way of knowing whether any recipients actually opened the message. If you choose Yes, you get a receipt report when each of the recipients reads your message. You can't choose Yes for some recipients and No for others if they are all on the same message. Figure 4-5 shows a typical receipt report.

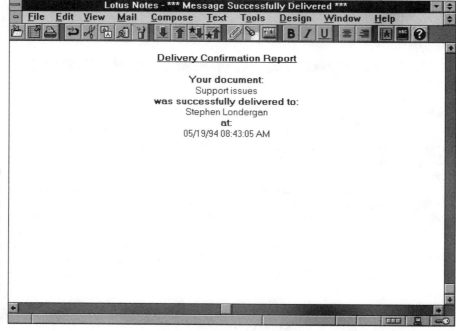

Figure 4-4:
A delivery confirmation report. This message got to the recipient's e-mail database.

Figure 4-5:
You get this
receipt
report if you
choose Yes
in the
Receipt
Report: field.

When you ask Notes for a receipt report, a message appears at the bottom of the recipient's screen saying that a receipt report was sent. Can you believe it — some people consider this to be rude. They don't like you to be checking up on them. Use this option sparingly if you work with sensitive people.

A receipt report doesn't mean that the message has been read; it only means that the recipients opened it or deleted it. They may close it immediately when they see your name or they may get distracted and forget to read it.

If you create categories for your messages, you can type in one or more of these categories in the *Personal Categories* field. Then you can place the memo in those categories once you save it. In Chapter 5, we tell you about categories.

Get me the manager

Chances are that you are not going to have much to say to the manager of your mail database — chances are that you don't even know who that is. Nevertheless, if you do have something to suggest or to complain about, choose Compose⇨Memo to Manager. The To: field automatically contains the proper address, and all the other fields are the same as they are in the Memo form, except that there is no cc: and no bcc: field.

If you want to ask for a raise or a day off (or more work), Memo to Manager won't do it. It does not send a memo to *your* manager but to the manager of whatever database is currently active. If you want to send a memo to your own boss, you have to type in the name yourself.

It's for you

The phone rings:

> *Caller:* Is Sally there?
>
> *You:* No, may I take a message?
>
> *Caller:* Tell her to be sure to get the report to me by 3:00 today.
>
> *You:* I'll tell her.

Now what happens? You jot the message on a piece of paper and shuffle it into the pile of stuff on your desk. Your attention goes to other things. Sally never gets the message. J.B. never gets the report, Sally never gets another paycheck.

Or you choose Compose⇨Phone Message and fill it in, just as the exemplary and responsible member of the organization did in Figure 4-6. The message is instantly sent to Sally's mail database so that she will see it as soon as she reads her mail.

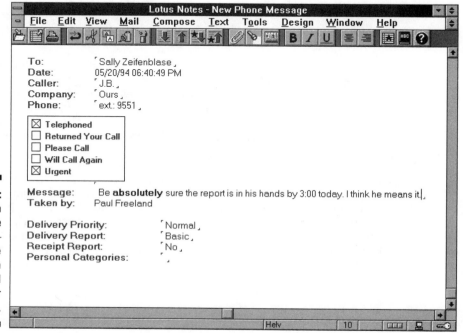

Figure 4-6: A filled-in phone message — much more reliable than the old paper system.

Of the two endings for our gripping drama, which one is the way that you would handle the phone call? Unless you like watching people getting their heads handed to them on plates, you might want to consider using Notes.

How shall I answer thee?

You have read a memo, it's still on the screen or it's highlighted in the view, and you have a few things to say in response. You could, of course, compose a whole new memo. It's a bit easier, however, to Choose Compose⇨Reply because then you don't have to fill in the To: field. The name of the person who sent the original memo automatically appears in the To: field and the subject of the original memo appears in the Subject: field. Fill in the other fields, type your reply in the Body field, and send it off.

Using the Reply button in the upper-right corner of the message you are reading is a little faster than using the menu. Clicking this button brings a reply memo form to the screen, already addressed to the sender of the original message.

Hey y'all — Reply to all

Of course, you may want the reply to go to everyone who got the original memo. In that case, choose Compose⇨Reply to All. The sender of the original message is in the To: field, and all the other addressees are in the cc: field.

Forward, memo!

On the subject of sending memos, there is one more choice — but it's not on the Compose menu. Suppose that you want someone who was not an original addressee to see the message. Or maybe you want to send the original memo back to the sender with some changes. Or you want to send to your whole department a memo that was originally addressed only to you. Or imagine that the sender of the original memo forgot what was in it, so sending a reply that just says "No" might be confusing.

When you are faced with any of these situations, use Mail⇨Forward. The To:, cc:, and bcc: fields are blank (Notes has no way of knowing to whom you are forwarding the memo), but the subject and body fields are filled — they contain the text from the original memo. You supply your own addressees, perform any edits in the memo, and then send it off. Figure 4-7 shows a memo that has some additional comments added and bolded so that they are clearly visible and won't be confused with the original text.

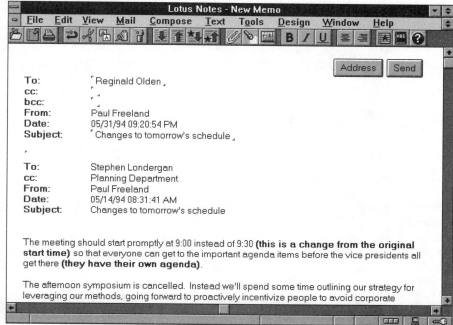

File   Edit   View   Mail   Compose   Text   Tools   Design   Window   Help

Address   Send

To: Reginald Olden
cc:
bcc:
From: Paul Freeland
Date: 05/31/94 09:20:54 PM
Subject: Changes to tomorrow's schedule

To: Stephen Londergan
cc: Planning Department
From: Paul Freeland
Date: 05/14/94 08:31:41 AM
Subject: Changes to tomorrow's schedule

The meeting should start promptly at 9:00 instead of 9:30 **(this is a change from the original start time)** so that everyone can get to the important agenda items before the vice presidents all get there **(they have their own agenda)**.

The afternoon symposium is cancelled. Instead we'll spend some time outlining our strategy for leveraging our methods, going forward to proactively incentivize people to avoid corporate

Figure 4-7:
This memo will be forwarded to Reg with some additions (in boldface).

If you are scattering comments of your own throughout the original body of the memo, consider changing the appearance of your comments by changing the text color or font or by bolding, italicizing, or underlining your comments. That way, your own brilliant additions are distinguishable from the original.

The Little Black Book — Company-Wide

If all went according to Hoyle, the first time you started Notes, you got — free of charge and with no obligation whatsoever — several icons: one for your e-mail database, one for your Personal Name and Address Book, and one for the Public (company-wide) Name and Address Book. This last database, the Public Name and Address Book, contains the names of everyone in the company who has a Notes workstation. Figure 4-8 shows an example of a Name and Address Book.

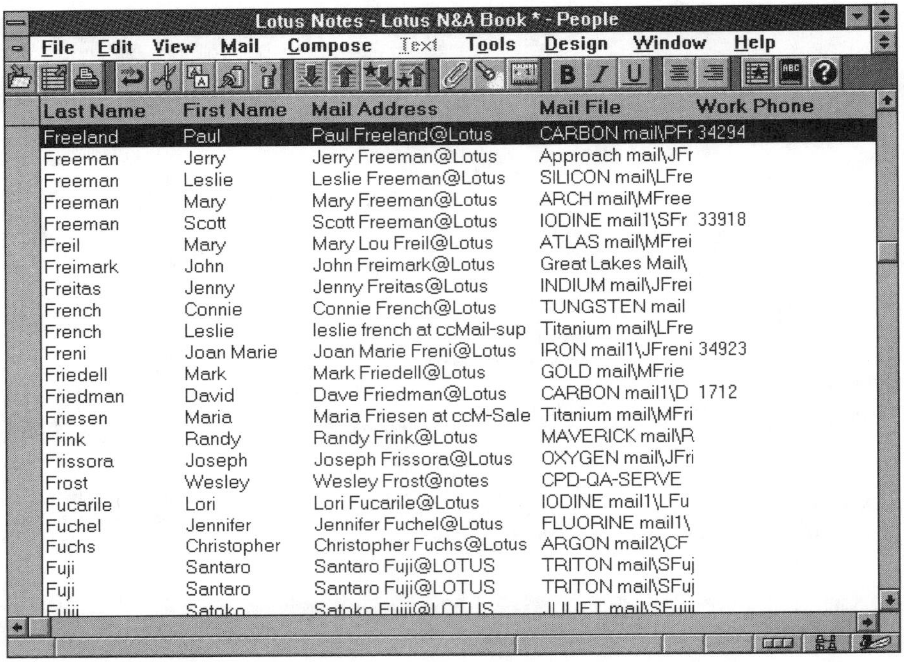

Figure 4-8:
This is a section of a typical Name and Address Book.

When you address a message, Notes looks in the Name and Address Book database. It checks to be sure that the spelling for each name that you typed is correct and that there is, in fact, someone in your organization with that name. If there isn't, Notes presents you with a dialog box like the one in Figure 4-9, asking what you want to do about your goof.

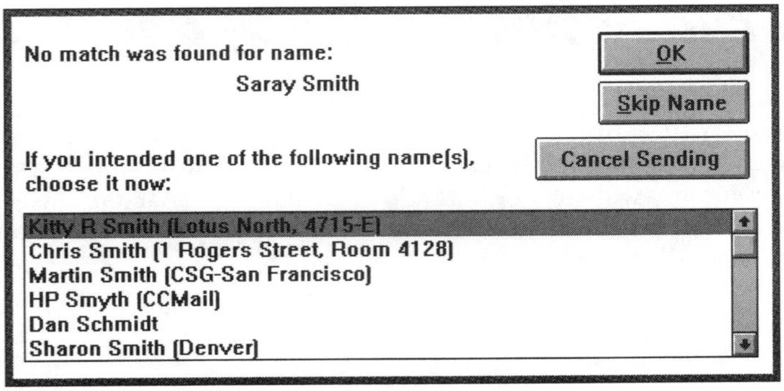

Figure 4-9:
If you goof up an addressee's name, this dialog box appears.

The following are several advantages to Notes checking all addressee names:

✔ You won't send a message to never-never land, thinking all the while that it'll find its way to the proper addressee.

✔ You won't insult someone by spelling their name wrong or forgetting an important part of their name — such as the fact that they hyphenate their last name.

✔ If there are several people with similar names in the organization, you have a lesser chance of sending the message to the wrong person.

While you're letting your highlighter do the walking through the Name and Address Book, you may notice that it takes a long time to get where you want to go. If the company has 4,000 employees, and you want to find a person whose last name is Tucker and you begin by looking at an employee named Allen, you have a lot of down-arrow keys to press. Pressing PgDn certainly will be a bit faster, but the fastest way of all is to type the person's last name. For instance, to move the highlight to a person named Tucker, you may only need to type **tuck** to move directly to that name. No, you don't need to type capital letters.

By the way, Notes maintains the data that you see about all the employees, but each of them may choose to make more information available. Double-click your name and you see a page of information about you. Figure 4-10 shows a page of information about one of the authors of this book.

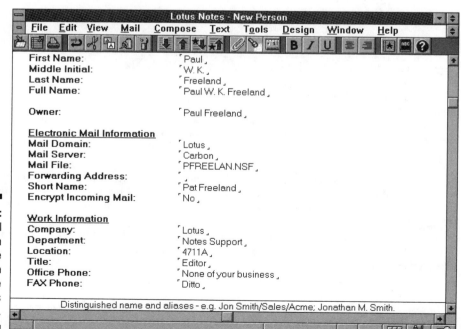

Figure 4-10:
Individual information about one person in the Name and Address Book.

The information in this form is updated only if you edit it, so don't forget to enter things about yourself that people need to know and then don't forget to update it if anything changes.

Save Me, Send Me

After you're finished writing, it's probably time to mail the memo. We say "probably" because if you wrote one of those hot-headed bombshells telling off your boss and threatening to quit, it's a good idea to wait a day or two (or more) before you send it. You may also want to look over a memo again tomorrow before you send it. In such cases, sending is not what you want — saving is.

If you decide to edit the message later, you can open it in the usual way (double-click it in the view) or highlight the message in the view and press Ctrl+E. E is for edit — this keystroke sequence calls the message to the screen and puts you in edit mode so that you can go on working on the message.

In any case, the easiest way to save or mail a memo is to press Esc. Then the dialog box in Figure 4-11 appears. You can choose to just Save, just Mail, or Save *and* Mail the memo. By default, both Save and Mail are checked although you can deselect one or the other. Click the box or press Alt+the underlined letter of the item to deselect it. (We cover Sign and Encrypt, the other two choices, in Chapter 6.)

Figure 4-11:
Press Esc
when you're
done writing
a memo.

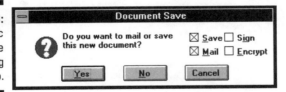

You don't need to supply a filename to save the memo — the memo automatically goes to your e-mail database. After you choose Yes, the memo is on its way — either to your e-mail database, the recipient's e-mail box, or both.

You don't need to send the message to yourself. Saving it puts it in your e-mail database.

If you pressed Esc by accident and you want to return to your memo, be sure to choose <u>C</u>ancel or press Esc again. Choosing <u>N</u>o tells Notes that you are not interested in this memo at all — you don't want to save it, you don't want to send it, and you don't want to continue looking at it on your screen. Therefore, Notes clears it off the screen right away and you can't get it back.

Here are some alternatives to pressing Esc when you're finished working on the memo:

- ✔ Choose <u>M</u>ail⇨<u>S</u>end. A dialog box appears giving you the chance to Si<u>g</u>n and <u>E</u>ncrypt the memo. See Chapter 6 for information on signing and encrypting messages.

- ✔ Double-click the command button (it looks like a minus sign or coin slot) in the upper-left corner of the memo. The <u>S</u>ave, <u>M</u>ail, Si<u>g</u>n, <u>E</u>ncrypt dialog box appears.

- ✔ Click the Save icon. This will save (but not send) the memo.

- ✔ Double-click the right mouse button (Windows and OS/2 only) anywhere in the memo. This has the same effect as pressing Esc.

- ✔ Click the Send button. A dialog box appears in which you can sign and encrypt the memo. Then you see another dialog box that asks if you want to save the memo.

Chapter 5

After the Reading — Managing Your Messages

In This Chapter

▶ Deleting unwanted messages

▶ Creating and using categories for your messages

▶ Searching for messages

▶ Printing Notes documents

After you read your messages, then what? Do they float off on the waters of time? Do you have to do something with them? Can you keep them, or do they disappear after you read them?

No, no, yes, and no. Any other questions? End of chapter.

The truth is that you really don't have to do anything with memos after you've read them. They continue to pile up in your e-mail database in just the same way that stuff accumulates on your desk. They don't automatically disappear after you read them. It would be awfully irresponsible of Notes to delete messages that you may need.

This chapter deals with the various things that you can do with a message or a group of messages after you read them.

The Scrap Heap of History

Most of the time you should seriously consider deleting your messages, unless you're one of those people who saves everything. To keep a message, you need to do absolutely nothing. Unless you actually punch the proper keys to delete a message, it's yours forever. Remember that every message you keep is that much more disk space you're using up on your Notes server.

If everyone in your organization kept three-year-old memos from Fred that say "Meet me for lunch," then your company would have to keep buying more hard disks for your e-mail server or someone would have to send out messages constantly asking people to clean out their e-mail databases, or else you and those who share your Notes server would run out of disk space and everyone would notice that the database was getting slower and s-l-o-w-e-r. You should find out what the policy is in your organization about the maximum size of personal e-mail databases.

How can you find out how large your mail database has become? Highlight your e-mail database icon or open your mail database. Then use File⇨Database⇨ Information. Figure 5-1 shows the dialog box that appears. Note that this irresponsible blot on society has an e-mail database that is more than 7.6 megabytes!

Figure 5-1:
Choose
File⇨
Database⇨
Information
to see how
large your
mail
database
has become.

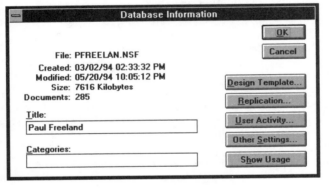

The most sensible course of action, of course, is to delete a memo as soon as you have read it if its message is something that you won't need ever again. If you don't delete memos right away, you will have to go back through one of the views every so often and delete old memos.

Of all the views to use when you choose the memos you want to lose on the scrap heap of history (say that five times fast!), the best is the All by Size view. The largest memos are listed first, so you should start there. In general, it is a good idea to delete any old, unused, dusty relics, because all memos add to the size of an e-mail database in several different ways. So deleting lots of little memos may be as beneficial as deleting one giant memo.

To delete a memo, do any of the following:

✔ *While the memo is visible on the screen, press Delete.* This marks the memo for deletion and opens the next memo in the view. It doesn't actually delete the memo; it only marks it for deletion. If you open the memo again, you will see word [Deleted] in the title bar.

✔ *While looking at a view, highlight the memo that you want to delete and press Delete.* This also marks the memo for deletion. You can in the view tell that it's marked for deletion because a little trash can appears in the leftmost column.

✔ *Highlight a memo and press the space bar or click in the far left column.* A check mark appears next to the highlighted memo, as in Figure 5-2. This is the best way to select a bunch of memos for eventual deletion. After you check all the memos that you want to delete, press Delete. A dialog box like the one in Figure 5-3 appears and asks which documents should be marked for deletion. Choose All Checked if you want to delete all the documents that have a check mark. Choose Only Current to mark only the highlighted message for deletion and leave the rest of the documents with just their check marks.

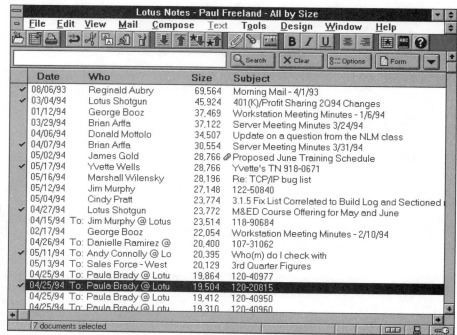

Figure 5-2: The check marks on the left indicate the selected documents.

Figure 5-3:
In this dialog
box, you tell
Notes which
memos are
going to get
axed.

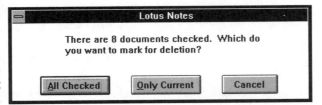

If there's a document that you changed your mind about and you don't want to delete it after all, now is the time to act. Highlight that document and press Delete — the trash can disappears. When any and all memos that you want to delete from your e-mail database have a trash can next to them in the left column, press F9. The dialog box in Figure 5-4 appears. Choose Yes to delete the documents *permanently and irreversibly* from your database. If you have any doubt about deleting documents, choose No; then, in the view, highlight each memo you don't want to delete by pressing Delete to remove the trash can in the left margin. After you have removed the trash can from the left column for documents you don't want to delete, press F9 again.

Figure 5-4:
This is your
last chance
to change
your mind
about
deleting
documents.

When you choose Yes, the documents are deleted. You already know this, but you do need to be aware that, after the documents are deleted, they are really gone. You can't get them back. There is no undelete, no undo, no disk utility, no act of Congress — nothing, nada — that will undelete a deleted document. Get the point?

If you do File➪Database➪Information after you have deleted some messages, you won't see any change in the size of your e-mail database. Notes holds unused white space for future use. However, if the white space is more than ten percent of the size of your e-mail database, eventually Notes will reclaim the space for other use — probably late at night while you're asleep.

Consider detaching attachments to memos and storing them on your hard disk and then deleting the attachment from the memo. Doing so reduces the size of the memo. Learn more about attachments in Chapter 6.

Another way to save server disk space is to create a local copy of your e-mail database on your hard disk and then copy and paste the older or larger memos to this local copy of your e-mail database. Then delete them from the database on the server.

A Place for Everything — Using Categories

Of course you are not going to delete all your messages; therefore, those that you keep ought to be arranged in some sort of system. Depending on the view you're using, all your memos may be arranged by date, size, or the person who sent them, but those arrangements may not be particularly useful for your day-to-day work.

When you're writing a memo, the two buttons you see on the screen are Address and Send. When you're reading a memo, you see two different buttons: Categorize and Reply. We cover the Reply button in Chapter 4, so here we'll put the Categorize button to use.

Just as you might use file folders for your important papers, you should use categories for the messages that you keep. Otherwise they'll all join an ever-growing list of messages that are arranged only by date.

If you are using the All by Category view to list your messages, you will notice that all new messages are listed as Not Categorized. That's because no messages have been categorized yet. To categorize a message, highlight it or open it and then click the Categorize button or choose Tools⇨Categorize. The Categorize dialog box, like the one in Figure 5-5, appears.

Figure 5-5:
The
Categorize
dialog box.
You should
create
categories
of your own.

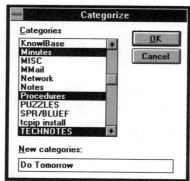

To categorize a message, you need to be in a view that uses categories. You have a choice of four: All by Categories, Drafts by Categories, Received by Category, and Sent by Category. If you try to categorize a message in another view, you'll get the error message that you see in Figure 5-6.

Figure 5-6:
This is what happens to people who try to categorize a message in an uncategorized view.

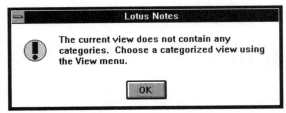

The first time you use the Categorize button, you won't see any categories listed in the dialog box. To join the thousands of satisfied category users, you have to create some of your own. Nothing's free in this world. Why doesn't Notes create some categories for you? The reason is simple — there is no way to know what categories are appropriate for you. Also, categories cease to exist when they are empty, so you can't have a category until you have a message to put in it.

To create a new category, make up a name and type it in the text box at the bottom of the dialog box. In Figure 5-5, the highlighted memo has four categories: Minutes, Procedures, TECHNOTES, and a newly created category, Do Tomorrow. This doesn't mean that four separate memos will be created — it just means that the one memo appears in four places.

If you want to assign a message to several new categories, type all the new names separated by commas. To take a message out of a category, click that highlighted category to deselect it. After you choose OK, the message is listed in all the highlighted categories and all the new categories. If you deselect all categories, the message will be listed as Not Categorized.

Meanwhile, back in the view, categories are listed in alphabetic order with the messages in them listed by date. (See Figure 5-7 for an example.) If you want to move the highlight to a different category, press the first letter in the category name.

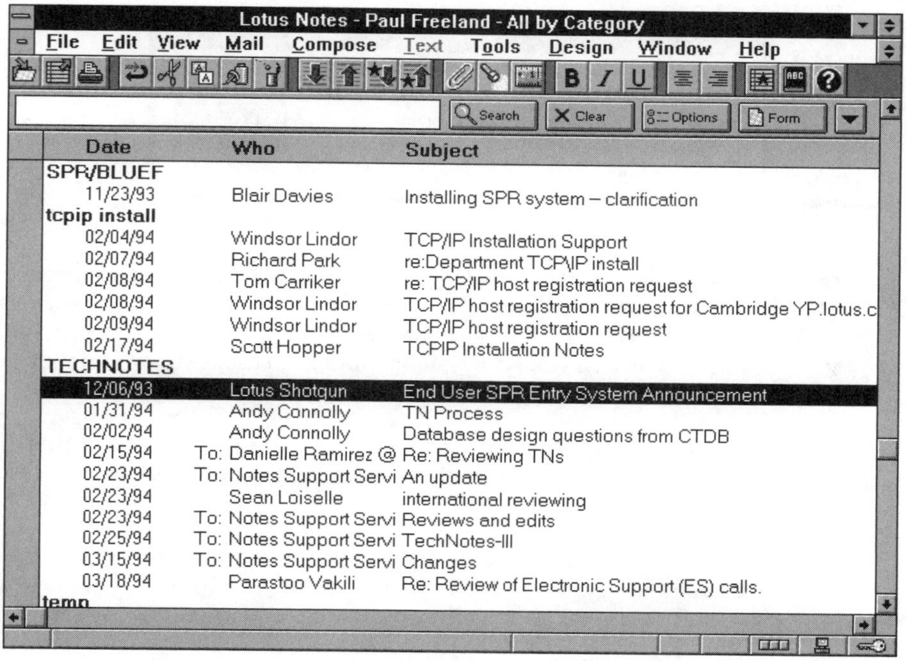

```
                    Lotus Notes - Paul Freeland - All by Category
   File   Edit   View   Mail   Compose   Text   Tools   Design   Window   Help
```

Date	Who	Subject
SPR/BLUEF		
11/23/93	Blair Davies	Installing SPR system – clarification
tcpip install		
02/04/94	Windsor Lindor	TCP/IP Installation Support
02/07/94	Richard Park	re:Department TCP\IP install
02/08/94	Tom Carriker	re: TCP/IP host registration request
02/08/94	Windsor Lindor	TCP/IP host registration request for Cambridge YP.lotus.c
02/09/94	Windsor Lindor	TCP/IP host registration request
02/17/94	Scott Hopper	TCPIP Installation Notes
TECHNOTES		
12/06/93	Lotus Shotgun	End User SPR Entry System Announcement
01/31/94	Andy Connolly	TN Process
02/02/94	Andy Connolly	Database design questions from CTDB
02/15/94	To: Danielle Ramirez @	Re: Reviewing TNs
02/23/94	To: Notes Support Servi	An update
02/23/94	Sean Loiselle	international reviewing
02/23/94	To: Notes Support Servi	Reviews and edits
02/25/94	To: Notes Support Servi	TechNotes-III
03/15/94	To: Notes Support Servi	Changes
03/18/94	Parastoo Vakili	Re: Review of Electronic Support (ES) calls.
temp		

Figure 5-7:
A category
for every
message
and every
message in
its category.

Oh Where, Oh Where?

Your e-mail database grows and grows as you add and categorize messages. Your system is almost foolproof, with everything right where you can find it. Then one day the boss calls and asks you to find some information that you received about one of the company's clients, Amalgamated Consolidated Enterprises. You look in all the likely categories and don't find anything on that client, but you know that you never delete messages about clients.

How will you ever find it?

That's right.

What's right?

Find!

Rest assured that if you didn't delete it, it's still there. You just need to check the contents of each message to find it. No, you don't need to *read* the contents of each message — Notes does that for you. At the view level, use Edit⇨Find. The dialog box featured in Figure 5-8 appears.

Figure 5-8:
Use
Edit⇨Find to
find a lost
memo.

Find		
Find: [ ]		**Find All**
☐ **Case Sensitive**	☐ **Backwards**	**Cancel**
☐ **Accent Sensitive**	○ **Search within View**	
☐ **Whole Word**	● **Search selected Document(s)**	

In the text box at the top of the dialog box, type the word or phrase that you want Notes to find. Use uppercase where appropriate and be sure that you also select Case Sensitive if you want the search to find matches with the same case. In other words, if you type "amalgamated" in the text box and then select Case Sensitive, the search will not find "Amalgamated."

Accent Sensitive allows you to find words containing symbols that are usually used in other languages. To find documents containing cañon but not canon, be sure to select Accent Sensitive.

Choose Whole Word if you want to find a group of letters only when they are surrounded by spaces. For instance, unless you choose Whole Word, searching for "soft" will yield documents containing "software" and "soften" as well as "soft."

You can use Backwards only if you have a document open. Choosing this tells Notes to search the document from the end to the beginning.

The last two items have radio buttons because you must choose one or the other. If you choose Search within View, Notes only looks at the characters that appear in the view and not at the contents of the documents. On the other hand, with Search selected Document(s), Notes reads through every document in the view for the text you are hoping to find, unless you have specifically selected some documents for it to search.

Got all that? Then you're ready to click Find All. If you have a lot of memos in your database, the search may take a few seconds. When it's done, all documents containing the text that you want will have check marks in the leftmost column.

What do you do with all these check-marked documents? That's up to you: you can read them one by one, delete them all, or print them. See the next section for instructions on printing.

In the little scenario that we created earlier, your boss wanted you to find any information about a client. If you found four memos containing the specified phrase (and those four are still check-marked), you can use Mail⇨Forward to send them to your boss all bundled into one memo. Pat yourself on the back and go have a cup of coffee.

By default, you see a Search button on the Full Text Search bar right below the SmartIcon palette in the view. You can't use it unless you have indexed your mail database. Don't index unless you don't need to use your computer for a while, because making an index can take a bit of time (hours if it's a big database). See Chapter 16 for information on creating an index. You can hide the Full Text Search bar until you are able to use it; choose View and deselect Show Search Bar.

Using Edit⇨Find on your e-mail database will result in a *limited search*. A *Full Text Search* requires an index. Indexing a database is very much like indexing a book; the database uses the index to know where every occurrence of a word is. In an indexed database, Edit⇨Find allows you more flexibility in your search. For instance, you can find words or phrases that only occur near other words or phrases. You can index the databases on your own computer, but the manager of a database on a server must create the index.

All the News That's Fit to Print

Notes is supposed to allow the world to enter the information age and eliminate the use of paper. The world hasn't reached that goal yet — we're still using enough paper to bury the Empire State Building every year. So, it stands to reason that sooner or later you will want to print something from Notes.

You can print a single document, such as the one that you happen to be looking at on your screen or the one currently highlighted in your view, or you can select a bunch of documents in a view and print them all.

 If you want to print the document that's visible on the screen, click the Print SmartIcon or choose File⇨Print and watch for the dialog box in Figure 5-9.

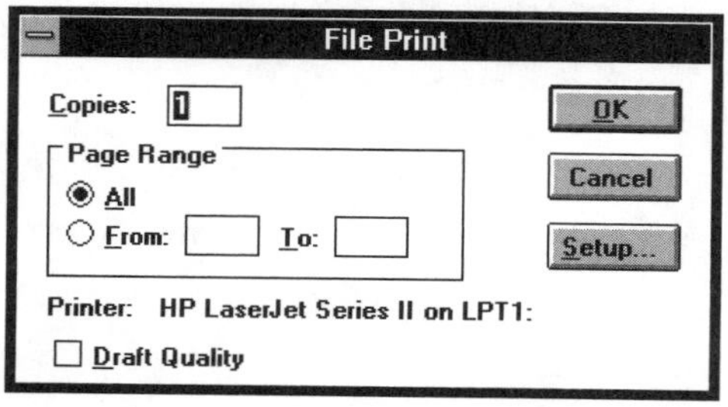

Figure 5-9:
The File
Print
dialog box.

File Print

Copies: [1]

Page Range
⦿ All
○ From: [   ]   To: [   ]

OK
Cancel
Setup...

Printer: HP LaserJet Series II on LPT1:
☐ Draft Quality

This dialog box doesn't require too many decisions of you — just whether you want to print all pages or only selected pages, and whether you want a quicker but plainer printout by choosing Draft Quality. Choose OK and head for the printer.

If your search for Amalgamated Consolidated Enterprises was successful (Notes found several documents and put check marks next to each one in the view), you may want to print them all for the boss. Choose File⇒Print or click the Print SmartIcon, and this time you see a different dialog box, like the one in Figure 5-10.

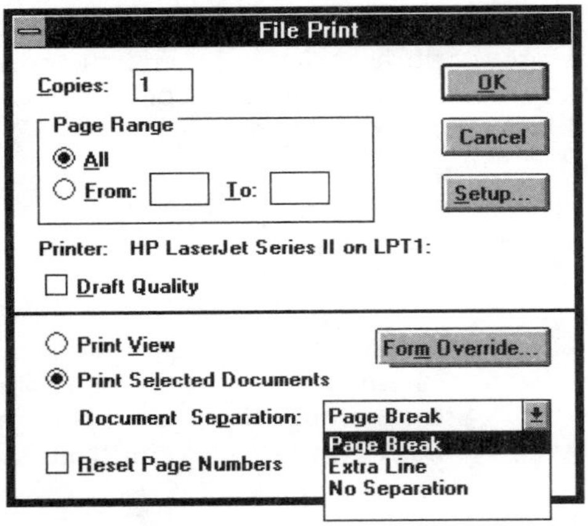

Figure 5-10:
A different
File Print
dialog box,
complete
with the
drop-down
box for
Document
Separation.

Again you have to decide whether you want all pages and whether you want draft quality printouts, but major decisions await you below the dividing line in the dialog box. You can elect to print the view by selecting — yes, you guessed it — Print View. Only the fields that show in the view will be printed.

If you want all the contents of the selected documents, choose Print Selected Documents. Now, how do you want the four documents separated? Here are your choices when you choose Document Separation:

- ✓ Page Break — Each new document will start a new page.

- ✓ Extra Line — Between each document Notes will print a line.

- ✓ No Separation — Each document follows the one before it, with no separation.

If you choose Page Break, you may also decide how to number the pages (assuming that you are numbering the pages; see Chapter 12 if you are). If you select the Reset Page Numbers check box, then every time a new document starts, its page number will be set to 1; otherwise, pages with new documents get the next page number in order.

Chapter 6
Power Memos

· ·

In This Chapter

▶ Including other files in memos

▶ Security measures — signing and encrypting

▶ Using custom forms

▶ Reading mail on a different computer

▶ Creating and using group names

· ·

*I*n an age of power ties and power lunches, it stands to reason there should be power memos. After a few meet-me-for-coffee-at-10:00 memos, you may find yourself saying, "There must be more to memo writing than this. I'm getting sick of coffee." For sure you can do plenty more with memos than just arranging meetings. With your dazzling memos, you can be the talk of the office, a legend among your coworkers.

Enclosed Please Find

One reason for writing a memo is to discuss some information that already exists. For instance, you might want to get some feedback on a report that you are writing in Microsoft Word. Do you have to retype the whole report into your Notes memo? No way! This is the nineties! Notes, that high-tech marvel, comes to the rescue. You have several options for getting around the chore of typing the whole report again.

I'm gonna paste you

If you've spent any time copying and pasting, you're familiar with the Clipboard. When you copy information, Notes holds it in the Clipboard so that you can paste it into other files, documents, or applications. The simplest way to get information from a separate program into Notes is by using the Clipboard.

You could be writing a memo about a section of a report written in Microsoft Word. Copy and paste that section from the report right into your memo and then add your own comments in and around the pasted text. Of course you can paste an entire file, unless it's too big to fit in the Clipboard. For more information about copying and pasting, see Chapter 15.

Attaching attachments

If you write a paper memo that explains a report that you have written, you might decide to paperclip the report itself to the memo so that the recipient can see what you're writing about. That's what an *attachment* is: a file attached to a memo. Figure 6-1 shows a file attachment. If you're a keen observer, you notice that the attachment is a symbol or icon in the memo, often showing the attachment's native program. You can't actually see its contents in the memo when you attach it.

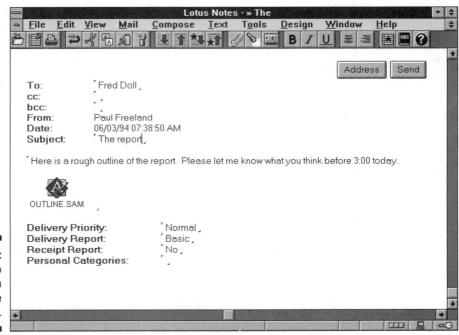

Figure 6-1:
A memo with an Ami Pro file attached.

Feel free to attach virtually any type of file to any Notes document — binary files, compressed files, executable files, graphics files, files created in other programs, and even entire Notes databases from your local disk. The only things you can't attach are databases stored on a server, Macintosh folders, or PC directories. Keep in mind that a large attachment makes a large memo and increases the size of your database. "But," you may ask, "what happens to the original file when I attach it to a Notes document?" Fret not; the attachment is only a *copy,* so the original file is unaffected.

You can only attach a file in a rich text field. This is no problem in the body field of a memo, because it is a rich text field. In other memo fields and in other databases you may run into trouble. How do you know if it's a rich text field? Put the cursor in the field and check the File menu. If Attach... is grayed out, then the field is not a rich text field.

 To attach a file to a memo, put the cursor where you want to place the attachment and select File⇨Attach... or click the file attachment SmartIcon. The Insert Attachment(s) dialog box that you see in Figure 6-2 appears. This is where you choose the file or files to attach. If the file that you want is on another drive, select the correct one in the Drives box. By the same token, if you need to use a different directory, designate the proper one in the Directories box.

You may want to narrow your search to only one type of file. For example, to find only WK4 files created in Lotus 1-2-3 for Windows, enter ***.wk4** in the text box under File Name. Only files with the WK4 extension will appear in the File Name list box.

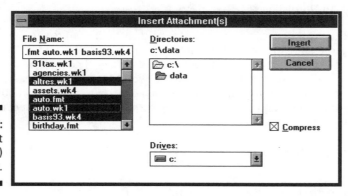

Figure 6-2:
The Insert
Attachment(s)
dialog box.

By default, the Compress box is checked. That squeezes the file as it's attached so it will be smaller. It may be compressed by as much as 80 percent. Now the memo itself takes up less disk space and will take less time to send. The only reason not to compress files is that the attachment process takes a little longer. Your recipients will not know whether you compressed it or not, because the attachment automatically decompresses when it gets detached. So don't worry about someone complaining about receiving a squashed file.

In the File Name box, highlight the proper file name and press Enter or click Insert. Can you attach more that one file? Yes. Can you attach them all at once? Yes, if they are all in the same directory. Highlight the first file and then hold down Ctrl while you select the other files that you want to attach. To select several consective files, highlight the first, Shift+click the last one, and all files in between are highlighted.

In Windows, as an alternative to the File menu, you can use File Manager to click and drag a file or group of files to the memo.

I got an attachment — now what?

Imagine getting a memo with an attachment — and nothing else. What is it? What program did it come from? What are you supposed to do with it? Sensible questions all, and ones that you ought to answer for the recipient when you send an attachment with your memo. Don't leave the person guessing. Also, be sure that the recipient has the program that the file was created in. If you send a WordPerfect for Windows file and the recipient doesn't have WordPerfect for Windows, the file is useless.

If you are using Release 3 of Notes and send an attachment to recipients who are using Release 2 of Notes, they will get an error message saying Document contains an unrecognized feature (possibly from another version of this product). If you know that some recipients do use Release 2, mention the error message in your memo and assure them that they will be able to use the attachment anyway, and that they should not be disgruntled, chagrined, or otherwise discouraged.

What should you do if you receive a memo with an attachment? You have a choice.

Chances are that you'll want to see what's in it. Double-click the attachment or select it and choose Edit⇨Attachment⇨Information. You'll see a dialog box like the one in Figure 6-3. In addition to giving you choices about what to do with attachments, this dialog box also tells you the filename and file size of the attachment and the last date and time that somebody saved it. The number in parentheses after the file size tells you how much the file has been compressed.

Figure 6-3:
Double-clicking an attachment calls this dialog box to the screen.

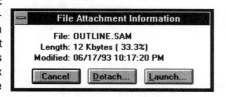

If you got into the dialog box by accident, choose Cancel. Otherwise, choose Detach to put a copy of the attached file on your hard disk or choose Launch to open the file and use it.

Remember that to launch the file you must have the appropriate application (the program that the file was created in). When you choose Launch, the application used to create the file starts and opens the file, accompanied, of course, by the short delays and screen changes that we all have come to love and to associate with the festive opening of a software program.

If you want to put a copy of the attached file on a local disk, choose Detach. You'll see the dialog box in Figure 6-4. Don't mention this to the folks at Lotus (we don't want to hurt their feelings), but it would be clearer if they had used the word *Save* rather than *Detach*, because it creates the impression that the file is actually detached when it isn't. A copy of the file is saved to a disk, but the attachment remains attached to the memo.

Use the File Name text box to give the attachment a different name from the one it had when it was attached, or, if you're happy with the filename of the attachment, leave it alone. Use the Drives list box to determine which drive gets the privilege of storing the detached file. Use the Directories list box to set the directory where the attachment will go. When all is in readiness, choose Detach. The file is decompressed and saved to the disk and directory that you chose.

If a message has several attachments, you may want to detach all of them at once. Click and drag across them all and then choose Edit⇨Attachment⇨Detach. Designate the directory and drive in which to save the files and choose OK.

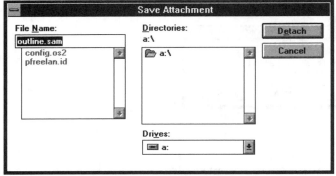

Figure 6-4:
The Save
Attachment
dialog box
appears
when you
choose
Detach.

After you have saved the attachment to your local disk, you ought to consider deleting the attachment so that the memo doesn't take up so much disk space. You may also want to delete an attachment if you attach the wrong file to a memo you're writing. You need to be in edit mode to delete an attachment. Then press Ctrl+E or choose Edit⇨Edit Document. Highlight the attachment and press Delete or Enter. Take a second to ponder the message box that appears in Figure 6-5.

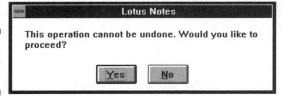

Figure 6-5:
Think before
you jump!

Undo usually allows you to reverse the most recent action. Deleting attachments is an exception — it is irreversible. If your boss sends you a memo with an attached file and you delete it before reading it, you'll have to ask sheepishly for another copy. Of course, if you don't save the document after you accidentally delete an attachment, you can retrieve it again (if it was previously saved) and the attachment will still be there.

Importing files

What if you want the recipients of your message to actually see the contents of a file when they open the memo? Attaching files is not good for that, because all they see is a symbol of the file. *Import* is the command to use because it brings the contents of a file into your message in readable form.

Choosing File⇨Import converts a file that was created in another program into a format that can be read in a Notes document. You may not be surprised that the files you import have to be some sort of data file, with real words or numbers or graphics that people can look at. You can't, for instance, import executable files (files ending with the extension EXE) because they are program files, not data files.

Place the cursor in the spot where you want the imported document to appear and then choose File⇨Import. The dialog box in Figure 6-6 appears.

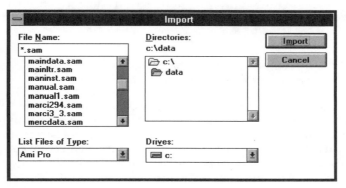

Figure 6-6: You can import an Ami Pro document right into your Notes memo.

Use the Drives and Directories boxes to specify where Notes can find your file. Then, in the List Files of Type list box, specify a file type (Ami Pro, for instance). Now only files with the extension SAM appear in the File Name list box. Highlight the file you want to import, select Import, and as quickly as your hard disk can spin, you will have the file in your Notes document.

Feeling a bit confused? Don't know whether to import or attach or use the clipboard? The list below will help clear up the confusion:

- ✔ Use the clipboard when you want to put only part of a file in a Notes document.

- ✔ Use the clipboard when you want the reader to see the contents of the file but you are unable to use Import. You'll know because the file type you need does not appear in the List Files of Type list box.

- ✔ Use the clipboard if the recipient does not have the software necessary to open an attached file.

- ✔ Use File⇨Import when you want the readers of your message to see the actual contents of the file in the message.

- ✔ Use File⇨Import when the readers don't need to have a copy of the file itself on their local disk.

✔ Use File⇨Import when you are not sure if the recipients have the software necessary to open the file you want them to see and you can't use the Clipboard, when you're using a DOS product, for instance, or when there is too much information to fit in the Clipboard.

✔ Use File⇨Attach... when the file can't be imported, such as for executable files.

✔ Use File⇨Attach... when you want the recipient to have an actual copy of the file to keep on a local disk.

Another couple of ways to include data from other files in your memos are DDE and OLÉ, or Subscribe on the Macintosh. We explain these in Chapter 15.

Can You Keep a Secret?

Sure enough, plenty of busybodies, bad guys, and spies are around. You may be sending your messages over less-than-secure media — if you use the modem, you'll be sending your message over phone lines, where a person up to no good might be able to read them. This is no problem for your meet-me-for-coffee messages, but if you send a message that includes sensitive corporate data or information that you don't want anyone else to read, you had better *encrypt* it.

Encrypting a message is easy. Notes does all the work to scramble the body of a message or a specified field in another database so that only the people you send it to can read it. From the time it leaves your mail database until the recipient opens it, the message is encrypted. So if some low-life snooper does intercept your message, the only things he or she will be able to read are the addresses and the subject line.

When you press Esc after finishing a memo, you see a dialog box that allows you four — count 'em — four choices. You can Save, Mail, Sign, and Encrypt the message. If you click the Send button, you see another dialog box, which allows you to Sign and Encrypt the message. We'll talk about signing in the next section. To encrypt the body of the message, you'll have to be sure to check the box next to Encrypt. That probably comes as no surprise unless your mind is wandering, but the main point is that selecting Encrypt is all you have to do. When you send the message, the encryption is done behind the scenes for you, and when the recipients open the message, they'll see the plain text just as you wrote it. Only intended recipients with the proper User IDs can read the encrypted part of the message. The only one who will see the actual encrypted version is the poor spy who intercepts the message in transit.

Think about it — who can read your e-mail if it's open and visible on your screen and you're away from your desk? If you guessed "anyone who walks near your computer," you may have a bright future in the spy business, because you're absolutely right. If you leave a highly sensitive message visible and go for a cup of coffee, forget about your bright future in the spy business. The message is decrypted while it is open. So when you leave your desk, close the message and your mail database and then press F5 to disable your access to Notes. After that, the next time you try to use Notes you'll have to enter your password — and so will anyone else. Get it? To learn how to set a password, check Chapter 13.

Sign Here

The company president calls you and complains about a memo you sent that demanded shorter working hours and a raise for the whole department. Try as you will, you can't remember sending a memo like that. Are you senile? Is your memory failing? Maybe, but it's also possible that someone sent a memo in your name. Anyone with the know-how can write a memo that has your name in the From: field, even though it isn't really from you.

The way to avoid being blamed for messages that aren't really from you is to *sign* them. You sign messages for the same reason that you sign checks or official documents: to show that they're really from you. You don't need to sign a meet-me-for-coffee memo, but when you send a message with crucial or sensitive information, you may want Notes to prove that the message really came from you.

We're talking computers here — obviously you can't scratch your signature on the screen at the bottom of a memo. You'd just end up with a scratched screen. You sign a message by choosing Sign from the dialog box that appears when you send a message.

The signature you use in Notes is even more difficult to forge than your own John Hancock; it's a numeric code added to the message when you send it and checked by the recipient's computer when they open the message. There is no actual signature on the memo, but this message appears at the bottom of the screen:

```
Signed by David Witter on 09-11-94 08:30:46, according to
                 Amalgamated Industries
```

Mail Is More Than Just Memos

Most of the time when use your e-mail database, you use the Compose menu to write a memo. In some organizations, however, someone behind the scenes may have created special forms for everyone to use. For instance, suppose that you need to order some more staples. Or suppose that you need to reserve the conference room for your Monday morning poker game. Possibly some genius has created a Staple Order Form or a Conference Room Reservation Form. There may be forms for special announcements, special requests, status reports, or information sheets.

These don't come with Notes; they only exist if someone where you work has specially created them, so don't be disappointed if you choose <u>M</u>ail⇨<u>C</u>ompose⇨ <u>C</u>ustom Forms and get the message

```
File does not exist: FORMS.NTF
```

On the other hand, choosing <u>M</u>ail⇨<u>C</u>ompose⇨<u>C</u>ustom Forms may open a menu of customized forms that you can use for special occasions. They may even be already addressed so you don't have to run around trying to find out who is in charge of ordering staples or reserving conference rooms or scheduling vacations.

Reading Your E-Mail on a Friend's Computer

You get to work and realize that you forgot the key to your office. Your computer is in the shop. Your section of the building is closed for cleaning. The network in your area is not working. These are only some of the many heart-breaking reasons why you may not be able to read your e-mail on your own computer. Is all lost? Do you have to wait until tomorrow when you remember your key? Of course not — if there were no hope, this section of the chapter would not exist.

May I see some identification, please?

The solution, in case you missed the title, is to read your mail on someone else's computer. The only thing you need is your User ID on a floppy disk. We've already said that the User ID is your key to using Notes, and without it you don't even exist as far as Notes is concerned.

You can use File Manager in Windows to copy your User ID to a floppy, or, if you are using a DOS-based computer, use the DOS copy command to copy your User ID to a floppy disk from the Notes directory. Then keep it in a safe, accessible place. The DOS command is

```
COPY C:\NOTES\YOURNAME.ID A:
```

Substitute the actual name of the User ID file for YOURNAME.ID.

You may be tempted to keep your User ID in a network directory. That's not a good idea, because anyone can get hold of it there and then use it to read your e-mail or send messages using your name. They can even sign them for you if they have your User ID.

Your User ID is probably on your computer's hard disk, your laptop (if you have one), and a floppy disk (for safe-keeping, in case your computer goes on the blink). Regardless of where you keep your User ID, you should protect it with a password so that if it falls into the wrong hands, it can't be used for dirty low-down tricks. Use Tools⇨User ID⇨Password⇨Set to associate a secret password with your User ID. When choosing a password, remember the following:

- ✔ Passwords are case sensitive.

- ✔ Your password ought to be at least 8 characters and can be up to 31 characters, in any combination of letters and numbers.

- ✔ It should not be easy for someone else to figure out. Don't use your birthdate, social security number, or name, for instance.

- ✔ It should be something that you won't forget.

- ✔ As you type it, only *X*s will appear on the screen, so no one can see what you typed.

So, to read your e-mail on a different computer, start Notes on the other computer, insert the floppy disk that has your User ID, and then choose Tools⇨User ID⇨Switch To. . . . You'll see the Choose User ID to Switch To dialog box, like the one in Figure 6-7. Choose the proper drive and directory, select the filename for your ID file, and then choose OK.

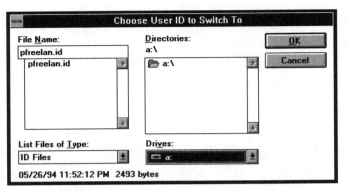

Figure 6-7:
This dialog
box lets you
use your
own User ID
at a different
computer.

Now the icon, please

You must add your own e-mail database to the desktop if you want to read your e-mail, so be sure you remember the name of your mail server. To add your icon to the Notes desktop of the computer you are using, use File⇨Open Database. Double-click your e-mail server in the Server list box, then highlight your e-mail database name in the list box below that. Choose Add Icon to place the icon for your e-mail database in the desktop.

After you have added your e-mail database icon, you can proceed as though you were using your own computer. When you're done, be sure you don't leave your User ID as the current one — others could use the computer and your User ID as though they were you. To log off Notes, do one of these:

- Have another user switch to his or her User ID using choose Tools⇨User ID⇨Switch To. . . . That logs someone else on and so logs you off.

- Exit from Notes. Whoever starts Notes the next time will have to either enter your password or switch to another User ID.

- Press F5. This logs you off Notes so that when you (or anyone else) try to use Notes, you'll have to enter your password again.

If this is the only time you plan to use this other computer to read your e-mail, you should remove your e-mail database icon when you're done. Highlight the icon and press Delete. When the prompt asks `Remove selected icon(s) from your workspace?`, answer by choosing Yes. After all, it's just common courtesy to clean up after yourself.

Don't forget to take your floppy disk with you when you leave.

Making a List, Checking It Twice

Tired of typing long addresses like Susan Brown @Apex @abcd.com @Wirenet? Has typing the same list of names for many memos gotten you down? Are you fatigued, disgruntled, looking for a way to ease your burden? Then you've come to the right place, friend, for this is your lucky day. No more need to carefully copy a complicated address only to find that you missed one little keystroke and the message never got delivered. No more hours in front of a hot computer repeatedly typing the same old list of names.

Join the group!

Groups to the rescue! Like satisfied Notes users everywhere, you too can just type Susan Brown and be confident that Notes will supply the rest of the stuff to send your message across the intervening gateways and network connections. Now, with a few keystrokes, you can send a memo to a long list of recipients. "But," you may ask, "how can this miracle be possible?"

The answer is to create your own groups. Open your Personal Name and Address Book (not the Company Name and Address Book) and choose Compose⇨Group. A blank form appears in which you enter the name of the group, the name of the owner of the group (that's you in this case, because it's your own database), an optional description of the group, and finally, of course, a list of the members of the group.

As long as you were careful to enter the names correctly in the list as you typed them, you can now simply address a memo to the group name and it will be sent to all members of the group.

If you also open the Company Name and Address Book, you can copy names out of it and paste them into your group. That way you can be sure that you pick the right person, use the correct name, and get the spelling right. You can also copy and paste the name in the From: field of a memo that someone sent to you.

In Figure 6-8 we have created a group for the sales force at the company headquarters.

In your group, you can even include other groups — up to six nested levels.

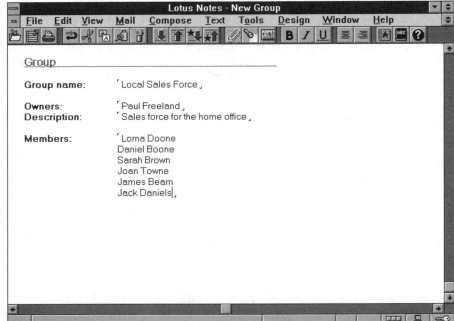

Figure 6-8:
You can use the group name instead of typing the whole list each time you send the members a memo.

Ooh, my aching wrists!

If you're getting carpal tunnel syndrome typing Susan Brown @Apex @abcd.com @Wirenet, consider creating a person document. Highlight your personal Name and Addresss Book and choose Compose⇨Person. In the First Name field, enter the first name of the person as you plan to type it. If you might use Sue, Suzy, and Susan at different times, enter all of them separated by commas. Enter the optional middle initial and the Last Name, in the Full Name field, add the last name, type the fill Notes address (in this case, it's Susan Brown @Apex @abcd.com @Wirenet). That's the last time you'll have to type that tangle of symbols. Now, when you want to send her a memo, just enter Susan Brown (or Sue Brown, or Suzy Brown) and Notes will supply all that other junk.

Part III
Entering the Brave New World of Notes Databases

The 5th Wave   By Rich Tennant

"THIS SECURITY PROGRAM WILL RESPOND TO THREE THINGS:
AN INCORRECT ACCESS CODE, AN INAPPROPRIATE FILE REQUEST,
OR SOMETIMES A CRAZY HUNCH THAT MAYBE YOU'RE JUST
ANOTHER SLIME-BALL WITH MISAPPROPRIATION OF SECURED
DATA ON HIS MIND."

In this part...

OK, you've read all your mail (and, we're sure, quickly responded to each and every message). A whole other world of Notes applications is just waiting for you. After all, e-mail is just e-mail — Notes databases are what really demonstrate the power and possibilities of Notes.

Chapters 7 through 10 show you how to do the things you need to do in Notes databases. We show you how to add database icons to your desktop, how to deal with the views you may encounter, and what you can do with a database's documents.

More good news: if you're comfortable using your e-mail, you won't have any trouble learning how to use Notes databases. The only real difference between your e-mail database and all the other databases that you encounter is their audience. Your mail database is yours and yours alone, but in this part we discuss the databases that whole groups of people use — groups that may be all around the world.

Chapter 7
Database Basics

In This Chapter

▶ Some basic terminology

▶ Using Notes servers

▶ Finding and opening Notes databases

▶ Getting some help

*R*eady to jump on the groupware bandwagon? The Notes databases that you'll be using will really demonstrate the true power of the program. In the simplest terms, a Notes database is nothing more than a collection of documents. But, in not-the-simplest terms, Notes databases represent a way for you to share information with other Notes users. These other Notes users may be your buddies around the corner, the purchasing department up the street, or your customers all over the world.

A Notes database might be a collection of purchase orders (yawn . . .), or it might be a discussion in which people predict future trends in your industry (wow!). One way or the other, you'll find that Notes databases allow you to interact with people in ways you've never thought of — and with people you've never thought of, either.

Words You'd Better Know by Now

Let's get some more jargon out of the way:

▶ A *database* is a collection of information. Most of the Notes databases you'll use aren't on your computer, but are instead on a Notes server somewhere.

▶ A *document* is what's in a Notes database. Notes documents are composed by people, at least one of whom looks just like you. You will read documents that have been composed by other people. Depending on the type of database you're using, you may also compose and edit your own documents.

- ✔ A *form* is a part of a database that you use to view, compose, and edit documents.

- ✔ A *view* is a summary of the documents in a database. A view displays documents in a database, but not necessarily all of them. Because a database can have many views, you might have one view that shows just your customers in California and another view that shows just your customers in Michigan.

- ✔ A *lemming* is a small Arctic rodent with a short tail and fur-covered feet. Unless you are a zoologist, you won't encounter too many of these animals when you use Notes.

Opening a Notes Database — Nothing Could Be Simpler

To open a Notes database, find the database's icon on your desktop and double-click it. Couldn't be simpler. If you're a little rusty on how to use the Notes desktop, refer to Chapter 2.

I Haven't Got the Icon: Finding a New Notes Database

Your boss calls you (or maybe sends you an e-mail), and tells you that you have to start using a new Notes database to respond to customer inquiries. Although you've heard other people in the department talking about this database, you've never used it before. What do you do?

You ask her where the database is. A Notes database could be on your computer, but if it were, it wouldn't be accessible by your co-workers. (That's not called groupware; that's called my-ware.) More often than not, the databases you need are on a Notes server somewhere, and you had better ask your boss for both the database's name *and* the server's name before you try to find it.

Notes databases are either on your hard disk or (more likely) on a Notes server. Databases aren't *yours*; they're *ours*.

Whenever you need to open a database that you haven't used before, you choose <u>F</u>ile⇨<u>O</u>pen Database. You'll get the dialog box displayed in Figure 7-1.

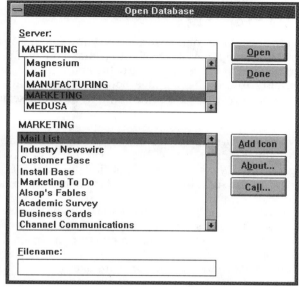

Figure 7-1:
Use the
Open
Database
dialog box
to find
a new
database.

The first item in the list will always say Local. That's where you look if you want a database that's on your own hard disk. On a Mac, it says Notes Data Folder instead of Local. After Local, you'll see one or many Notes server names, depending on how your administrator has set up Notes at your company.

To see a list of the databases that are on a server (or on your local hard disk), choose File⇨Open Database and then double-click the name of the server. You can also click the name of the server and then use the Open button.

If you don't see the name of the server you're after, use the top scroll bar to see the entire list. After you have selected a server (by double-clicking its name), you can also use the filename scroll bar to see all the database names.

If your company has more than one Notes server, your administrator collects them into *groups*. When you choose File⇨Open Database, you see the servers in the same group as your Home Server (the server that has your mail database on it). There may be other Notes servers at your company that are in different groups; their names won't appear in the File⇨Open Database dialog box. If you are trying to find a server that's not there, try typing the server's name and clicking Open. If that doesn't work, contact your administrator.

Servers, servers, everywhere

You're on a quest to find a Notes database and you know that it's on a server. But which server? Most companies have more than one. Your company might have one server that has databases belonging to the marketing department, and another for sales, and so on. You get the idea. Some companies have hundreds of Notes servers, some have a few, and some may only have one server (for now).

When you are trying to find a new Notes database, it's tough to know where to start looking. If your boss didn't tell you which server to use, be adventurous: just start looking on the various servers until you find the database in question. You just might come across some other Notes databases that interest you, too.

The server names you see in the File⇨Open Database dialog box are the whim of your administrator. The names might be very functional (and grown-up) like "Marketing," "Sales," and so on. Or the names might be more imaginative (and fun) like "Apples," "Oranges," and "Limes." When push comes to shove, though, you should ask someone which server you are supposed to use.

Digging into directories

Just as you have subdirectories on your hard disk to help you organize your files, your administrator may have set up subdirectories on the server to help organize the databases. As you poke around on your Notes servers, you will eventually encounter one of these subdirectories. If your server has subdirectories, they will appear at the bottom of the list of database titles, as the directory named "ADMIN" does in Figure 7-2.

To see a list of the databases in that subdirectory, double-click the directory's name. The item in the list that looks like two periods can be used to return to the parent directory on the server (as in Figure 7-3).

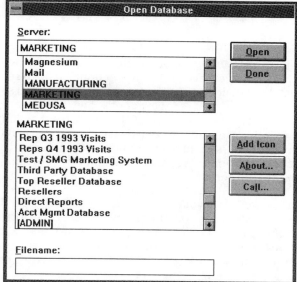

Figure 7-2:
Subdirectories always appear at the bottom of the list of databases [enclosed in square braces].

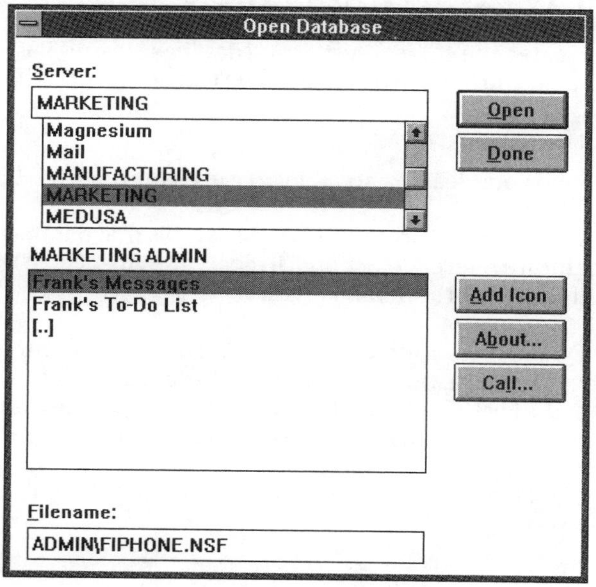

Figure 7-3:
The double dots in the list of database titles takes you back to the parent directory.

I hear you knocking — certification problems

As you may imagine, your administrator has all kinds of tricks to determine which people get to use which servers. If you ever double-click a server name in the File⇨Open Database dialog box and get an error message that says either `Your ID has not been certified to access the server` or `You are not authorized to use the server`, it probably means that your administrator has to do something to allow you to use that server. You can't do anything to fix this problem, so send your administrator an e-mail to ask for access. Make sure you cc your boss so that your administrator knows that you're not kidding around here.

To be able to use a server, both your User ID and the server's User ID have to have a common certificate. Giving out these certificates is one of the many jobs your (no doubt highly-paid and well-trained) administrator does all day. So if Notes ever tells you that you don't have the right certificate to use a particular server, contact your administrator, who should be able to fix the problem.

To open or to add, that is the question

When you have located the correct server and database in the File⇨Open Database dialog box, you have two choices. You can do one of the following:

- Open the database right away.
- Add the icon to your desktop so that you can easily open it later.

If you click Open, Notes does three things. First, it adds that database's icon to your desktop for future reference. Second, it closes the File⇨Open Database dialog box. Finally, it opens the database you chose.

When you click Open, Notes adds an icon for that database to your desktop. That way, the next time you want to use the database, you won't have to go searching for it in the File⇨Open Database dialog box. You'll be able to just double-click the database's icon right from your desktop.

When using the File⇨Open Database dialog box, you can just double-click a database's title to open it.

If you click <u>A</u>dd Icon, Notes adds that database's icon to your desktop but does not open the database. Instead, it leaves you in the <u>F</u>ile⇨<u>O</u>pen database dialog box so that you can add some other databases to your desktop. This button is useful if you need to collect a few databases and you want to get them all in the same trip to the <u>F</u>ile⇨<u>O</u>pen Database dialog box.

What Am I Going to See When I Open the Database?

That depends.

When you double-click a database's icon, you will usually see one of the views in the database, as you see in Figure 7-4. You will normally see the view that you were using the last time you were in that database, because Notes is pretty good about remembering what you were doing last time you were there.

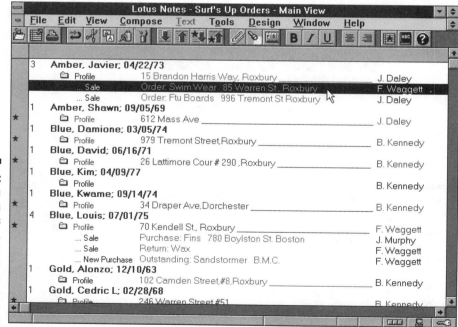

Figure 7-4: When you open a Notes database, you will usually see one of the database's views.

If you're opening a database for the first time ever, you'll see the database's Policy Document instead of one of the database's views. Read it very, very carefully (in other words, most people ignore it entirely) and then press Esc to close it and get to work in the database. The next section covers Policy Documents in greater detail.

Welcome to my database

When you open a database for the very first time, Notes presents you with what is officially known as the database's *Policy Document*. A Policy Document is nothing more than a little introduction to the database; it will usually tell you what the database is used for, who created it, whom to contact in case of an emergency, and so on. You can see a sample Policy Document in Figure 7-5. Close a Policy Document the same way you close any Notes document — by pressing Esc.

The person who creates the database writes the Policy Document, and some database designers are more conscientious than others. Some Policy Documents will be more instructive than others. In fact, a lazy database designer might not create one at all, so don't be surprised if you occasionally don't see any Policy Document when you open a new database.

Figure 7-5:
The first
time you
open a
database,
you will see
its Policy
Document.

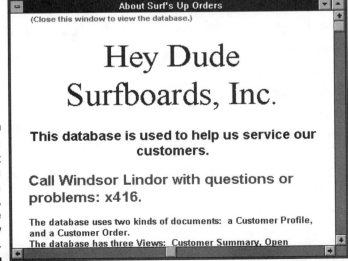

About Surf's Up Orders

(Close this window to view the database.)

Hey Dude
Surfboards, Inc.

This database is used to help us service our customers.

Call Windsor Lindor with questions or problems: x416.

The database uses two kinds of documents: a Customer Profile, and a Customer Order.
The database has three Views: Customer Summary, Open

Out of sight, out of mind: How do I find the Policy Document later?

Because the Policy Document has lots of useful information, it should be easy to find if you want to refer to it later. However, once you use a database for a couple of months, you probably forget all about the Policy Document, since you only saw it once on the first day you used the database.

If you need to reread a database's Policy Document, you can always choose Help⇨About *the database name,* and — bingo — there it is.

When You Need Help

Sometimes you get stuck and don't know where to turn. Or you try to do something but can't remember which button to press. Or maybe you are trying to figure out how to do something that you've never done before. Notes has a bunch of ways to give you help:

- ✔ Notes' built-in help
- ✔ The help screen that's in every database
- ✔ Your Notes manual
- ✔ This book
- ✔ Your friends
- ✔ The documentation databases
- ✔ The Koran/Talmud/Bible (admittedly, these books aren't exactly chock-full of Notes tips, but they may be a good source of comfort for your non-Notes related problems)

Using the Notes help system

There are two ways to use the Notes help system: you can ask for help about the particular activity you're stuck with or you can peruse the entire Notes help database.

Using context-sensitive help

Press F1 anytime, anywhere, for help about wherever you are stuck.

Good news: Like most software these days, context-sensitive help is always just a keystroke away in Notes. Whenever you get stuck, you can always press F1 (or the help key on a Mac), and Notes will do its best to show you a help screen that's related to whatever you are doing at the time. Like always, you press Esc to close the help document.

Bad news: The context-sensitive help in Notes may be less useful than the help that's available in other programs. That's because the help that comes with the program is only about how use the Notes program but not about how use any particular database. When you have a question about the particulars of an application you're using, you'll have to get to the database's own help screen. Getting database-specific help is covered later in this chapter.

Reading the help database

Got a few minutes before your next meeting? All the screens that you see when you press F1 come from a Notes database, called, appropriately enough, "Notes Help." You can rifle through the documents in the help database the way you read any other database. They have lots of information that you might never even think to ask about.

The icon for the help database is probably already on your desktop, so you can just double-click it and go to town. If the help database's icon isn't on your desktop, use the File⇨Open Database dialog box to find it. You can use the help database that's on any one of your Notes servers.

Using a database's help

Remember our earlier section about Policy Documents? Every database has another, similar document called the *Help Document*. Like the previously described Policy Document, this document is created by the person who designed the database and is intended to help you figure out how use the database. To see a database's Help Document, you have to open the database in question and then choose Help⇨Using Surf's Up Orders. (Of course, your database won't be named Surf's Up Orders, right?) Check out Figure 7-6 to see a sample Help Document.

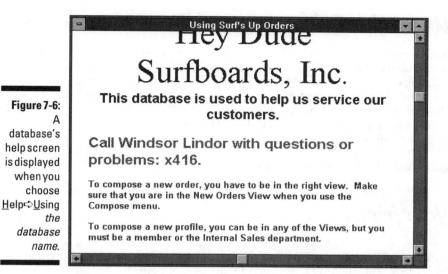

Figure 7-6:
A
database's
help screen
is displayed
when you
choose
Help⇨Using
the
database
name.

Some application developers (but not the good ones) are lazy, so don't be surprised if you occasionally see a dialog box that says No help is available for this database when you try to see a database's Help Document. If it happens to you, call up your administrator and complain loudly.

Notes documentation

Of course, we can't ignore the Notes manuals, which contain everything you ever wanted to know about Notes. Come to think of it, they probably contain *more* than you ever wanted to know about Notes. If you didn't get a set of Notes manuals when you got the program, give a call to your administrator.

When all else fails, read the manual.

Using this book

Well, if you got this far, you know how to use this book! The point is that we hope you'll use it as a reference all through your career with Notes, and our intent was to organize it so that you can quickly find the information you need. You should tell your friends, your co-workers, and your boss about this book. Shouldn't everyone in your company have a copy? *Lotus Notes For Dummies* makes a great gift, too. Maybe you should buy a couple of extra copies, just to be on the safe side.

This book is the best computer book you have ever read.

Your friends

Given the fact that Notes is *group*ware, it's safe to say that there's a whole group of people who use Notes at your company, and any one of them (or at least the friendly ones) can be a great resource for help and tips about using the program. Don't discount their importance! You can call them, e-mail them, or ask them in line in the cafeteria.

Lots of companies even have a special Notes database just so people can ask each other how to use Notes. If your company doesn't have one of these, maybe you should suggest it to your administrator. If you tell your administrator that one of these databases would keep you from calling the help desk as often, we'll bet that the database will appear within the hour!

Last, but not least, using the documentation databases

Another place you can look for help is the Notes documentation databases. You'll find them on just about any Notes server, in the DOC directory.

Don't overwhelm yourself — these documentation databases are *not* for the faint of heart. Unless you're destined to be a power-user of Notes, and unless you'll be doing stuff like creating your own databases and installing Notes servers, you probably don't have to bother with them.

Chapter 8

Once You're in the Database

In This Chapter

▶ Using views

▶ Navigation

▶ Categories

▶ Unread documents are usually red documents

*W*hen you double-click a database icon to open it, you see a *view*. (Check out Chapter 7 for more information about opening databases and using the icons and stuff like that.)

Every database has at least one view — most databases have several. A database view does three things:

✔ It *summarizes* the documents that are in the database.

✔ It *sorts* the documents in the database.

✔ It *selects* documents in the database.

I Was Just Thinking of View

Figure 8-1 shows a view in a database that's used to track travel requests. The view is showing (or *selecting*) only the travel requests that are still in process. This implies that there are other kinds of documents in this database that don't appear in this view — probably the ones that are *closed*. The view sorts the documents by the city to which the employee hopes to travel and then sorts by the name of the employee. A lot of the employees at this company seem to be going to New Jersey. (We've heard that New Jersey is lovely in the summertime.) The view also summarizes the documents — it's probably a safe bet that each of the documents has more fields than this particular view actually displays in its columns.

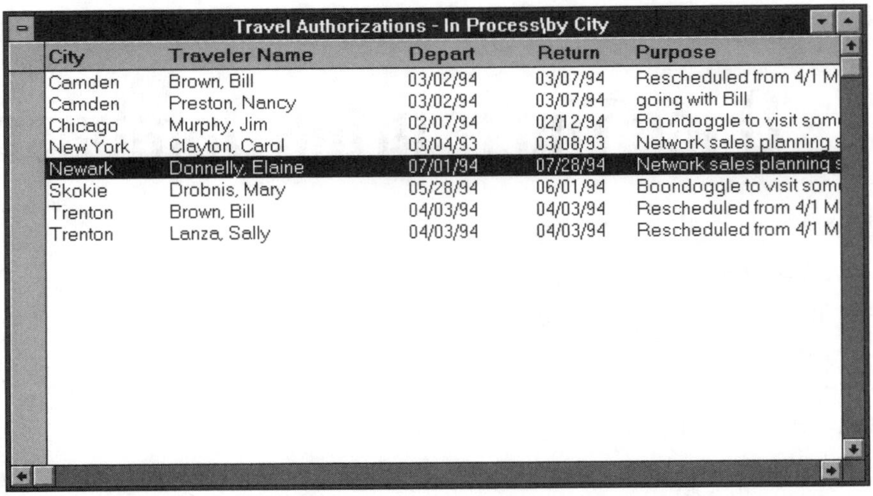

City	Traveler Name	Depart	Return	Purpose
Camden	Brown, Bill	03/02/94	03/07/94	Rescheduled from 4/1 M
Camden	Preston, Nancy	03/02/94	03/07/94	going with Bill
Chicago	Murphy, Jim	02/07/94	02/12/94	Boondoggle to visit som
New York	Clayton, Carol	03/04/93	03/08/93	Network sales planning s
Newark	Donnelly, Elaine	07/01/94	07/28/94	Network sales planning s
Skokie	Drobnis, Mary	05/28/94	06/01/94	Boondoggle to visit som
Trenton	Brown, Bill	04/03/94	04/03/94	Rescheduled from 4/1 M
Trenton	Lanza, Sally	04/03/94	04/03/94	Rescheduled from 4/1 M

Figure 8-1:
A view is the way Notes summarizes, sorts, and selects documents.

What's in a View, Anyway?

Each line in a view represents an individual document, and each column represents values from the fields in that particular document. (We discuss the nitty-gritty details of documents and fields in Chapter 9.)

Each column in a view displays the value of a particular field in the document. For example, back in Figure 8-1, the first column displays the name of each city that the employees want to visit, the second column has the employee names, the third column has the date they will leave, and so on.

Sometimes, Notes database designers decide to show off by putting little pictures in some of the columns, like the little paper clips you can see in the first column of Figure 8-2. There are five of these little pictures:

The Picture	What It's Supposed to Look Like
	A document or page
	A folder
	A person
	A couple of people
	A paper clip

Date	Who	Subject
★ 07/17/94	Jim Hines	Re: Out of the Office / Scott, Jim, Gary
★ 07/17/94	Jim Hines	Performance Reviews for 92 and 93 G&Os
⊘ 07/17/94	To: Mary Peterson	Budget YTD
07/17/94	Jim Hines	Out of the Office / Scott, Jim, Gary
Friends		
07/17/94	Pablo Martinez	His Anecdotes about his life in the boy scouts
07/17/94	David Driscoll	My direct n# @ PowerPlace: (508) 276-1134
Newsletter		
07/17/94	Jennifer Smith	Network was down, but not out
Orders		
01/16/93	Anthony Gatta	Item Ordered
Personal		
07/17/94	To: David Cole	Biography
Plans		
07/17/94	To: Jim Haney	Training Plan: Items for Discussion at 10:00
⊘ 07/17/94	Jamie Ostron	FY94 budget Data I sent to Mary
Training Plans		

Jim Hansen's Mail - All by Category

Figure 8-2:
An icon in your mail database means that the file has an attachment.

Database designers sometimes use these icons to provide a visual clue for you. If you see a view that has the little face icon, the documents are probably about people. If you see the folder icon, maybe the documents in that view have embedded Microsoft Word documents. You'll definitely see one of the icons in your mail database next to any message that has an attachment.

The paper clip icon usually signifies that the document in question has an attachment.

In many databases, Notes tracks which documents you have read and which ones you haven't. This distinction is particularly helpful in a discussion database, where you don't want to waste time on the documents that you've read before. You can *usually* tell a document is new it will be a different color than the rest of the documents. It will *always* have a little star next to it, in the left-most column of the view. Check out Figure 8-3.

Date	Topic
★ 05/18/94	**Intel MDM drivers (DAVID JONES, 1 response)**
★ 05/19/94	Intel 14.4. MDM file (Peter Manfield)
05/20/94	**Where to get Notes (Carl Farmly)**
07/31/94	**Spelling checking (Frank Bobson, 2 responses)**
08/19/94	Some answers to your questions (Barbara Dansly)
08/20/94	Ah ha (Frank Bobson)
08/20/94	**Notes Classified Ads (Phillip Melund, 6 responses)**
08/23/94	Great Application! (Rob Wallas)
★ 08/23/94	Give us a full path to the file (Jim Menlo)
★ 09/25/94	Request Granted (Phillip Melund)
★ 08/26/94	Answers #1 (Phillip Melund)
09/01/94	You can now edit ads (Phillip Melund)
09/11/94	How about remote? (Lee-Ann Smith)
★ 08/31/94	**Indented Categories (Lori Heading, 1 response)**
★ 09/10/94	It is supported in Notes (Pete Ziggs)
09/15/94	**Can Notes remember ALL of my categories in Mail? (Steve Harper, 4 r**
10/09/94	I don't think so (Ann Sturdivant, 1 response)

Support Conference - Main View

Figure 8-3:
Unread documents always have a star next to them and are usually a different color, too.

Usually, unread documents are red, but don't be surprised if in some databases they're some other color. The database designer decides what color they'll be.

Changing Views

If you are using one view in a database and want to switch to another, or even if you just want to see what views are available in the database, you use . . . you guessed it, you use the View menu. We can't tell you exactly what to choose from the View menu, because the names of the views vary from one database to the next. We can tell you that the view names in a particular database appear below the line in the View menu, as indicated in Figure 8-4. Don't worry; you'll find out what the stuff *above* the line does later in this chapter.

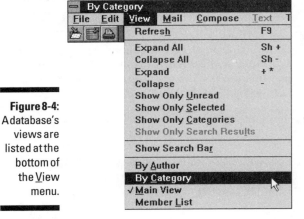

Figure 8-4:
A database's views are listed at the bottom of the View menu.

Categories

As we mentioned earlier, one of the things a view does is sort the documents; that is to say, it lists the documents in some particular order. A view in our travel database might list the documents sorted by the destination city, and another view might list the documents sorted by the employees' departments.

Some views, though, are not only sorted but also *categorized*.

In a *sorted* column, the documents are listed in order according to what they have in that field, and they each show what they have in that field, even if it's the same as the document above them. On the other hand, a *categorized* column still sorts the documents, but a particular field value is listed only once, followed by all the documents that have the same value in that field.

Confused? It's easier to see than it is to read. Take a look at Figure 8-5, in which you can see a database that tracks questions for a company's help desk. There are two calls for Ben Thompson: one about something called Api Development and the other about Tech Support. In this view, the documents for Ben have been categorized under his name. In a sorted view, his name would appear next to each call, but in this categorized view, his name is listed only once, with his calls below his name. In fact, his calls are categorized yet again (along with Fran Yee's calls) under the category Acme Corp. In a sorted view, every line would have the name of the company *and* the name of the person.

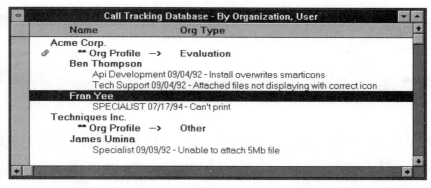

Figure 8-5:
A
categorized
column in a
view is just
a fancy way
to sort.

Expanding and Collapsing Categories

One of the reasons that views have categories is that it makes the view a little neater and easier to look at. You can also use the categories to further neaten up a view by *collapsing* and *expanding* them.

In Figure 8-6, the HR Policies category has been collapsed. That means that the detail for the HR documents is now hidden. The documents are still there, and they'll appear like magic when the category is expanded.

OK, how do you do it? Easy. Use the arrow keys to select the category in question and choose View⇨Collapse. Bye-bye, documents. Get them back again by choosing View⇨Expand.

You can also collapse and expand a category by double-clicking the category or by using the cursor keys to select the category and then pressing Enter.

Ready to go for broke? Consider View⇨Collapse all, and its cousin, View⇨Expand all. These two commands do just what they sound like they do; they collapse (or expand) all the categories at once.

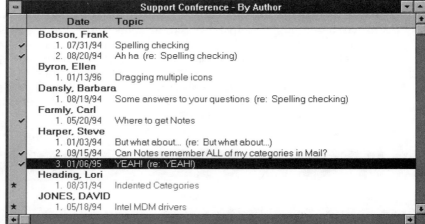

Figure 8-6:
A collapsed
category
does not
show the
documents
in that
category.

So, What Can You Do with the Documents in a View?

You can do four things with the documents in a view:

- ✔ Select them
- ✔ Read them
- ✔ Print them
- ✔ Delete them

Selecting documents

You can do all kinds of things to the documents in a database — you might need to print them, maybe delete them, or perhaps even forward them as e-mail messages. First things first, though — you gotta know how to *select* them.

How to select them one at a time

In a word-processing program, if you want to make a word bold, you first select the word somehow and then use the command to make the word bold. This same concept applies to selecting documents in a view. If there are a couple of documents in the view and you want to do something to them — print them, or delete them, or re-categorize them — you have to select them first.

By now, you've probably noticed that big black bar that's running across the screen whenever you have a view window open. It's called the *selection bar*, and it's used to highlight an individual document. Whatever document is in that black bar is hereby *selected*.

But what if I want more than one?

Funny you should ask. Let's say that you want to print five documents in a view. Sure, you'll use the selection bar to select them, but how do you tell Notes that you want more than one? The easiest way is to select the first document in question and then press the spacebar. When you do, you'll notice that the document gets checked off in the far-left column of the view, as you can see in Figure 8-7.

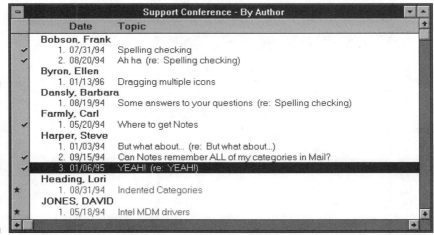

Figure 8-7:
When you select a document, Notes checks it off in the left-hand column.

If you need to select a few documents, select each one and press the spacebar. If the documents you want are one after the other, just hold Shift while you move the selection bar over the documents using the cursor keys. Notes checks them off.

Better yet, if you use a mouse, you can select a bunch of documents all at once by clicking and dragging over in the left column where you saw the check marks appear.

Finally, you can deselect a document that you mistakenly selected (oops!) by using any of the methods that you used to select it in the first place. In other words, if you have already checked off the document, then selecting it again unchecks it.

Reading documents

You don't have to read paragraph after endless paragraph to find out how to read a document! When a document in a view catches your eye, select it and then press Enter to read it. If you have a mouse, you can just double-click to open the document for reading. One way or the other, it's bye-bye view and hello document. The view disappears and the document appears. You can then press Esc to close the document and return to the view.

Printing from a view

When you have a view open (as opposed to a document) and you choose File⇨Print, you get the dialog box shown in Figure 8-8.

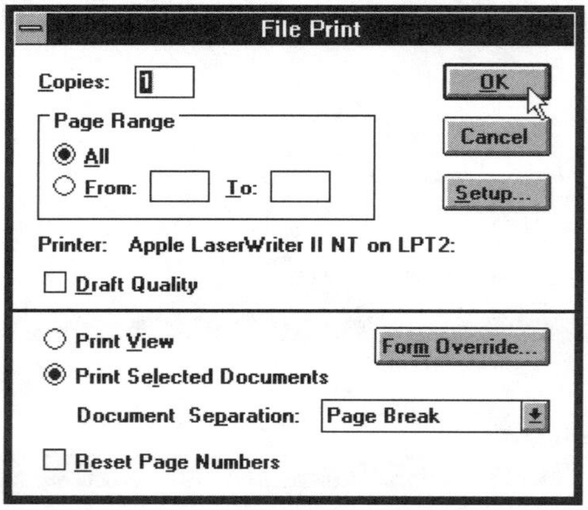

Figure 8-8:
Choose
File⇨Print
to print the
documents
in a view.

There's a lot of stuff in that dialog box — and you may have even *more* options, because what you see depends on the kind of printer you have.

The most important buttons in the dialog box are the ones under the line: Print View and Print Selected Documents. Use these buttons to specify whether you want to print the view as it appears on the screen or, instead, print the actual documents that you have selected.

Use the other buttons to determine what the headers and footers should look like, whether Notes should reset the page numbers for each document it prints, and so on. Check out Chapter 5 for more information about printing.

Deleting documents

To delete documents, select the document (or documents) that you want to get rid of and press Delete. When you do, the documents do not actually disappear, but each get marked with a little trash can, as you can see in Figure 8-9.

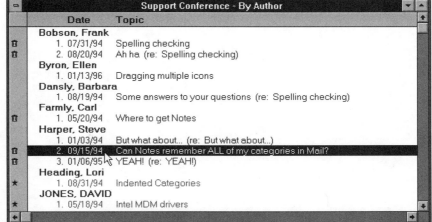

Figure 8-9:
A trash can means that the document is marked for deletion.

To actually get rid of the marked document, do one of the following:

✔ Press F9.

✔ Choose View➪Refresh.

✔ Close the database.

When you do one of those actions, Notes makes you confirm that you're going to delete some documents with a Yes/No dialog box. That's good, because you can choose No (if you goofed) and Notes won't delete the documents after all.

If you've marked a document to be deleted and you decide that you don't want to delete it after all, select the document again and press Delete again. The trash can disappears. You can stop worrying, because that document's not going anywhere.

Of course, you can't necessarily delete a document just because you know how to use the Delete key. In fact, in most databases you can only delete a document if you are the person who composed it in the first place. So that means that you can't delete anybody else's documents, and you don't have to worry about anyone else deleting your documents, either.

Chapter 9

Using Documents

In This Chapter

▶ Reading documents

▶ Figuring out what's in a document

▶ Composing and editing your own

▶ Printing and deleting

*T*he heart of any Notes database is the documents that are in it. (If you have ever used a program like dBASE or Lotus 1-2-3, documents are like records.) A document is all the information about a particular — well, a particular whatever. If the database you're using is a purchase tracking system, you may have one document for each customer and one document for each order they've placed. If we're talking about your e-mail database, each document is a message. If you're using a discussion database, each document made by each person is a separate comment on the topic at hand.

The Makings of a Document

When you open a document, you see all kinds of things: words, pictures, icons, even *objects*. If you're going to be a Notes big shot, you'd better know what they're all about. Here's what you'll see in your travels:

- ✔ Static text
- ✔ Fields
- ✔ Buttons
- ✔ Popups
- ✔ Doclinks
- ✔ Objects
- ✔ Icons

Static text

The kind soul who created the databases that you use no doubt included some *static text* on the forms. Static text can be the title of the form, field names, or maybe some instructions about how to use the form. It's called *static* because you can't change it, not because it gives you a shock when you rub your feet on the rug. Take a look at Figure 9-1 to see some examples of static text.

Fields

Fields are where the action in a document is. They contain the information that matters, and they contain the information that you *can* add and change when you're composing or editing a document.

Maybe you can put away your calculator: Editable vs. computed fields

In most cases, when you compose a new document, the fields are empty. You're expected to enter the new customer's name, address, and so on. However, you may occasionally encounter a *computed* field. A computed field is a field for which the program automatically calculates the contents.

For example, let's say you're using a database that tracks customer orders and it has three number fields: a Quantity field, a Price field, and a field named Extended Cost. This Extended Cost field would probably be a computed field. That means that when you enter a value in the Quantity field and then enter a value in the Price field, Notes automatically multiplies the two together and puts the answer into the Extended Cost field. Pretty neat, huh?

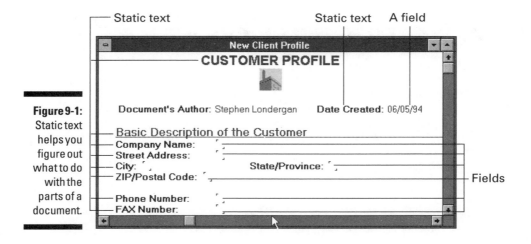

Figure 9-1: Static text helps you figure out what to do with the parts of a document.

Computed fields are often non-editable. In the preceding example, if your $4,000 computer is already automatically calculating the Extended Cost field, why would you want to change it?

It's really true — computers can't make mistakes. Only people can.

What default with de-field?

On the other hand, some other computed fields are, in fact, editable. The person who created your database may save you some time (and typing) by including default values in some fields.

Let's say that most of your customers are from California (hey, dude!), which explains why, every time you compose a new Customer Profile, the State field already says *California*. You can change the State field if you want — after all, not all your customers are from San Francisco — but think of all the typing you *don't* have to do for the people who are in California. Think of default values as being suggestions.

Lots of Notes databases have default values in fields that hold things like area codes, state names, and author names. That's good, because they can save you mucho time and typing.

All the myriad fields

Notes has several field types, and you'll be using each in your new career with Notes. The Notes field types are as follows:

- ✓ Text
- ✓ Rich text
- ✓ Date/time
- ✓ Keywords
- ✓ Numbers
- ✓ Names
- ✓ Sections

When you are entering a new document, it really is hard to know what the fields' data types are — in other words, it's hard to tell just by looking if a field is a date field, or a number field, or even a text field. Just use common sense; if the field's name is something like Quantity or Price, it's a safe bet that Notes expects you to enter a number. If the field is Address, you can bet it's a text field.

Text fields

A *text field* is just what it sounds like. A text field can contain any combination of characters: letters of the alphabet, digits, punctuation, you name it. A text field might contain a customer's name, your colleague's street address, or a description of property that's for sale.

A text field can contain a maximum of seven thousand characters. That's more than you'll ever need to put in a text field, so don't worry about it!

There's another (special) kind of text field called a *keyword* field. A keyword field is just a text field in which the possible entries have been "pre-ordained" by the person who created the database. That's good news, because it means that (a) you don't have to type a keyword field's contents, because you get to pick from a list of the possible values and (b) you don't have to worry that you'll make a mistake in the field. Figure 9-2 shows an example of each of the three kinds of keyword fields.

Keyword fields come in three flavors:

- ✔ Radio buttons
- ✔ Check boxes
- ✔ Standard

In a *radio button field,* you can only choose one of the options in the list, and you select the value you want by clicking it. You can also use the arrow keys to highlight the option you want and then press the spacebar to select it.

In a *check box field,* you can make more than one selection. Click as many of the values as you want — or highlight them with the arrow keys and use the spacebar to select them.

Last but not least, there's the *standard keyword field.* This field is sometimes hard to distinguish from a "regular" text field because the list of options doesn't appear until you move the cursor into the field and press Enter. Once you do, a dialog box appears from which you can make your selection(s).

If you are using a standard keyword field, you can also press the spacebar to "cycle" through the options that are available. (It's a little faster to use the spacebar than the dialog box.) You can also type the first letter of any of the options to choose it, which is even *faster.*

How do you tell the difference between a regular text field and a standard keyword field? In most cases, your database designer will have put some kind of hint on the screen (like the one we're sure you noticed in Figure 9-2). If there's no hint and you're not sure which one it is, get the cursor into the suspected field and press Enter. If a dialog box full of options appears, it's a keyword field. If a list of options *doesn't* appear, it's a regular text field.

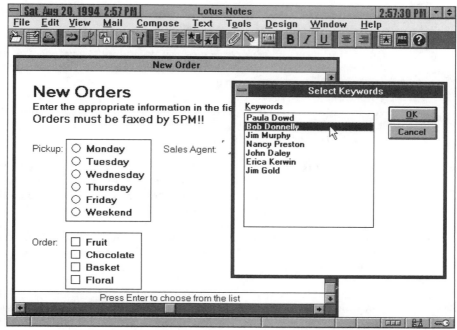

Figure 9-2:
Keyword
fields save
you time and
typing,
because you
just pick
from the list.

Rich text fields

A *rich text field* is what separates Notes from all the rest of the database programs in the world. Rich text fields are like regular text fields in that they often contain words and numbers. So why are they so "rich"? Well, in a rich text field, you can use the Format menu to make certain words bold, or italicized, or larger. Just try that in a program like dBASE or Paradox — or in a regular text field, for that matter.

So how do you tell the difference between a rich text field and a regular text field? You probably can't, or at least you can't by just looking at it. When you are composing a document, text fields don't *look* different from rich text fields. If you really want to tell the difference, you'll have to be adventurous. Type a few characters in the field you're trying to identify and then try to make them bold. If you can boldface the characters you just typed, it must be a rich text field. If Notes won't let you make them bold, or italicized, or anything fancy, the field you're in must be a plain text field.

What's even more intriguing (well, moderately intriguing, anyway) is that a rich text field can contain information that came from other programs. Using the powers of *Object Linking and Embedding*, you can use a rich text field to store the contents of a Lotus 1-2-3 spreadsheet or perhaps an MS-Word document right in the middle of your Notes document.

Habla OLÉ? For some strange reason, Object Linking and Embedding is called OLÉ, even by people who aren't Spanish.

One of the latest computer buzzwords is *compound document*. A compound document is a document that has several objects included in it. For example, you might put a document in a database to show your colleagues the progress you've made on a project you've been working on. In the body of the message, you include a Lotus 1-2-3 spreadsheet, a Freelance chart, and an audio recording of the new jingle. That's a compound document. Notes can include all that fancy stuff in one rich text field.

Rich text fields can also contain attachments. You use attachments to include a computer file in a Notes document. In the old days, you would do your expenses in Lotus 1-2-3, print the spreadsheet, and then give the piece of paper to your boss for approval. Now, because you're using Notes, you can actually *attach* the spreadsheet to an e-mail message and get it to your boss electronically. We're one step closer to the paperless office! (Do you think people will use floppy disks instead of napkins to wipe their mouths in the paperless office of the future?)

Any rich text field can hold many, many megabytes of information — you can send someone an e-mail and include in it a Lotus 1-2-3 worksheet, *and* a Microsoft Word document, *and* a copy of your AUTOEXEC.BAT file, *and* a scanned picture of your new baby.

Date fields

Date fields hold (you guessed it!) dates. You might be surprised to learn that you can also enter times in a date field; if you're using a database that tracks customer calls, you might need to enter a date (or time).

The format you use to enter a date or time depends on the way your computer was set up. If, upon trying to save a document, you get the error message `Unable to interpret time or date`, you probably used dashes when you should have you used slashes. Or maybe you used slashes when you should have used dashes!

Number fields

Number fields hold numbers, pure and simple. Don't try to enter any characters besides numbers in a number field — like slashes, dashes, letters, or smiley faces.

Name Fields

Name fields are special because they hold a person's name for some kind of security reason. For example, most Notes documents have a computed field that automatically records the name of the person who composed the document. This is done so people who read the document will know who wrote it, and so Notes itself will know who should be able to edit the document later. (In most databases, you can only edit a document if you composed it yourself.)

You will occasionally encounter editable name fields; a database might have a field where you must enter the name of the person who should receive your purchase requisition, for example. If you do find your cursor in a name field someday, just type the person's name as it would appear on their birth certificate: "Pat Freeland" or "Jimmy Carter."

Section fields

The last, and fanciest, field type is the *section*. Application designers use sections to set up parts of their forms so that only certain people can edit the fields in that part of the form. Imagine a database that's used to process travel requests — whenever you need to take a business trip, you fill out a document in the database detailing your destination, purpose, and so on. Once a day, your Vice President of Purchasing reviews the documents in the database to approve or deny that day's requests.

The part of the form that your Vice President of Purchasing uses to approve or deny the trip might be set up as a section. You, the person who wants to go somewhere, can edit the fields at the top of the form (the date field, destination, and so on), but only the boss can edit the part of the form that has the approval field. As much as you'd like, you can't approve your own trips! Unless, of course, you *are* the boss, in which case we hope you enjoy the trip, and don't forget to send us a postcard.

You'll know when a section begins on a form, because a big fat horizontal line will split the screen, as in Figure 9-3. You can double-click the line itself to see the names of the people who can edit the fields in that section.

Buttons

In addition to the static text, fields, and sections that you'll come across in Notes, you'll also come across *buttons*. Buttons help you do things quickly.

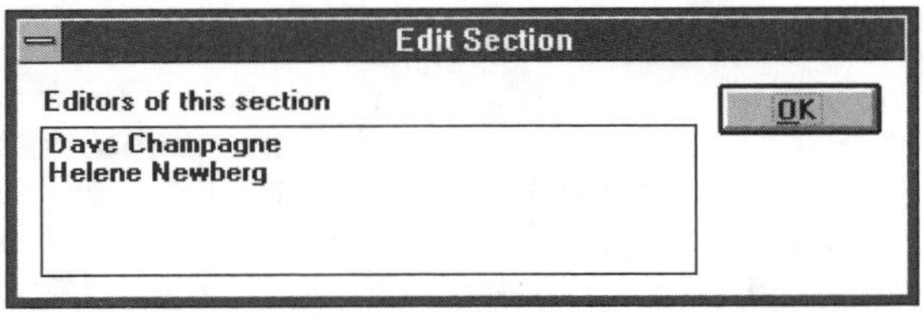

Figure 9-3:
Finding out
who can
edit the
fields in the
section.

Edit Section

Editors of this section

Dave Champagne
Helene Newberg

OK

For example, there's a button on the forms in your e-mail database that you can use to compose a reply, as shown in Figure 9-4. If you are reading an e-mail message and want to reply, you *could* choose Compose⇨Reply, but you could more easily just click the Reply button at the top of the form.

What happens when you click a button depends on what the database designer has programmed it to do.

Figure 9-4: A
button you'll
often use is
the Reply
button in
your e-mail
database.

re: That idea you had

Categorize   Reply

To: Stephen Londergan
cc:
From: Scott Sinnott
Date: 06/04/94 1:50:32 PM
Subject: re: That idea you had

Hey Steve-

That idea for the '94 benefit is great. I'll call Mary and see what she thinks. Do you want to serve those finger sandwiches we used last year?

Let me know!

- *Scott*

If you're not sure what's going to happen when you click a button, press Ctrl while you click a button to get a dialog box that shows you the exact formula or macro that the button will perform. Don't get worked up about the syntax of a formula and macro; just look at it and you'll probably get an idea of what's going to happen if you click it for real.

Popups

Pop-ups give you a reminder, a hint, or more information about a particular word or sentence. You know that a word has a popup associated with it because a little green box encloses the word(s), as you can see in Figure 9-5. Press and hold down the mouse button anywhere in the green box to see the popup. (In Chapter 12 you see how to create your own popups.)

Doclinks

A *doclink* is just a quick cross-reference to some other Notes database. Let's say you are using your company's Q&A database to ask someone in Human Resources about whether you get to take Veteran's Day as a holiday. Unbeknownst to you, though, someone else asked the very same question last week. Rather than answering your question (and duplicating the answer given last week), your HR rep might instead compose a response document and include in it a doclink to the original answer. You can see an example of a doclink in Figure 9-6.

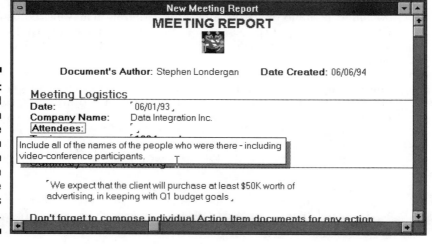

Figure 9-5:
Press and hold down the mouse button anywhere in the green box to see the contents of a popup.

Doclinks are represented by a small, gray icon that's supposed to look like a page. Click it once to see where it's going to take you; double-click a doclink to actually go and see the document being cross-referenced. When you've read the linked document, press Esc to return to the document that you were reading in the first place. Skip ahead and read Chapter 12 if you want to see how to create your own doclinks.

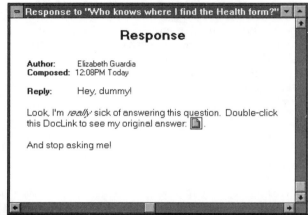

Figure 9-6:
Double-click a doclink to see the cross-referenced document.

Objects

Sometimes when you are reading a document you'll see that it contains an *embedded object* (which is usually just called an *object*). More specifically, the document contains data from some other program; it may be a Lotus 1-2-3 worksheet, a couple of pages from an MS-Word document, or a QuickTime movie. Figure 9-7 shows a document that has one of these fancy-shmancy embedded objects.

There are two cool things about objects. First, the object is displayed in its original format. In other words, if someone has included an Excel spreadsheet in an e-mail, it looks like an Excel spreadsheet. Second, through the wonders of Object Linking and Embedding (also known as OLÉ), when you double-click the object itself, Notes starts the program that created the original object and lets you review it (and maybe edit it) there. Awesome!

You must have the originating program installed on your computer to activate and edit an embedded object. In other words, you can't double-click a Lotus 1-2-3 spreadsheet to open it in Lotus 1-2-3 if you don't have that program installed on your computer.

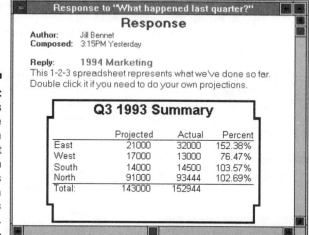

Figure 9-7:
An object is
just some
data from a
different
program
that is
included in
a Notes
document.

Icons

Another way to include data from other programs in Notes documents is to use an *attachment*. If you are reading a Notes document and stumble upon an icon like the one in Figure 9-8, you've found an attachment.

An attachment is a little bit like the embedded objects that we discussed earlier, in that it represents a file created in some other program. The difference is that with attachments, you mostly detach them (copy them onto your computer) to have for your very own. With embedded objects, you usually just read them, without keeping a copy for yourself.

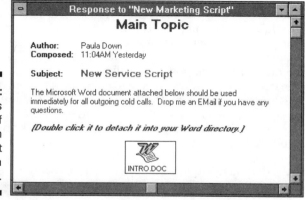

Figure 9-8:
You see this
icon if
there's an
attachment
in a
document.

To detach an attachment (that's a fancy way of saying "to copy the file onto your computer"), double-click the icon in the document. Notes presents you with the attachment dialog box, shown in Figure 9-9. Click Detach to make the file your own.

When you double-click an attachment icon, you can also choose to *Launch* the attachment. Launching an attachment means that Notes starts the program that created the attached file and then loads the attached file into it. Just like Embedded objects, you must have the originating program installed on your own computer to be able to launch an attachment.

If you want to save a copy of the file you just launched, you'll have to use the *other* program's File⇨Save command to get it onto your hard disk.

Figure 9-9:
Use this
dialog box to
put a copy
of the file
onto your
computer.

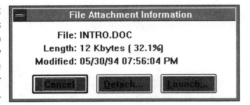

File Attachment Information

File: INTRO.DOC
Length: 12 Kbytes [32.1%]
Modified: 05/30/94 07:56:04 PM

Cancel   Detach...   Launch...

Come on in and Join the Party!

You've read a bunch of documents in a Notes database and now you want to jump into the fray and make your own contribution — you're going to add your own new document.

Before you start messing around with the Compose menu, Notes needs to know in which database you intend to compose a document. More often than not, you'll already have a database open when you decide to compose a new document, and when you go to the Compose menu Notes will present you with a list of the documents you can compose in that database. Sometimes, though, you might be in one database when you decide to compose a document in *some other* database. If that's the case, you had better open the "right" database before trying to compose a document, or else you'll end up composing a document in the wrong place. Ditto if you don't have any database open when you decide to compose a document.

You have to open the database in question before trying to compose a new document.

Using the Compose menu

When you choose Compose, Notes gives you a list of the documents that you can compose in that database, as shown in Figure 9-10.

It just stands to reason that the list will vary from one database to the next. In your mail database, you can compose a Memo, a Reply, or a Reply to All, but in a different database you can compose different kinds of documents. We can't give you examples of their names, because the names of the documents depend on the databases you use.

What if you can't contribute?

Just finding the Compose menu doesn't mean that you can actually compose documents in a given database. Some databases only allow you to read documents without allowing you to compose your own. (Don't take it personally.) If you're not sure whether you're allowed to compose documents, open the database in question and look in the very lower-right corner of your screen. If you see a little picture of eyeglasses (shown in Figure 9-11), you can forget about the Compose menu — you only have *Reader* access to that database and consequently can only read the documents that other people have composed.

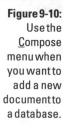

Figure 9-10:
Use the
Compose
menu when
you want to
add a new
document to
a database.

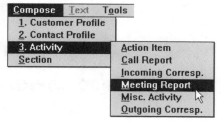

Figure 9-11:
If you see
eyeglasses,
you have
Reader
access only.

Call your administrator if you want to add documents to a database in which you only have Reader access.

Assuming you have a level of access to a database higher than Reader, Compose all you want. Refer to Chapter 10 to learn more about all the various database access levels.

Does it matter which document is open when I compose a new one?

The answer to the preceding question is a definite "maybe." Many databases have documents that rely on a feature called *Inheritance*. Inheritance is a way for Notes to pass information from a document that's already in the database to the new one you're about to compose.

Let's use our hackneyed customer service database example again. In it, you can compose two types of documents: a Customer Profile and a Customer Order. The database is already set up so that when you compose a new Customer Order, Notes automatically fills in the name of the customer and other information about them. Notes accomplishes this feat of wonder by inheriting the values from the address fields of the Profile document that you had selected when you composed your new Order. So, you better have the right Profile open (or highlighted in the view) before you try to compose a new order — if you have the wrong Profile open, you'll get the wrong address in your Order.

The moral of the story is that if you're using a database that relies on Inheritance to compute some fields when you make a new document, you must have the right document open when you compose your own.

Moving around in your new document

This is easy. As you are entering values in your new document, use Tab to move from one field to the next. You can also use the arrow keys and the mouse to get from one field to the next.

You can't use Tab to move from a rich text field to the next field. You have to use the arrow keys or the mouse instead.

Saving your new document

When you are done filling out the fields in your new document, press Esc. Notes presents you with the dialog box shown in Figure 9-12. Choose Yes to have your document saved in the database.

Figure 9-12:
This dialog
box appears
every time
you press
Esc after
composing
a new
document.

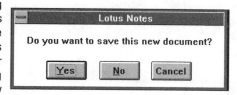

 You can also save a document by choosing File➪Save. It's a good idea to save the document often while you are composing it, in case you screw up, there's a power failure, or your computer falls out of the window. We don't recommend putting your computer on the windowsill, anyway.

Abandoning your new document

What's that? You say you blew it? You started composing a new document and now you've changed your mind and don't want to save it? Just press Esc and choose No from the Save dialog box. Presto — it's gone!

Play by the rules

The person who created the database may have set some rules for the fields; perhaps you can't leave certain fields empty, or perhaps there's a rule making sure that you enter one of the "approved" two-character state abbreviations. When you save a document, Notes validates what you have entered in the various fields against the rules (if any) that the database designer has set up. Don't be surprised if you get a dialog box (like Figure 9-13) when you try to save a document. It's telling you that you made a mistake and that it's not going to let you save the document until you fix the problem. No big deal: click OK, fix your mistake, and then try to save the document again.

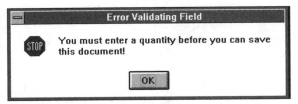

A Document Catches Your Eye

Besides reading documents and entering new ones, there are some other things you can do with a document. You can print a document, edit it, delete it, and mail it.

Print it . . .

To print the document that you have open, click the Print SmartIcon (or choose File➪Print). You'll get the File Print dialog box, as you see in Figure 9-14. You can decide if you want more than one copy, which pages you want to print, and whether to print in draft quality. Once you've made up your mind, click OK. And out it comes!

If you use a laser printer, don't bother with the draft quality check box, because it won't print any differently. If you don't use a laser printer, you can use the draft quality box to have Notes print your document a little more quickly.

Figure 9-14:
The File
Print dialog
box.

Edit it, maybe . . .

If you want to edit the document that you have open, choose View➪Edit Mode (or press Ctrl+E). Assuming that you are, in fact, allowed to edit the document, Notes puts you in *edit mode*, and you can change any of the field values. When you're done making your changes, save the document just like you were saving it for the first time. (Press Esc and then choose Yes.)

Of course, being able to read a document doesn't mean that you can also edit it. In fact, most databases only allow you to edit a document if you are the document's original author. (You wouldn't want somebody else to edit your document and take all the credit for your great ideas, would you?) If Notes won't let you edit a document, either (a) you aren't the person who composed the document in the first place or (b) Notes doesn't think you're the document's author, even though *you* know you are.

In scenario (b), you'll have to contact your administrator, who will fix the problem so that you can edit your documents or will explain to you why you aren't allowed to edit your own documents. Although there is occasionally a good reason to prevent you from editing a document once you have saved it, in most cases your administrator will fix the database so that you can edit your documents.

Delete it, maybe . . .

To delete the document you have open, press Delete. When you do, Notes closes the document you were reading, marks it to be deleted it, and then takes you to the next document in the database. Notes won't actually delete the document until you update the view or exit the database, so you do have a chance to change your mind and not delete the document if you decide you've made a mistake. Refer to Chapter 5 to learn more about deleting and undeleting documents.

In most databases, after you compose a document, you (and you alone) control its destiny. You're the only person who can edit it and/or delete it. (That's good — otherwise, your rivals would be deleting your documents all day long. And that would make you look bad.)

Hey Bob, did you see this?!

You can turn any Notes document you see into an e-mail message — anytime, anywhere. If you're reading a document and decide that you want to forward it to your friend, choose Mail⇨Forward. Notes takes the document and stuffs it into a new e-mail message that you can send to your buddies. You address it as you would any other message and send it off. Refer to Chapter 4 if you need help using Notes e-mail.

And When Things Get Sensitive

We didn't exactly save the best for last in this chapter. It's not that the following two features are bad, it's just that you'll hardly ever use them, if you ever use them at all. In fact, you should only read the rest of this chapter if you absolutely have to — only if you've been told that you'll be *encrypting* fields and/or hiding documents.

Using encryption to make fields private

Notes has a feature called *field encryption* that is an extremely secure way to make certain field values private. (And we mean private! If a field has been encrypted and you are not one of the people who is allowed to see the field's contents, there is *nothing* you can do to spy on the field.)

OK, so why would you ever use encryption? Let's say your company has a database that tracks information about employees. It has fields like Employee Name, Office Location, Phone Number, and Yearly Salary. The whole company uses the database as a kind of corporate directory; people use it to look up other employee names and phone numbers and stuff.

Would you want all of your colleagues to be able to see how much money you make? We want the whole company to use the database, but we want to make the salary field protected, so that only you, your boss, and the Human Resources department can see the salary field. (Your salary is surely so high that it'd breed all *kinds* of discontent and resentment if everybody could see it! We can't have that, now can we?)

When a field has been encrypted, you need a special *key* to see the field's contents. If you read a document in which there is an encrypted field and you have not been given the key to the field, you will *not* be able to see the contents of the field. Notes stores these keys in your User ID.

It's the database designer's job to create these keys and distribute them to the appropriate people. (In this example, that would be you, your boss, and the HR department.)

When composing a document that contains an encryptable field (or fields), it's not enough to just save the document the way we described earlier. Before you save it, you have to tell Notes that you want the encryptable field(s) to be encrypted — and you do this by choosing Edit⇨Security⇨Encryption keys. Look at Figure 9-15 to see what the resulting dialog box looks like.

You can tell that a field is potentially encryptable because the little brackets around the field are be red instead of black.

Select the key you want to use to encrypt the field and click Add. (Your User ID may have more than one key, in the unlikely event that you use encryption in two different databases.) *Now* you can save the document as we discussed earlier in this chapter. You can be sure that the only people who can see that salary field are the people to whom the database designer gave the key that you used.

This is pretty heavy stuff, isn't it? Remember, most people never even use this fancy security feature, so you can probably let it all go in one ear and out the other.

Your administrator or database designer will tell you if you have to worry about encryption keys. Unless you hear differently from either of them, don't worry about field encryption!

Figure 9-15:
Use the
Encryption
Keys dialog
box to
choose the
keys you
want Notes
to use for
the encrypt-
able fields.

Hiding a document altogether

Last but not least, when you compose a document, you can decide that you only want certain people to be able to read the document. By creating a *Read Access Control List* before you save a new document, you can be very specific and particular about the people who are able to see your document. People who use the database but are not listed in your document's Read Access Control List will never even know that the document is there!

Just before you save a document that you want to make private, choose Edit⇨Security⇨Read Access List to get the dialog box shown in Figure 9-16. Click the radio button that says "Only the following users" and then enter the names of the chosen few in the text box at the bottom of the dialog box, clicking Add after you type each name. When you're done entering the names of the people who can read your document, choose OK and then save the document the way you would normally.

If you add a Read Access Control List to a document, don't forget to include your name in the list; otherwise, even *you* won't be able to see the document!

Figure 9-16:
You can make sure that only a few users can read your document by using the Read Access Control List dialog box.

Read Access Control List

Document may be read by
○ All users
◉ Only the following users: Remove

Jim Gold
Mary Kuppens
Stephen Londergan

OK
Cancel

Add access list entry
People, Servers, Groups and Roles: Add
Marketing

Chapter 10
This Old Database

· ·

In This Chapter
▶ Creating a new database
▶ Using a database template
▶ Modifying forms and views to make them your own

· ·

You say you'd like to try your hand at creating a database? Maybe you're considering a career as a Notes database designer? Then this chapter's for you, because it's about how you begin to create a new Notes database.

If you're a Notes Express user, you probably *don't* need to read this chapter.

As you can probably guess, database design is pretty serious business, and there's no way we can do the whole topic justice in this one chapter. We hope, though, that we can at least get you started in your new career.

Why Reinvent the Wheel?

The good news is that most of the work has been already done for you — maybe. When you installed Notes on your computer in the first place, you got a whole pile of *database templates*.

A database template is a special kind of database that you can copy. The idea is that you make a copy of one of the templates and then modify the forms, fields, and views to suit your purposes. There's still some work to do in the customization of the database, but at least you don't have to create every single field, form, and view from scratch, right?

Lotus Notes comes with 17 database templates — and they're free! Refer to Appendix D for a detailed description of each. You may also find that the application designers at your company have created database templates, too.

For this chapter, we're going to create a new database based on the Things To Do template.

Creating the New File

To start off your new database, choose File➪New, and you'll get the dialog box displayed in Figure 10-1.

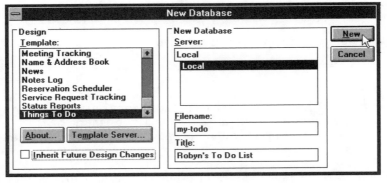

Figure 10-1:
Use
File➪New to
create a
new
database.

Use the Template list to see all the templates that are available. After you have highlighted any one of the template names, you can click About to see the database's Policy Document. You can check out Appendix D of this book for a more detailed description of each of the templates.

Use the Template Server button to tell Notes which of your company's servers you want to check for templates. If you know that one of the servers at your company has a special template on it, you can use this button to tell Notes that you want to see a list of the templates on that server.

Use the Server list to tell Notes where you want the new database to be created. At many companies, you cannot put a new database on the server without first getting special permission from your administrator. If you find yourself in that boat, you can always create the new database on your local hard disk.

Even if a bunch of people will (eventually) share the database you're creating, start out by creating it on your workstation. Wait until it's finished to put it on the server.

Tell Notes the database's Filename — follow the standard rules for filenames for your particular operating system. Use the Title field to tell Notes what you want to call the database.

The database's filename is what the database is called on the disk, but the title is how the database is known in Notes. Because the title appears in the database's icon on your workspace, you should be more imaginative and descriptive in the database's title than you can be with the database's filename.

When you finally click <u>N</u>ew, Notes grinds its gears for a minute or two and creates the new file. You know you're ready to continue when you see the database's Policy Document.

Customizing Your New Database

After you click <u>N</u>ew, the database is created, and you may not need to customize it all. In many cases you can just use it the way it is — no assembly required.

But because it's your database and you own it, you can make structural modifications to the new database — maybe add a new field to the forms, change some colors, or perhaps modify the way some of the views work.

As we mentioned earlier, this is pretty serious business, but at least we can whet your appetite!

Peeking Under the Hood: Changing the Forms and Fields

In our Things To Do database example, we copied the Task form that came with the template (see Figure 10-2). It already has fields for the project name, status, and priority, among others.

That's all well and good, but we decide (for the sake of argument) that we want to make a couple of modifications to the form:

  - ✔ Add a title
  - ✔ Change the background color
  - ✔ Add a field for names of people who are helping with the project
  - ✔ Change the options for the Priority field
  - ✔ Make the Status field bright, candy-apple red

To change the Task form, choose <u>D</u>esign⇨<u>F</u>orms and then click <u>E</u>dit. You'll see the form as you've never seen it before — now you're designing the form, not using it to compose or edit a document. Check out Figure 10-3.

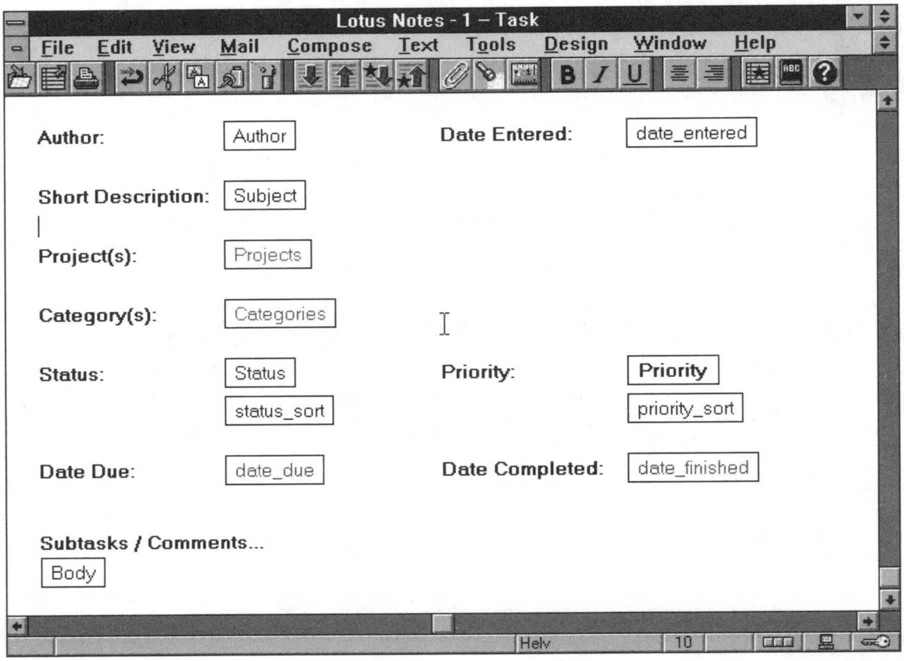

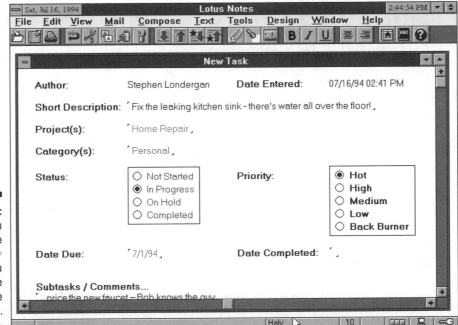

Figure 10-2:
The Tasks form from our new database.

Figure 10-3:
When you use Design➪ Forms, you can change the way the form works.

When designing a form, you include two things:

- ✔ Static text
- ✔ Fields

Use *static text* to give instructions, label the fields, and lead the user through the form. In Figure 10-3, the words *Short Description* and *Subtasks/Comments* are examples of static text. It's called *static* because it doesn't change as you use the form to compose and edit documents.

Fields, on the other hand, are the parts of the form in which you enter values when you compose documents. As you are designing the form, a block represents each field. For example, you can see in Figure 10-3 the little block with the word *Subject* in it — that represents the Subject field.

Adding some static text to the form

First, we want to add a title to the form. We position the cursor at the top of the form and type the title. In Figure 10-4 we also used the Text⇨Font and Text⇨Alignment options to beautify the title.

You format the Static text on a form the same way you format any text — by using the Text menu.

Changing a field's color

Next, we make the Status field a different color. This is actually pretty easy, because changing a field's color is the same as changing any word's color: highlight the field in question and then choose Text⇨Font. Use the Font dialog box to change its color, as in Figure 10-5.

1 – Task

To Do Item

Author: [Author] Date Entered: [date_entered]

Short Description: [Subject]

Project(s): [Projects]

Category(s): [Categories]

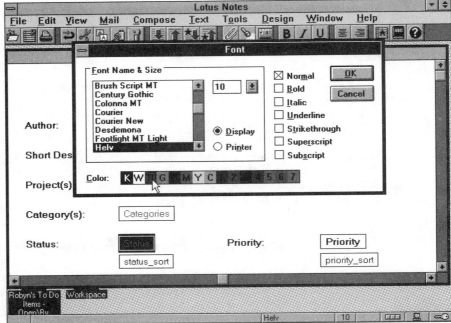

Figure 10-5:
To change a
field's color,
highlight the
field and
choose
Text⇨Font.

Adding options to a Keyword field

One of our departures from the template is to add a new classification to the
Priority field. The field is already on the form — we're just going to change it.
You just double-click the field in question to get the Field Definition dialog box.
If you don't use a mouse, you can highlight the field in question and press the
spacebar. The Field Definition dialog box is shown in Figure 10-6.

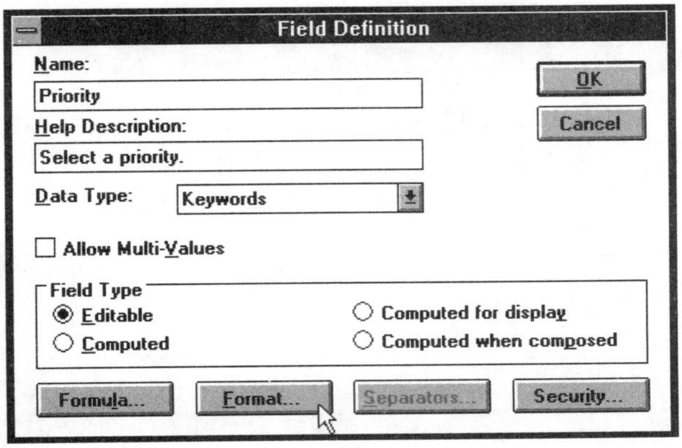

Figure 10-6:
The Field
Definition
dialog box.

There's a lot to see in the Field Definition dialog box: the name of the field, what kind of field it is, and so on. But if you're only interested in adding to the keyword list, choose Format to get the Design Keyword Format dialog box, shown in Figure 10-7.

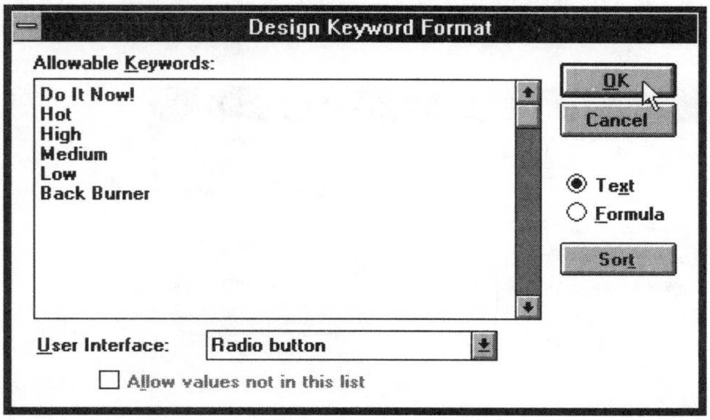

Figure 10-7: To change the keyword list, double-click the field and choose Format.

After you've added the new keyword, click OK twice to get back to the form. From now on, whenever you compose a document with this form, your new keyword will be on the keyword list, as you can see in Figure 10-8.

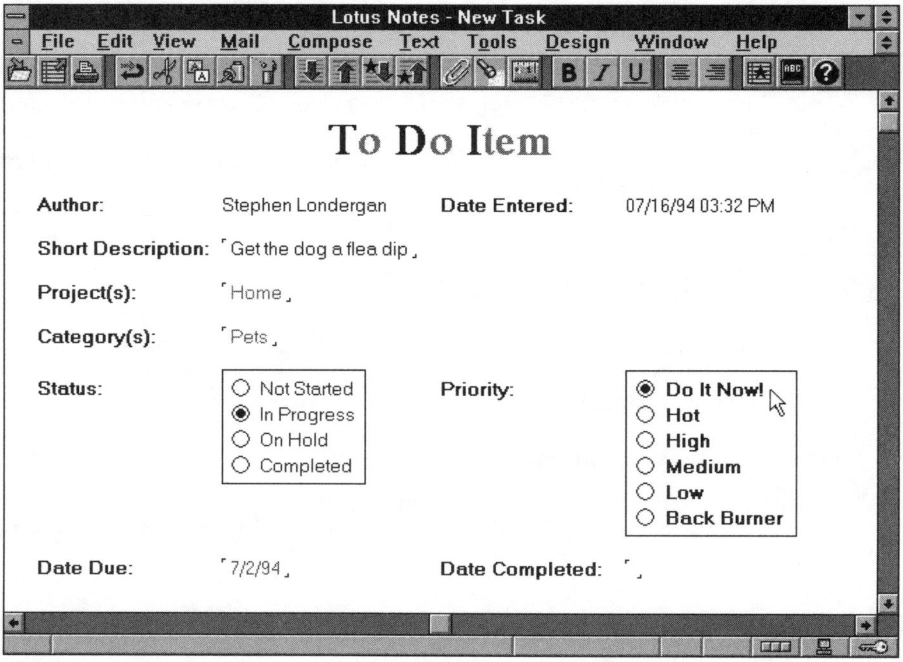

Figure 10-8: The new keyword list.

Changing the form color

To change the background color of the form, choose Design⊏>Form Attributes. As you can see in Figure 10-9, you can use the Color list at the bottom of the Design Form Attributes dialog box to change the background color. We chose G, which is a lovely pale yellow. Choose OK to save your change to the form's color.

```
┌──────────────────────────────────────────────────────────┐
│  ▄                  Design Form Attributes                 │
│  Name:  [1 -- Task | Task                    ]   ┌──OK──┐  │
│  Type:  [Document                         ]▼│    │Cancel│  │
│  ☒ Include in Compose Menu                                 │
│  ☒ Include in Query by Form           ┌─Read Access...─┐   │
│  ☒ Default database form              ┌Compose Access...┐  │
│  ☐ Automatically refresh fields                            │
│  ☐ Store form in documents            ┌─Encryption...─┐    │
│  ☐ Inherit default field values       ┌Object Activation...┐│
│  ☐ Mail documents when saving                              │
│  ☐ Updates become responses                                │
│  ☐ Prior versions become responses                         │
│  Color: A B C D E F G H I J K L M N O P Q R S T U          │
└──────────────────────────────────────────────────────────┘
```

Figure 10-9:
The Design Form Attributes dialog box.

Be careful about changing any of the other options on the Design Form Attributes dialog box — you could really screw up the way the database works.

On the subject of form background colors — be careful there, too. If you make the background color of your form dark blue, and the static text and fields on the form are all dark blue, too, you won't be able to see them! It's a good rule of thumb to make the background color one of the lighter selections and make the fields and static text a darker shade.

Adding a new field

The last modification we want to make to the form is to add a brand-new field so that we can record the names of people who will be helping with the projects we're tracking. When you want to add a new field to a form, do the following:

1. Position the cursor.

To position the cursor, you just click the place on the form where you want the new field to be. You might have to press Enter a couple of times to make room for the new field.

2. **Type some static text to describe the field.**

   Type the static text the same way you typed the title (if you added a new title) to your form.

3. **Insert the new field.**

   To add the new field, leave a little room after the static text (maybe two or three spaces or press Tab) and then choose Design⇨New Field. A dialog box appears, from which you should choose Create field to be used only within this Form. Trust us — you don't need to know what that means!

   The Field Definition dialog box expects you to give the field a Name, a Help Description, a Data Type, and a Format, as you see in Figure 10-10.

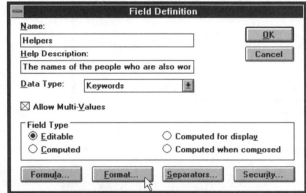

Figure 10-10: The Field Definition dialog box, for adding a new field to your form.

You also use this dialog box to determine if the field is Editable or Computed. If you want to add computed fields to your form, you'll need some help, because being able to write the formulas that calculate the contents of a computed field requires some pretty serious training. Ask your administrator for help if you need a fancy formula.

Although there are nine different field types available, you'll only use about three of them:

   ✔ Text
   ✔ Number
   ✔ Keywords

In our example, we chose Keywords for the field type, because there are only so many people who can work on the project, and we don't want to have to type their names every time we enter a new Task document in the database. To define the items for a Keyword list, choose Format.

In the dialog box shown in Figure 10-11, you enter the items for the keyword list and decide on the field's User Interface.

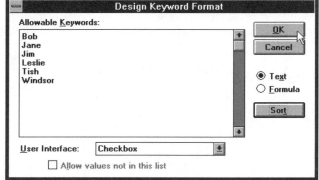

Figure 10-11:
The Design
Keyword
Format
dialog box is
where you
define a
field's
keywords.

Refer to Chapter 9 for more information about the three options available for the User Interface.

Use the Sort button if you want Notes to alphabetize the items you enter in the list and choose OK when you're done.

Saving the new and improved form

When you finish making your myriad changes to the form, press Esc and choose Yes — you want to save the form.

That's it! Now whenever you compose a document using the form, you'll get to see all your pretty colors and all your new (and changed) fields.

Views You Can Use

Our database came with a bunch of views — seven, to be exact. But if you've modified a form to include a new field, none of the views will include your new field. But that's OK, because creating a new view that has your new field, or even modifying an existing view to add your field, is an easy undertaking.

Creating a new view

The easiest way to create a new view for your database is to take one of the existing views, copy it, modify it, and save it.

To steal one of the existing views, choose Design⇨Views and watch for the dialog box shown in Figure 10-12.

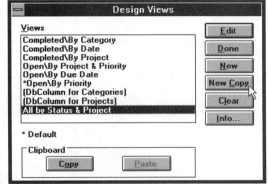

Figure 10-12:
The Design
Views
dialog box.

In our case, we select the All by Status & Project view and choose New Copy to make a new view based on that one.

After you choose New Copy, you'll get a behind-the-scenes look at the view, as you see in Figure 10-13. Each of the columns is shown across the top of the window; you can double-click any one of them (or use the spacebar) to see the formula that's being used to define the contents of the column.

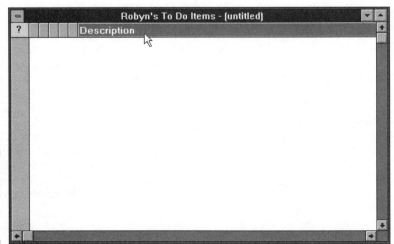

Figure 10-13:
Working on
a view
behind the
scenes.

Changing a column's definition

To change any one of the columns in the view, select the column in question by either double-clicking it or using arrow keys and the spacebar. After you have selected a column, you'll see the Design Column Definition dialog box, as you see in Figure 10-14.

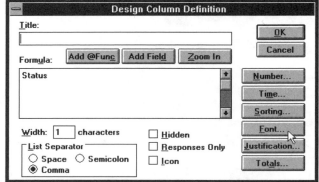

Figure 10-14:
The Design
Column
Definition
dialog box.

In our case, we're making a cosmetic change — we want to change the font and color of the Status column, which is the second from the left. To change the font, choose Font and then pick the appropriate typeface, size, and color.

Be careful about changing any of the options for a column other than the colors and fonts; unless you know how to write Notes formulas, you run the risk of trashing the column and/or the view. As always, contact your administrator if you need to do anything particularly fancy with the columns.

Changing a column's width

You can change a column's width in two ways. The first way is by using the Design Column Attributes dialog box, which has a Width field in which you can enter the exact width for the column. (Double-click the column in question to see the dialog box.)

The second way to change the column width is to use the mouse and avoid the dialog box. When you move the mouse pointer around in the tops of the columns in the view, you'll notice that occasionally the pointer changes to a vertical bar with two arrows on it (see Figure 10-15). If you want to change a column's width, you can roll the mouse pointer to the right edge of the column in question until the pointer becomes this little bar, click, and then drag to the new column width.

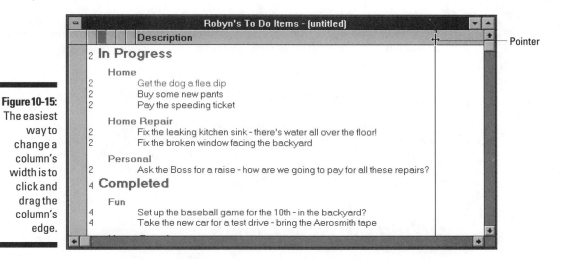

Pointer

Figure 10-15:
The easiest
way to
change a
column's
width is to
click and
drag the
column's
edge.

I'll have a new column, please

To insert a column, select the column that's to the immediate left of where you want to place the new column and choose Design⇨New Column. You'll see the same dialog box as in Figure 10-14, only it'll be empty. You have to supply the Title, Formula, Width, and so on.

The column's title can be any words you want; whatever you type in the Title field will appear at the top of the column.

The Formula field is the most important, because that's the field that determines what is displayed in this column for each of the documents that appears in the view. In our case, we're going to write the simplest formula possible: just the name of the field we want to display, as shown in Figure 10-16.

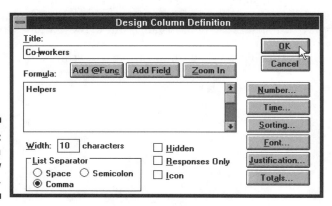

Figure 10-16:
Defining a
new
column.

The formulas that determine the contents of a column can get pretty complex. We're copping out again and recommending that you contact your administrator if you have to do anything particularly fancy in your view's columns.

Checking your progress

Notes does *not* re-display the contents of the view as you make each change to the view. Whenever you want to check your progress and have Notes display the view, press F9. You'll see all the columns as you have defined them so far. This is a good way to see if your formulas are correct, if you made the columns fat enough, and just generally to check up on yourself.

Giving the view a name

People have names, forms have names, and this view needs a name, too. To tell Notes what to call your progeny, choose Design⇨View Attributes and enter in the Name box the name that you want to appear in the View menu.

Saving it

When you're done with your modifications, press Esc and choose Yes to save the view. Just like the form in the previous section, your new view will now be an option in the View menu for the database.

The Icon

No database would be complete without a pretty picture. If you feel like you have a Picasso up your sleeve, choose Design⇨Icon. You can then use the mouse to draw the picture that will represent your database. You're out of luck if you don't have a mouse; designing an icon is one of the few times that you have to have a mouse in Notes. When you're done with your masterpiece, click OK. We describe other buttons in the Design Icon dialog box shown in Figure 10-17.

Turn Erase mode on

Turn Draw mode on

Draw only straight lines

Spray-fills a bigger area

Paint Roller-fills an area

Fills one pixel or erases one pixel, depending on whether you are drawing or erasing

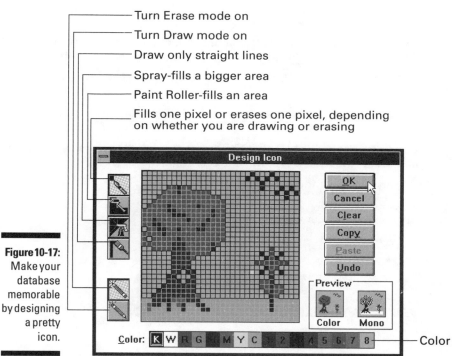

Figure 10-17: Make your database memorable by designing a pretty icon.

Color

You can use the Copy and Paste buttons to steal an icon from another database, or to paste in a picture from another program.

Deciding Who Can Do What in Your Database

If your ultimate goal is to put your database on a server so that others can use it, you'll need to define the Access Control List. To do that, choose File⇨Database⇨Access control.

If you're the only person who will be using your database and the database will be on your computer (and not on the server), you don't have to set the Access Control List.

As you can see in Figure 10-18, you have seven levels of access available:

- ✔ **Manager:** Can do anything to the database, including deleting the file entirely. Most important is the ability to change the Access Control List.
- ✔ **Designer:** Can do everything the Editor can do, plus change the forms and views.
- ✔ **Editor:** Can do everything the Author can do, plus edit the documents that other people created.
- ✔ **Author:** Can do everything the Reader can do, plus compose new documents and edit or delete his or her own documents.
- ✔ **Reader:** Can read the documents in the database.
- ✔ **Depositor:** Can only compose documents in the database. Cannot read other people's documents.
- ✔ **No Access:** Can't even open the database.

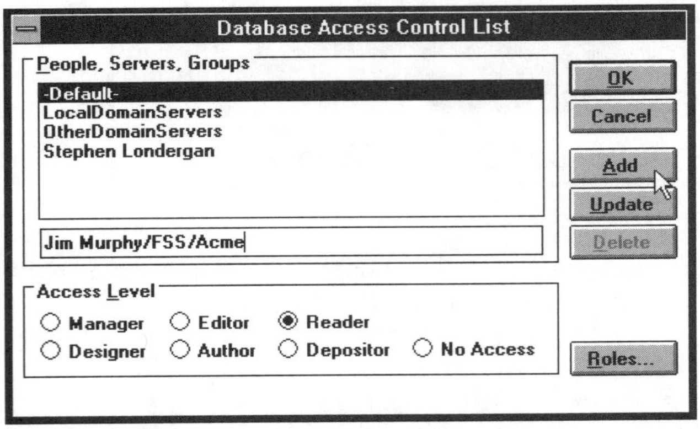

Figure 10-18:
The
Database
Access
Control List
dialog box.

> **Database Access Control List**
>
> People, Servers, Groups
> -Default-
> LocalDomainServers
> OtherDomainServers
> Stephen Londergan
>
> Jim Murphy/FSS/Acme
>
> Access Level
> ○ Manager ○ Editor ● Reader
> ○ Designer ○ Author ○ Depositor ○ No Access
>
> OK
> Cancel
> Add
> Update
> Delete
> Roles...

To set up the Access Control List, enter the names of the people who will be using the database, choose the level of access they'll get, and choose Add. When you finish adding names, choose OK.

Your administrator can help you define the Access Control List for the database, particularly if you want to use group names (instead of individual's names) in the list.

Put It on the Server

If you want other people to be able to use your new database, you need to put it on a Notes server. You can do that by using the File⇨Database⇨Copy command.

Make sure you have put your own name in the database's Access Control List before you copy the database onto the server. If you forget, you may not be able to even open the database at all, much less make any future design changes!

You may have to solicit special dispensation from your administrator to be able to copy your database to the server.

The 5th Wave — By Rich Tennant

"THAT'S RIGHT, DADDY WILL DOUBLE YOUR ALLOWANCE IF YOU CREATE MORE DATABASES FOR HIM."

Part IV
Fine-Tuning the Way Notes Works

The 5th Wave   By Rich Tennant

"IT'S AN INTEGRATED SOFTWARE PACKAGE DESIGNED TO HELP UNCLUTTER YOUR LIFE."

In this part...

The last time you bought a car, could you tell them that you wanted the driver's seat facing backwards, or that the car should be a station wagon with a convertible top and should have a refrigerator in the back seat? Right, it's impossible. After you got the car in your own garage, could you switch transmissions or add another seat? Of course not. When you get it home, it's pretty much the way it's going to be until you trade it in, except for the rust spots, of course.

Notes gives you much more flexibility than your car does. You can make lots of changes even after you install it on your hard disk. No, it doesn't come with a cigarette lighter or air conditioning, but it does allow you to change some of the functioning: the appearance of the documents you create, the way text looks on the screen and when you print it, and the way you use the program. And it never rusts, it never pollutes the air, and you don't have to have insurance to use it. Of course, you may find it a bit difficult to drive to church on Sunday morning but you can't have everything.

The chapters in this section tell you how to add a personal touch to your documents, make databases easier to use, modify the functioning of the program for your special needs, and make Notes behave when it works with other programs. There's even a chapter about taking Notes out on the road.

Chapter 11
Adding a Personal Touch

* *

In This Chapter

▶ Selecting text

▶ Changing the appearance of text

▶ Formatting text as you type it

▶ Creating non-keyboard characters

▶ Changing margins and setting tabs

▶ Setting pagination

▶ Setting alignment and spacing

▶ Using paragraph styles

* *

*W*hen you send a memo or create a document, don't you want people to notice it? Of course you do. Otherwise you wouldn't have written it. If one sentence or phrase is more important than other text, don't you think that you should change it in some way so that it will stand out? Naturally.

Of course, you could make the text pink and huge, and when you are finished with this chapter you will know how to do that, but perhaps something a bit more subtle will do the trick.

Changing Characters

All truly great documents are composed of individual characters. In fact, *all* documents are composed of individual characters, and this section deals with changing them, one at a time or in groups — like words, sentences, or paragraphs. You can change the appearance of a bunch of characters before you even type them, or you can pour out your thoughts onto the screen and then go back and make the changes when the typing is done.

You may want lots of fancy changes to your text, and that's fine with Notes as long as you play by the rule. There's only one rule — the text has to be in a rich text field. You'll know if a field is not a rich text field because trying to change the text won't work. It's as simple as that. *You* can't make the field a rich text field; the database designer did that in his laboratory in the dark of night. Unless you wield considerable influence or are good at bribery, if it's not a rich text field you'll have to forget trying to change the appearance of the text.

You're it!

Lots of times you'll type text and then decide to go back and change it. Before you can change its appearance, however, you have to let Notes know what it is you want to change. The act of selecting the text you want to change is called, well, *selecting*. What you can do to the text comes later; right now you can just work on selecting it.

There are three terms you had better get straight right now: *I-beam, cursor,* and *insertion point*. The I-beam is the vertical line that moves around the screen as you move the mouse. It's called an I-beam in Notes because it looks like an I-beam used in building construction — a vertical line with little horizontal tails at the top and bottom. If you don't have a mouse, don't bother looking for the I-beam; it's not there. The cursor and insertion point are the same thing. They are names for the thicker vertical line that winks at the place where something you type will appear. The I-beam is always visible on the screen, but if you use the mouse to scroll up or down, the cursor may scroll off the screen. Then, if you move the cursor by pressing any cursor movement key (like an arrow or PgUp or PgDn) or if you type something or press the spacebar, the screen display changes to show you where the insertion point is.

The easiest way to select text is to click and drag across it with the mouse. When text has a dark box around it, that means it's selected. The dark box is called *reverse video* (light letters on a dark background rather than vice versa). If you don't have a mouse, you can select text by moving the cursor to the beginning or the end of the text, holding down Shift, and pressing a directional arrow to move over the characters that you want to select. If you press the left- or right-arrow key, you will stretch the highlighter one character to the left or right. If you press the down- or up-arrow key, you will highlight to the same point in the next or previous line. The point is that pressing Shift while using any cursor movement key combinations moves the cursor and highlights text on the way.

Here are some additional tips about selecting:

- Use Ctrl along with Shift and the cursor movement keys to speed up the process of highlighting. Ctrl+left- or right-arrow moves the highlight one word at a time. Ctrl+down- or up-arrow moves the highlight to the beginning or end of the next or previous paragraph.

- Double-click a word to select it.

- If you want to select all the text in the current field, you're in luck — you can use the menu to choose Edit⇨Select All or just press Ctrl+A.

- If you want to select text in more than one field at a time while you are in edit mode, you're out of luck. Regardless of the method you choose to select text, you can only select text in one field at a time.

- If you want to select two separate chunks of text, you're out of luck. You can only select one bit of text at a time.

- If you survey all you selected and find you selected the wrong text, simply select other text to correct the mistake.

- If you selected some text but meant to select more, hold down Shift and then click at the farthest end of the additional text or use a cursor movement key combination. All text between the currently selected text and the place where you click is added to the selected text.

- To select a big chunk of text, put the cursor at the beginning of the text you want to select and then use the mouse and the scroll bars to scroll until you can see the other end of the text you want to select. Finally, Shift+click at the other end of the text. All the text in between is selected.

- To select all text from the cursor to the beginning of the field, use Shift+Ctrl+Home. To select all text from the cursor to the end of the field, use Shift+Ctrl+End.

During sales all selections will be final, all major credit cards accepted, please wait for the next available salesperson, have a nice day.

Now that I have your attention

After you've selected the text, the time has come to change it. You can remove it completely, change its appearance, change its location, move or copy it elsewhere, or check its spelling. Not only are there lots of things you can do with the text, there are often several ways to do each one. Table 11-1 includes information about what to do and how to do it. Don't get nervous about trying to learn all the different ways to do things; learn the method that works best for you and forget the rest.

Table 11-1		Text Changes		
Action	*Icon*	*PC Keyboard*	*Mac Keyboard*	*Menu commands*
Italic	*I*	Ctrl+I	⌘+I	Text⇨Font⇨Italic
Bold	B	Ctrl+B	⌘+B	Text⇨Font⇨Bold
Underline	U	Ctrl+U	⌘+U	Text⇨Font⇨Underline
Normal style	No icon	Ctrl+T	⌘+T	Text⇨Font⇨Normal
Delete		Delete	Delete	Edit⇨Clear
Cut to Clipboard		Ctrl+X	⌘+X	Edit⇨Cut
Copy to Clipboard		Ctrl+C	⌘+C	Edit⇨Copy
Paste		Ctrl+V	⌘+V	Edit⇨Paste
Append to Clipboard	No icon	Ctrl+Shift+Insert	None	No menu item
Change Font		None	⌘+K	Text⇨Font⇨Font Name and Size
You may also use the Status Bar to change this feature.				
Change Font Size		F2/Shift+F2	⌘+K	Text⇨Font⇨Font Name and Size
You may also use the Status Bar to change this feature.				
Change Font Color		None	None	Text⇨Font⇨Color
Align Paragraph		Ctrl+J	⌘+J	Text⇨Alignment⇨Left, Right, Center, Full, or None
Indent Paragraph		F7/F8	F7/F8	Text⇨Paragraph⇨Margins
Note: F7 for first line only, F8 for all lines.				
Outdent Paragraph	None	Shift+F7/F8	Shift+F7/F8	Text⇨Paragraph⇨Margins
Note: Shift+F7 for first line only, Shift+F8 for all lines.				
Strikethrough		Ctrl+K	⌘+K	Text⇨Font⇨Strikethrough
Superscript		Ctrl+K	⌘+K	Text⇨Font⇨Superscript
Subscript		Ctrl+K	⌘+K	Text⇨Font⇨Subscript

The Ctrl key on IBM-style keyboards and the Command key (⌘) on Macintosh keyboards work with other keys to streamline the things you do most often. Don't be careless about whacking at these key combinations for one simple reason — if you pick the wrong one, you may be really sorry. For instance, suppose you made lots of changes to some text and then accidentally used Ctrl+T. You would be removing all the formats you just applied!

If you do use a key combination by accident, remember one more useful one — Ctrl+Z. That will *undo* (reverse) whatever was the most recent action.

Some of the SmartIcons work as soon as you click them. The bold SmartIcon, for instance, makes selected text boldface without any more effort on your part. However, if you're a keen observer, you have noticed that the icon for strikethrough is the same as the icon for subscript, superscript, font, font size, and for font color. How can one icon do all that? It doesn't — it calls to the screen the Font dialog box (the same one you get when you choose Text⇨ Font), and the same one that we show in Figure 11-1. After the dialog box appears, you can choose all sorts of changes for the text you selected, including giving it a large font size and coloring the letters pink.

Some key combinations work the same way, too. For example, pressing Ctrl+K calls the Font dialog box to the screen so you can make selections to enhance your text.

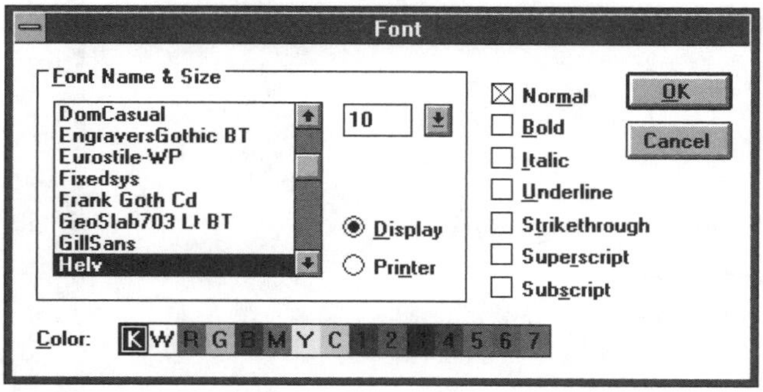

Figure 11-1:
The Font
dialog box.

Sometimes there are two different lists of fonts that programs use — one list is fonts available for screen display and the other list is fonts available on the printer. The Display/Printer option in the Font dialog box allows you to select from one of those two lists. Most of the time you'll find that the lists are very similar, or even identical.

One little quirk is worth keeping in mind. Imagine this situation — or try it if you're feeling adventurous. You want to italicize a phrase in the middle of a sentence. By accident, you don't select all of the phrase, so only half of it gets italicized. If you now select the whole phrase and click the italic SmartIcon, the italicized half of the phrase looses the italics while the other half becomes italicized. If you need to add an enhancement to more text, select only the part that you didn't already change, or change it all to Normal using Ctrl+K+Normal and then start again.

A really useful habit to get into is using the Status Bar. It is sometimes called the live Status Bar (which sounds as though it's going to bite you if you step on it) because you can use it to make changes. Next time you're hanging around a rich text field, stop by the Status Bar by clicking in the box containing the name of the current font. In Figure 11-2 you can see the results of clicking in the font box in the Status Bar. The variety of fonts you have available depends upon the software and the printer you are using.

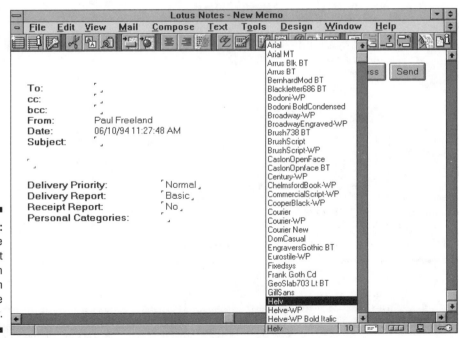

Figure 11-2:
These are
fonts that
you can
select from
the live
Status Bar.

Figure 11-3 shows the available font sizes at the Status Bar. The fonts and sizes available are the same whether you use the Status Bar, the font SmartIcon, or Text⇨Font. The Status Bar is just a faster way of making a selection. If you select a bunch of text and then look at the Status Bar, you will normally see the name of the font used in that selection. Sometimes you won't see the name of a font, though. Why not? If the text that you select uses two or more fonts, there won't be a font name or size in the Status Bar. But don't fret — even if the font name or size box is empty, you can still use the Status Bar to choose one font for the whole selection.

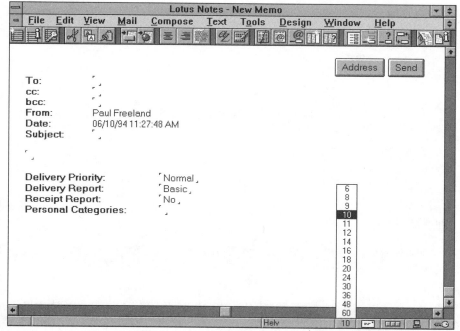

Figure 11-3:
These are the font sizes available at the Status Bar.

Putting it all together

Say you are writing a memo to the department inviting them to a party on Friday afternoon to celebrate a birthday. You type the text first and then you decide to realign and enhance some of the text. You quickly learn that just putting your cursor at the beginning of a word and clicking the bold SmartIcon is not enough. Selecting the text and then choosing bold is the only way to enhance text once you've typed it.

After you do get the hang of enhancing text, you can make your memos much more interesting and professional. Figure 11-4 shows an invitation/memo written by someone with no interest in improving memos, or who has a lot to learn about Notes. There's nothing wrong with the content — it's just not very interesting.

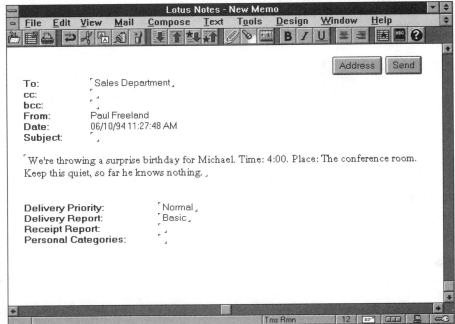

Figure 11-4: This is a dull (yawn) memo.

It only takes a few keystrokes to improve the appearance of the memo with a new font, some italicizing, and centered lines. The same memo with some polishing, shown in Figure 11-5, looks a lot more interesting. If it's a good idea to do a little interior decorating with your party memos, it's even more important to be sure that you plan just as carefully the documents that you create in the line of work. Choosing the right words is only half the battle: the other half is making a document look good.

A little enhancing goes a long way. If too many words in a document are boldface, they don't seem so important anymore. If you plaster lots of different fonts and different font colors and sizes around the page, your document may look more like a circus poster than an official announcement.

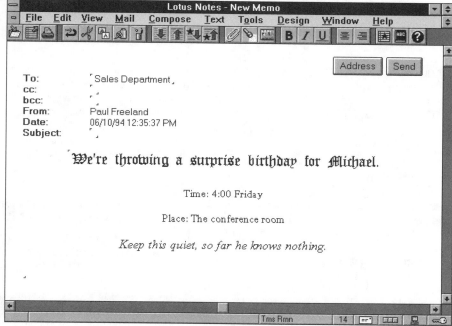

Figure 11-5:
It doesn't take much to turn a dull memo into an eye catcher.

Can it be bold if it doesn't exist?

Here are some of the more frequently asked questions about enhancing text:

Q: How can you select text you haven't even typed yet?

A: You can't.

Q: Can't you decide to enhance text before you type it?

A: Yes.

Q: What do you do to enhance text you haven't typed yet?

A: Funny you should ask. The keystrokes and icons described earlier work for text that you are about to type as well as for text you typed yesterday. If you are typing a sentence and know that the next few words should be bold, click the bold SmartIcon (or use one of the other techniques for bolding), type the text, and then click the bold SmartIcon to turn bold off and finish typing. If you want to center the next line you're about to type, click the center text SmartIcon and type. Voilà.

Q: Which fork should I use when eating prawns?

A: When unsure about which fork to use, eat with your fingers.

If your keyboard doesn't have six hundred keys

Our world is shrinking fast. Maybe that's why so many people are trying to lose weight. You can be in New York for lunch and France for dinner. Of course, all that eating won't do much for your weight in this shrinking world, but that's beside the point. "What is the point?" you may be wondering silently.

The point is that we are increasingly called upon to use words and symbols in our writing that come from other languages. You ignore the subtle differences between English and non-English alphabets at your peril. Don't say we didn't warn you. Ignoring the fact that an O and an Ø are two different letters can bring offense, squelch a deal, or even precipitate a food fight. Referring to the Bürgermeister (the mayor) as the Burgermeister (the man in charge of the burgers at a cookout?) is not the way to ingratiate yourself to His Eminency.

You may be wondering how you are going to type a U with an umlaut when there isn't a key on your keyboard for that letter. It's pretty hokey to type U". Notes, recognizing that you may need to type some non-English characters, has a large number of extra characters not available on your keyboard (or in stores). The LMBCS (Lotus Multi-Byte Character Set) includes all characters available in Notes.

The LMBCS includes characters available on the keyboard as well as non-keyboard characters — characters unique to foreign languages and such characters as © for copyright or £ for Pound Sterling. To see the list of LMBCS characters and the way to create them, check the documentation or use the help feature — use the index and choose Characters. The way to type one of these character sets depends upon whether you are using a Macintosh or IBM-style keyboard. If you are using Macintosh, you may not be able to see the character on the screen (depending on the font you're using). You'll have to print to see the character.

Mac users should use Keycaps for information on how to create non-keyboard characters.

As an example of the way to create a character, here are the keystroke sequences used to type the Ø. On a Macintosh keyboard, press Option+Shift+O. On the IBM-style keyboard, press Alt+F1, then O, and then /. If you want a particular character, look in help or in the documentation for its Alt+F1 sequence (also called the *compose sequence*). If you can't find it there, you need to use the LMBCS character code. Press Alt+F1 twice, then 0, then – (a dash), and then the LMBCS number for the character (like 157 for the Ø). If the LMBCS code has only two digits, 33 for instance, use 033. (This is all sort of like dialing a long distance number with your credit card, isn't it?)

After you've created the character, copy and paste it. When you need it again, it's faster than using the LMBCS or compose key sequences.

Paragraphs with Character

Armed with the skills necessary to change bits of text here and there, we turn our attention to paragraphs. After all, there are times when you want an entire paragraph to have a unique appearance or characteristic so it stands out from the others around it or behaves the way that you want it to behave.

Here are a few things you ought to keep in mind as you work with paragraphs:

✔ You can select a whole paragraph and change the appearance of all its characters in the same way that you changed individual characters, words, or groups of words in the previous section.

✔ Choosing Text⇨Paragraph opens the dialog box that you use to make changes to the format of the paragraph (other than the appearance of the text). Figure 11-6 shows the Text Paragraph dialog box.

✔ You can only apply paragraph formats to text in rich text fields.

✔ You can change the characteristics of one paragraph at a time simply by putting the cursor in that paragraph.

✔ If you need to change several paragraphs, you must select them all.

✔ If you need to change all the paragraphs in the field, use Edit⇨Select All.

✔ If you change one paragraph, only that paragraph will contain the changes. For example, if you set tabs in one paragraph, that is the only paragraph that will have those unique tabs.

✔ If you haven't typed anything yet, use the Text⇨Paragraph menu to set the characteristics you want all the paragraphs to have, and then start typing. All the paragraphs will have those characteristics until you use the menu to set some new characteristics.

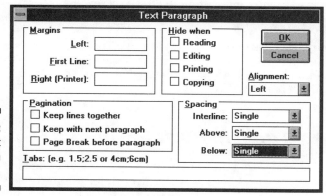

Figure 11-6:
The Text
Paragraph
dialog box.

All margins great and small

First on the list of changes you may want to make to a paragraph is to change the left or right margins. (Because the margins at the top and bottom of the page have nothing to do with paragraphs, they are in the File⇨Page Setup menu, covered later in this chapter.) There are three settings you can make:

- ✔ Left — sets the indent for all lines but the first one. The default is 1 inch if you are using Imperial measurements, or 2.54 cm if you're using Metric measurements. (You can switch from one to the other using Tools⇨ Setup⇨User⇨International.)

- ✔ First — sets the indent for only the first line if you entered a number for Left; otherwise (if there is no number entered in the Left text box), it sets the indent for all lines in the paragraph. The default is 1 inch or 2.54 cm.

- ✔ Right — sets the right margin for print only. This setting has nothing to do with screen display, so don't get mad when you set in a number and don't see a change on the screen. The default is determined by the size of the paper you are using in File⇨Print Setup⇨Setup⇨Paper Size.

To create a paragraph with a hanging indent, set the margin for the First line smaller that the margin for Left. Figure 11-7 shows some paragraphs with the first line margin set at 2 inches and the left margin set at 2.5 inches. If you use this technique for writing numbered paragraphs (an especially useful application of hanging indent), type the number and then press Tab. Even if you haven't set tabs, the cursor positions itself so that text in the first line is flush with all the other lines.

The right margin is measured from the left edge of the paper, so for a 2-inch right margin on paper $8^1/_2$-inches wide, set the right margin at $6^1/_2$. The right margin is automatically set at $7^1/_2$ (a 1-inch right margin). If that makes you happy, then don't bother to set it.

One paragraph, indivisible

When Notes calculates that the bottom of a page is at hand, it inserts a page break automatically where needed so that the printer will start a new page there. The place it chooses may not always be what you had in mind; you may prefer to have a paragraph stay together, even if it means a bit of white space at the bottom of the page. To protect the poor paragraph from being split, choose Text⇨Paragraph⇨Pagination (see Figure 11-8). Then choose one of the following:

- ✔ Choose Keep lines together to prevent Notes from breaking up a paragraph somewhere in the middle. Notes will either keep the paragraph on the current page or shove the whole thing to the next page.

✔ Choose Keep with next paragraph to be sure that a paragraph is always on the same page as the paragraph following it.

✔ Choose Page Break before paragraph if you definitely want the current paragraph to start a new page. This is useful when you want to start a new section on a new page.

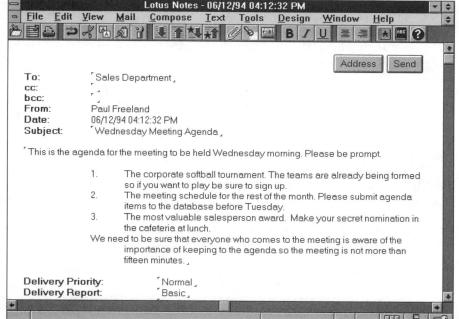

Figure 11-7:
This memo
contains
paragraphs
with a
hanging
indent.

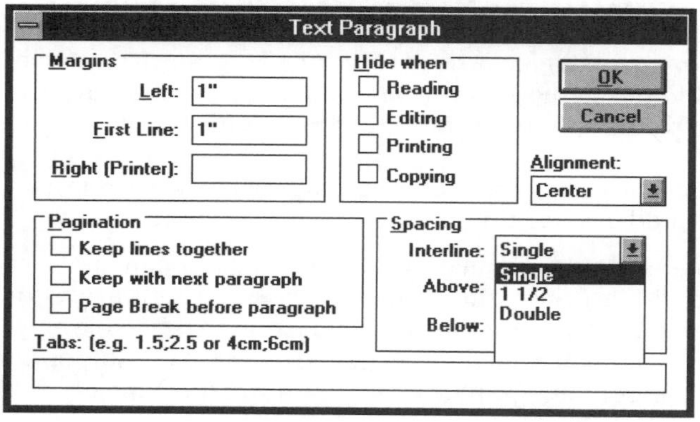

Figure 11-8:
The Text
Paragraph
dialog box.

Notes doesn't show text on the screen the same as it shows text when printing so you can't see how the document will look on the page. To get some idea of where the page breaks are, use View⇨Show Page Breaks.

Keeping tabs on your paragraph

Back at the factory, paragraphs automatically have their own tabs set at every half inch. This may be fine for you, in which case you don't have to set any tabs at all. If you are not happy with the preset tabs, use Text⇨Paragraph to set them where you want them. In the Tabs box, just type the distance (measured from the left edge of the paper) for all the tabs that you need. For that extra touch of variety, you may even enter some tabs in inches and others in centimeters. If you are using inches, you don't have to type any symbol, and if you want centimeters, just type **cm** after the number. You can't use yards, miles, quarts, or kilometers, though. Between each separate tab setting put a semicolon, not a comma. Notes complains if you use commas.

You may find it easier to use the ruler to set both margins and tabs. If you're rubbing your eyes trying to find a ruler on the screen, stop rubbing your eyes and use View⇨Show Ruler. You'll see the ruler at the top of the screen like the one in Figure 11-9. Click in the ruler where you want a tab, and a little T (which looks like an umbrella) appears. To get rid of an unwanted tab, click the T to remove it. The margin is a wedge near the left end of the ruler. Move it to a new position to set a different margin for the current or selected paragraphs. When you try to move the margin symbol, you may be surprised to find that it comes apart. Did you break it? No. The top part of the wedge corresponds to the First margin and the lower part of the wedge corresponds to the Left margin. (These are the ones you can also set by choosing Text⇨Paragraph⇨Margins.)

The incredible disappearing paragraph

The time may come when you need to hide a paragraph from some readers. If you want a hidden paragraph, you have four choices. You can tell Notes that the selected paragraph should be hidden for any of the following:

- ✔ *Reading.* The paragraph is only be visible when you are in edit mode. It will also be hidden for printing.

- ✔ *Printing.* As the word implies, when you print a document, paragraphs with the Hide While Printing attribute do not print. This is useful for suppressing the printing of paragraphs that you want to be visible only when the document is visible on the screen. You may also use this option when the paragraph contains graphics that slow down the print job.

✔ *Copying.* If you try to copy a paragraph with this attribute, you'll find that there is nothing to paste, but only when you copy while not in edit mode.

✔ *Editing.* The paragraph is visible when the reader is not in edit mode, but it disappears whenever someone tries to edit the document. This is a way to protect a paragraph from being changed by people who have the ability to edit documents. Be careful — after you have made this choice, you may never be able to edit the paragraph again.

There is a way around being unable to edit a paragraph — you can use it if you goofed and chose the Hide While Editing feature by accident, or if you want to get around someone else's use of this feature. While *not* in edit mode, highlight the paragraph that is hidden when you are editing, copy it to the Clipboard, and then get into edit mode and paste the paragraph into the document. This pasted paragraph will not have the hidden attribute so you will be able to edit it. Of course, when you are no longer in edit mode, the paragraph will appear twice unless you choose Hide While Reading.

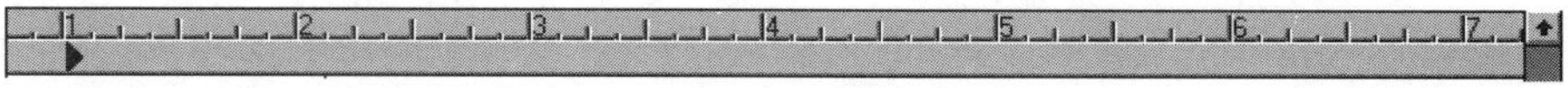

Figure 11-9:
This is the
ruler — a
quick way to
set margins
and tabs.

Get in align

Alignment refers to the arrangement of text in each line relative to the margins. You have five choices in this section of the Text Paragraph dialog box:

✔ *Left.* The text lines up with the left margin and has a ragged right edge.

✔ *Right.* The text lines up with the right margin and has a ragged left edge. Surely you're thinking that there is no right margin except for printing, so what can the text line up with? The answer is simple: the text lines up with the right side of the screen for display and with the right margin for printing.

✔ *Full.* The text is stretched from margin to margin so that the paragraph has no ragged edges. Full won't work if you type a really short line or if you press Enter at the end of a line.

✔ *Center.* Want to guess what this does? If you guessed that it centers the text on each line and gives lines ragged right and left edges, you may add ten points to your score and advance three spaces.

✔ *None.* Text starts at the left margin and goes to the right for ever. It doesn't wrap. Often when you import documents from other programs, you may be shocked to see that lines stretch off the screen and you have to scroll to the right and then scroll to the left, put your left foot in and put your left foot out, to see the rest of the text. Change the alignment to Left or Full to correct the problem. Then you do the hokey pokey and you turn yourself around — that's what it's all about.

Give me some space

Feeling cramped, squeezed, closed in? Do your memos seem to have too much stuff and not enough open space? Then you need to space out. The last item in the Text⇨Paragraph dialog box is Spacing, the way to spread out lines and paragraphs. When you want your memos to s-p-r-e-a-d out over more space or show more white space, select the paragraphs and choose Text⇨Paragraph⇨Spacing. Figure 11-10 shows the familiar Text Paragraph dialog box. Direct your attention to the lower-right corner and notice that there are three types of spacing and three choices you can make for each.

Interline puts 1, 1¹⁄₂, or 2 blank lines between each line inside the paragraph. Choosing Above or Below makes it possible for you to put some space above or below each selected paragraph. Choosing all three can be a heck of a mess; you may wind up with too much spacing. Practice a bit so that your screen isn't mostly white space with a line or paragraph appearing once in a while like an oasis in a white desert.

Figure 11-10:
Use Spacing in the Text Paragraph dialog box to space out your text.

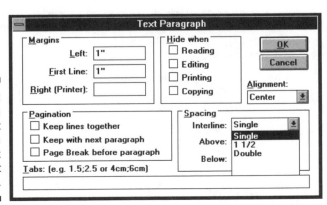

Figure 11-11 shows a memo that has 1¹/₂ line interline spacing and 2 lines of spacing above each paragraph.

Puttin' on the style

You have to make the coffee, you have to put paper in the copier, and now you have to jump all around your documents applying the same style over and over again to paragraphs. It's enough to raise your blood pressure (or your hackles).

Calm your hackles. You may still have to make the coffee, but you don't have to go through all the keystrokes again and again to format paragraphs scattered around your document. Imagine that you wrote a report with lots of sections and each section has its own title. You want the titles to be centered and bolded, have one line of space after them, and have a larger font with blue text. You can format one title and then use that style for all the other titles, thus saving lots of time and getting you home for dinner.

Applying styles also guarantees that you are consistent. After formatting 15 titles you're bound to get bored and careless, and you might forget to add boldface along with all the other formats to one of the titles. Then it will look a little different from all the others. Using styles guarantees that the same characteristics get applied to every paragraph you select.

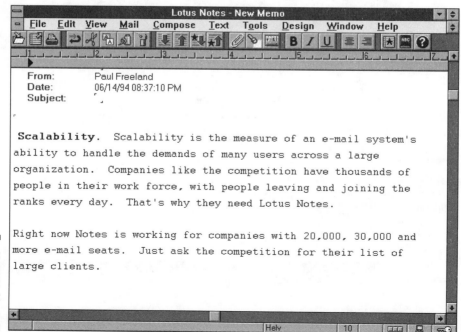

Figure 11-11:
Add spacing
to spread
out
paragraphs.

After you have written a title, centered it, colored it blue, bolded it, added the spacing, and changed the font, keep the cursor in the title and choose Text⬧Paragraph Styles. You need to give the style a name in the New Style Name text box. After you start typing the style name, the word New becomes usable (up until this point it was grayed out). In Figure 11-12, the formats applied to the title are being defined as a style called Title.

Clicking New defines the style. The name Title is associated with all the characteristics you put on the first title. Now put the cursor in another title, choose Text⬧Paragraph Styles, highlight the new style (Titles in this example), and then choose Apply. All the formats you used in the first title are applied at once to this title. What could be easier? I know, lots of things could be easier, but you have to admit that it's easier than applying each change individually to every paragraph.

What if you later decide to add a new feature to the style? Once again, choose Text⬧Paragraph Styles, highlight the name of the style you want to alter, and choose Paragraph. The Text Paragraph dialog box appears — make your changes and choose Done. As if by magic, all the paragraphs with that style change to show the latest update. You don't have to worry about looking all over the document and finding all the titles so that you can change each one.

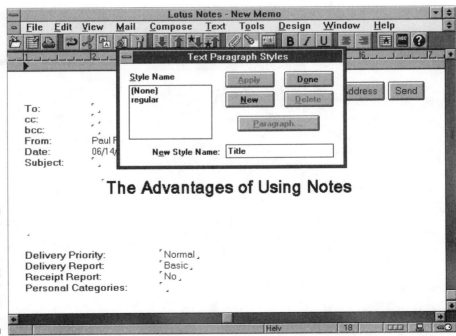

Figure 11-12:
Define and apply styles to format many paragraphs identically.

Chapter 12

Doctoring Your Documents

• •

In This Chapter

▶ Inserting page breaks

▶ Creating tables

▶ Modifying tables

▶ Adding and deleting rows and columns

▶ Adding headers and footers

▶ Changing the page setup

• •

*Y*our characters have character, your sentences make sense, your paragraphs have punch — all because you have added enhancements that changed their appearance. Now, what about the whole page and the whole document? This chapter takes you from concentrating on the individual characters to having a global view, seeing the big picture, and making the pages and the document a complete, professional, and well-done entity of which you can be proud.

While you are making neat changes to individual pages and making sweeping changes to the whole document, you may not see a single change on your screen. Is it time to lose your temper? No! Individual pages are what you see when you print. You don't see separate pages on the screen unless you use View⇨Show Page breaks. You don't see headers or footers, either, so the only way to see what a page will look like when it's printed is to print it.

Break It Up!

 Notes is a very smart program; it even knows when text is at the bottom of a page. When you print a document, it automatically puts a *page break* in the proper place. That way, you don't print text into the margin or off the page and into thin air. There comes a time in the affairs of folks, though, when they need to put a page break where Notes wouldn't. For instance, if a paragraph starts a new section and you want it to appear on a new page (even if the previous page isn't full), you can insert a page break. There are three ways to do this— keyboard, SmartIcons, or menu. Press Ctrl+L, click the page break SmartIcon, or choose <u>E</u>dit➪<u>I</u>nsert➪<u>P</u>age Break. The page break, if you choose to see it, appears as a solid line across the screen.

To remove a page break that you don't want anymore, place the cursor on the first character after the page break and press Backspace. If you delete a page break and it appears right back again, maybe one line before or after the place where it used to be, you are trying to remove a break that Notes put there all by itself because the text is at the end of the page. That's a page break you're going to have to live with.

 If you don't want a page break to appear in a particular paragraph, you can use the <u>P</u>agination part of the <u>T</u>ext➪<u>P</u>aragraph dialog box to determine where a page break will be, relative to existing paragraphs.

Let's Put Our Cards in a Table

If you're having dinner, a table is something on which you spill your gravy. When you're using Notes, a *table* is something that makes it a whole lot easier to keep rows and columns of information all lined up, without having to set up lots of tabs. A table is a spreadsheet you can place in your document with rows and columns of boxes into which you type information. One of the advantages of using a table instead of tabs is that tabs normally allow wrapping of text back to the beginning of the line, whereas tables keep text aligned in the column. Here comes a surprise — you can only put a table in a rich text field.

Put 'er there, pardner

Suppose for the sake of argument that you need to send a message that includes a schedule. The schedule itself would be a great candidate for a table — it involves small bits of data and needs to be in tabular format (unless you are trying to confuse your co-workers by typing the information in random order).

When you get to the place in the message where you are ready to place the schedule, use Edit⇨Insert⇨Table. Figure 12-1 shows you the Insert Table dialog box. You can see that you have to decide in advance how many rows and how many columns you want in your table. Yes, you can add more and delete some later if you goofed, but it's a bit easier to make the decision first.

The OK button in the dialog box is gray until you enter the number of rows and the number of columns you need for the table — it can't create a table with five rows but no columns. Left margin sets the distance that the left edge of the table will be from the left edge of the paper if you print it. It also indents the table from the left edge of the screen.

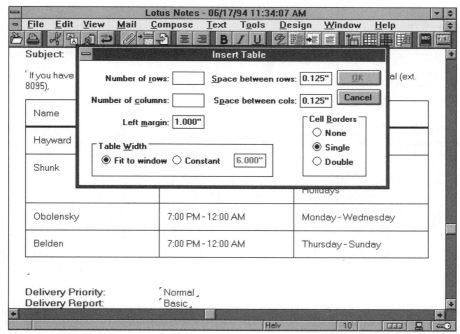

Figure 12-1:
The Insert
Table dialog
box.

Figure 12-2 shows a table with a schedule. A schedule is just one example of a good application for a table; if you try hard, you can think of lots of other examples. This table shows all the default settings; we'll add some changes soon.

The Fit to Window button (in the Table Width box) is useful if you plan to use a different size window for Notes as you are working, or if your readers are using many different displays. If you shrink the window with the document that has the table, the table will change so that you can still see the whole width of the table in the window. If you use Constant, you have to set a width. Then if you shrink the window you may only see part of the table at a time; that's a bit of a pain because you have to keep scrolling left and right to see different columns.

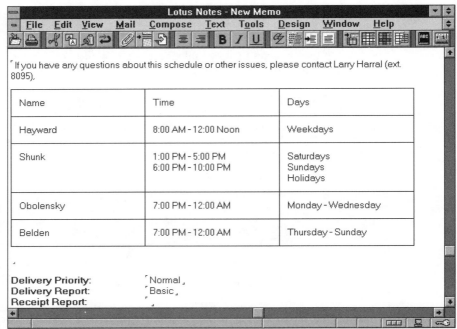

On the other hand, after you use Fit to Window, someone else looking at your table with a different screen, different operating system, or different fonts may have a lot of trouble making sense out of your hard work if the lines break in strange places. The text in the table may wrap at a place that makes the data harder to understand. It's your call — try it both ways if necessary and see which works best for that particular table. Figure 12-3 shows our table in a smaller window, but the data still makes plenty of sense even though it's rearranged slightly.

Space between rows and Space between columns allow you to change the distance between text in the columns or rows.

Cell Borders are not people who live in jail but are the lines that surround each cell. You may choose Single, Double, or None. Single and Double refer to the width (not the number) of lines forming the border, and None means there will be no lines in the table. Keep in mind that this Cell Borders setting affects every cell in the table. In a few paragraphs we'll tell you how to change a single border of a single cell.

After you have made all the decisions and set all the settings, click OK and after a few seconds a blank table appears where the insertion point was in the document. If you gasp with delight because your table has appeared exactly as

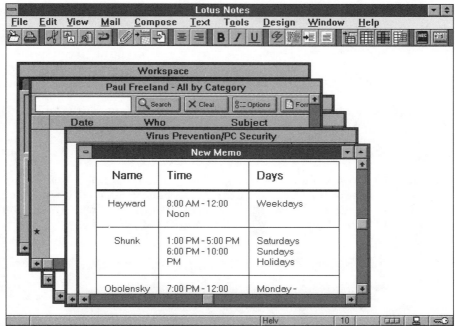

Figure 12-3:
With Fit to Window, the table shrinks to the width of the window.

you intended, then you are ready to put the cursor in a cell and type its contents. When you are done with one cell, move to the cell to the right by pressing Tab, to the cell to the left by pressing Shift+Tab, to the cell below by pressing the down-arrow key, or to the cell above by pressing the up-arrow key. Of course, you can click in a cell with the mouse to move to any cell in the table.

You have to use the menu, the ruler, or an icon to change the width of a column, but to change the cell height all you have to do is type. If there is too much text to fit on one line in the cell or if you press Enter, the height of the cell increases to accommodate the additional text. The whole row will be as tall as the cell with the most text in that row.

The tables they are a changin'

 If, on the other hand, you gasp with frustration because you made a mistake in your choices, you'll need to change the format of the table. Do you have to change the table before you enter data? No, you may change anything about the table at any time. The table in Figure 12-4 has the same data as the one in Figures 12-2 and 12-3. In fact, it *is* the same table, but after we added the data we made some changes.

Can you spot the differences? Take your time and examine closely the tables in
Figure 12-3 and 12-4. Hint: Column 1 is narrower, the data in Row 1 is bold, the
header of the middle column is centered, the bottom border of Row 1 is double,
and all data in Column 1 is centered. How did you do? If you spotted one
difference, put on your glasses; if you got two or more right, you may take the
rest of the day off.

 To change a table, be sure the insertion point is inside the table and then
choose Edit⇨Table⇨Format or click the table format SmartIcon. (You have to
have the cursor in a table for Edit⇨Table to be visible and for the table format
SmartIcon to work.) Either choice gives you the dialog box shown in Figure 12-5.

If Fit to Window made the data hard to understand, here's your chance to
change all that. Enter a width in the Column width box. Now if you change
window size, the table will not adjust. Also, if you want to change the indent of
the table, type in a new margin in the Left margin text box.

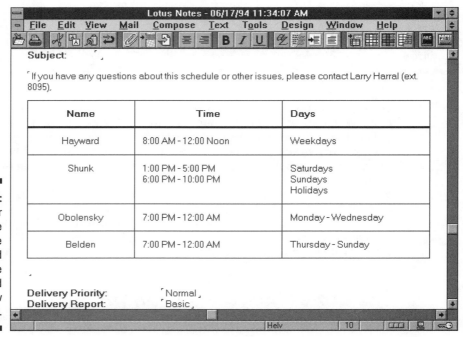

Figure 12-4:
After
entering the
data, we
decided
this table
needed
a few
changes.

Figure 12-5:
Use the Edit
Table
Format
dialog box
to make
changes to
your table.

```
┌─────────────────────────────────────────────────────────────┐
│                      Edit Table Format                        │
│                                                               │
│     Row  4   ▲▼          Column  2  ▲▼      ┌──────OK──────┐   │
│                                             ├────Cancel────┤   │
│     ☒ Fit to window        │ Justify Column │               │
│                                                               │
│        Left margin: 1.000"    Space between rows: 0.125"      │
│     Column width: 1.951"      Space between cols: 0.125"      │
│   ┌─Cell Borders─────────────────────────────────────────┐   │
│   │   Left        Right       Top         Bottom          │   │
│   │  ○ None      ○ None      ○ None       ○ None           │   │
│   │  ◉ Single    ◉ Single    ◉ Single     ◉ Single         │   │
│   │  ○ Double    ○ Double    ○ Double     ○ Double         │   │
│   └───────────────────────────────────────────────────────┘   │
└─────────────────────────────────────────────────────────────┘
```

How did we ever get that double line at the bottom of Row 1? Use the up or down-arrow key, to select a column and row (Row 1 and Column 1 for the cell in the upper-left corner, for instance) and then, under Bottom, select Double. You must change each border for each cell; you can't change borders for a whole row or column at a time.

If you choose None for a style of a border that an adjacent cell shares, you need to choose None for the other cell, too. Confused? Well, if you choose None for the bottom border of one cell, the border still won't go away if the top border of the cell below it is still there. So choose None for the top border of *that* cell, and (at last!) the border is gone.

Because Column 1 contains only last names, we decided that column could be a bit narrower. In the dialog box, click the up- or down-arrow key to select Column 1. This time it doesn't matter which row you select because you set the width for the whole column at once. Then type a value into the Column width text box. The width of the other columns will adjust to take up the extra space.

If you set the columns too wide, they may disappear off the screen, which is not terribly convenient because you will have to scroll back and forth to see them. Worse, though, is that the table may be broken up across several printed pages if it's too wide. One way around seeing your tables broken up for firewood is to put them on separate pages (using page breaks) and then print the pages with tables separately in landscape orientation. Use File➪Print Setup➪Setup➪Landscape.

While you're in the dialog box and while Column 1 is selected, you may as well click Justify Column and set the justification to Center. That, too, affects the whole column. Click OK to dismiss the dialog box when you have finished making changes.

What about centering the word *Time* and bolding all the words in Row 1? To change the justification and text enhancements of one cell, highlight the text in the cell and make the change. Put the cursor in the cell in Row 1, Column 2, and then center it. You'll have to highlight the text in each cell in Row 1 and bold them individually. Sorry, there is no quick way to do that.

Open table, insert row

You're done with the table and you're about to send it, when — "Eeek!" — you cry in frustration and disbelief. You forgot to include a column for Location. Is it tragic, is it sad, are you out of luck, is it difficult to add a column? None of these. Adding a column is as easy as clicking a SmartIcon, or if you prefer, making a menu choice.

 Be sure you are in the column where you would like the new blank column to be. (Of course, if you want to insert a row, then be in the row where you want to put it.) Click the insert row/column icon or choose Edit⇨Table⇨Insert Row/Column. Keep an eye out for the dialog box you see in Figure 12-6. In it you can specify whether to add a column or a row, how many to add, and whether to Insert them (at the place where the cursor is) or Append them at the bottom or right end of the table. To insert a column at the place where the cursor is, choose Column(s), leave the *1* in the text box, and choose Insert. Figure 12-7 shows the table with a column inserted for location.

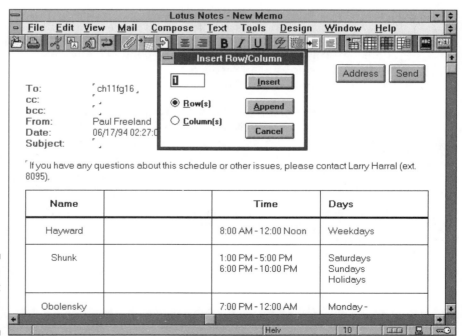

Figure 12-6:
The Insert
Row/Column
dialog box.

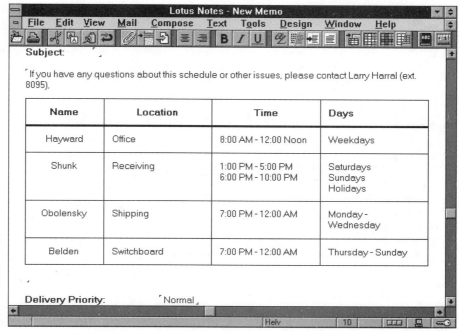

Figure 12-7:
The same
old table
with a new,
improved
Location
column.

If you insert several rows or columns, the new rows appear above the row where the cursor was, and new columns appear to the left of the column where the cursor was.

No more row four

We don't need Belden on the switchboard after all. In fact, we don't need that row any more. Got your eraser? Wait a minute, this is the computer age. There has to be a better way of getting rid of a row or column — something involving a SmartIcon or menu.

 Be sure to put the cursor in the row you want to delete. That sounds like a simple enough suggestion, but if you are not on your toes you'll wind up deleting the wrong row. Click the delete row/column icon or choose Edit⇨Table⇨Delete Row/Column. In the dialog box, be sure Row is selected (if you're deleting a row) and leave 1 in the number box (unless you want to delete more rows).

When you choose OK, you will see the warning in Figure 12-8. If you have the cursor in the wrong row or if you forgot to choose correctly between <u>R</u>ow and <u>C</u>olumn and then you choose OK, you can't get those deleted rows or columns back. So *be careful*. Because an ounce of prevention is worth two in the bush, here's a piece of advice. Save the document first; then do the deletion. If your deletion turns out to be a mistake, then dismiss the document without saving it and re-open it. Now try again and be *really* careful this time.

Figure 12-8:
Proceed
with
caution;
once the
row or
column is
gone, it's
gone
forever.

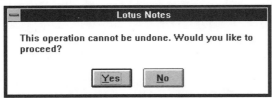

Trying to Get a Header

Imagine this heartbreaking situation. You print a 50-page monster report. A breeze blows through the open window just as the last page comes out of the printer, and your document blows all over the place. You pick up your document and try to put it in order. You have a tough time because the pages aren't numbered. Sad, isn't it? What's a body to do? Create a header and put page numbers in it, that's what.

One doc — one header

Page numbers appear in *headers* or *footers:* bits of text that appear at the top (header) or bottom (footer) of each printed page. You can choose to put other information in a header or footer, too, if you want. If a document is urgent or the kind of information spies and bad guys could really use against the company, put that information in the header. If every page says "URGENT!!" or "DON'T SHOW THIS TO BAD GUYS," the reader is likely to get the message, even if one page gets separated from all the others. Remember, you won't see headers on the screen because they are only supposed to be seen on the printed page.

To create headers and footers, choose Edit⇨Header/Footer. When you do, you see the dialog box featured prominently in Figure 12-9. In the big box next to Header is the place where you type the header. By the same token, you would type the text for the footer in the box next to Footer.

"What," you ask, "can the Notes user put in a header or footer?" The following list answers that question:

✔ Text — Type anything you want. Remember that a header or footer is only one line, so don't get carried away typing your entire life history, unless you have lived a very short or uneventful life.

✔ Page Numbers — Choose Page from the list at the right side of the dialog box. Only the page number appears. To be a bit fancier, type **Page** and then choose Page. The header or footer will look like this: Page &P. The &P turns into the proper page number when you print, so on page 5 you'll see Page 5. Now if the document gets blown around, putting it in order will be much easier. Of course, you can close the window and avoid the problem altogether.

✔ Time — Choose Time, and the header or footer shows the current time (according to the computer's clock) each and every time you print your document. Time is printed in a format like this: 03:48:42PM.

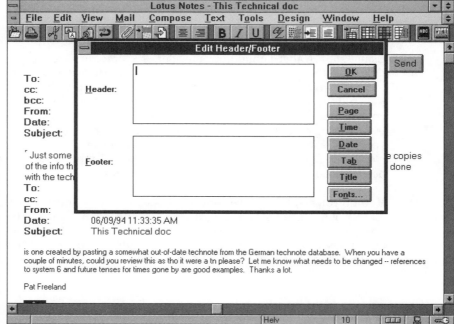

Figure 12-9:
Headers and footers can contain original text or standard bits of information (like page numbers).

✔ Date — Choose <u>D</u>ate, and the current date appears each time you print and it looks something like this: 12/25/94. Printing the time or date in a header or footer is handy if the reader needs to tell which is the most recent printout among a lot of printed copies of the same memo.

✔ Title — The window title of a document appears in the header or footer.

Two choices that look like things you would see in the header or footer are really ways to change their appearance. Fo<u>n</u>ts sets the font and font size for the whole header or footer. Ta<u>b</u> determines the placement of the text in the header or footer as follows (the vertical bar is the symbol for tab placed there by Notes when you click Tab):

This is a Header | | — Left-justifies the header or footer text.

| **This is a Header** | — Centers the header or footer text.

| | **This is a Header** — Right-justifies the header or footer text.

So, putting it all together, you could type

This is a Header | Page &P | &W

and you would see on the printout

This is a Header   Page 1   Daily Schedule

A header for all docs

Using <u>E</u>dit⇨<u>H</u>eader/Footer puts a header or a footer *in the current document only.* Note the dramatic use of italics to show you that when you open a document and create a header, it only applies to the document that you are editing right at the moment. You might, instead, prefer to create a header or footer for any document that is printed in the current database. Although there are no eye-catching italic words in the previous sentence, it is important to note that you can create a header or footer for every document that you print in the current database. Documents printed from other databases do not have a header unless you create one for that database too.

How do you create a header for every document in a whole database and not just for one document? Use the <u>F</u>ile⇨Page Setup menu. Figure 12-10 shows the dialog box that appears, and you've probably noticed that a big part of this dialog box is about headers and footers. Use the same steps we described in the previous section to create a header or footer.

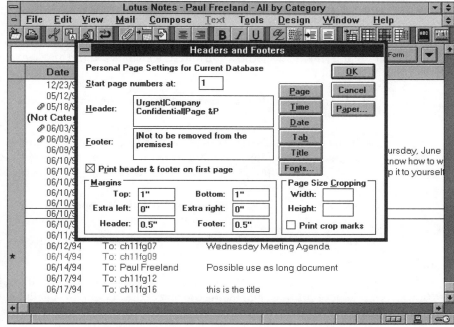

Figure 12-10:
The
Headers
and Footers
dialog box
controls
more than
just headers
and footers.

There are two extra little choices you may make for database headers that you can't make for individual documents:

✔ Start page numbers at: makes it possible to give the first page a different number from what it would normally get (which, of course, would be one). Why would anyone want to do that? Well, suppose documents from this database are included in a larger document, and the first page of the documents from this database appears on page three of the larger document. Start numbering with three so that you can add the first two pages from elsewhere and wind up with the correct page numbers on all pages.

✔ The check box Print header and footer on first page allows you to leave the header and footer off the first page if you want. If the first page already contains the information you want in the header or footer, why have it appear twice? Click this box to remove the X, and the header and footer will start on the second page.

Set 'Em Up, Boys

As long as you're in the Headers and Footers dialog box (the one you get by choosing File➪Page Setup), you may as well look around and see what else is there to improve the document.

At the bottom of the dialog box is a place to set the margins. Use it to set any of the following:

- ✔ Top and Bottom margins — measured from the top and bottom of the paper, respectively. The margins work with the page size setting (set using File➪Print Setup➪Setup) to determine the actual place where the text is printed on the paper.

- ✔ Extra left: and Extra right: add space to the left and right margins that you already set with Text➪Paragraph➪Margins.

- ✔ Header: and Footer: margins determine how far from the top or the bottom of the page the header and footer will be.

If you set the header margin larger than the top margin, you will wind up with your header printed right inside the text of the document. Yuck! The same goes for footer margin and bottom margin.

Now, if you're not confused yet, try this. You can also *crop* your documents by indicating a different printing area on the paper. If the printouts from your databases are going to be sent out to be professionally printed on different size paper, you can crop the printed data on the page by setting the length and the width of the area on the printout where text should appear (measured from the top and left side of the paper).

Are you saying to yourself, "What the heck is the difference between margins and cropping?" It's a good question, and the answer is a resounding "Not much." The one difference is that by choosing to crop and then selecting Print crop marks, you can cause lines to appear on the paper where the printers should crop the paper.

The page settings dialog box is different for a Macintosh, so you can expect to see the usual Macintosh page setup choices:

- ✔ Paper Size
- ✔ Percentage reduction or enlargement of text
- ✔ Print orientation (landscape or portrait)
- ✔ Special printer effects

Search and Rescue

Everybody makes mistakes. Remember — to err is human, to forgive is divine, and to make the same mistake again is inevitable. So in the spirit of mistake-making, you type up a long memo and then find that some text you typed was wrong. Of course you made the mistake over and over again. You may, for example, have referred to Sue when she prefers to be called Susan.

The time has come to find all the Sues in the document and change them to Susan. Use Edit⇨Find and replace or Ctrl+F. Watch for the dialog box that you see in Figure 12-11, which we have already tailored to our specifications.

Searching for text in order to rescue your document takes a bit of planning if it's to work right. Notice, for example, that we choose Whole Word so that we won't find the "sue" in suede. It would look silly if the document included words like Susande.

We also chose Case Sensitive so that if the document includes the word "sue" (the legal action), we won't replace that with Susan's name. If a word contains a diacritical mark like an accent, a circumflex, a cedilla, or a freckle, find and replace will look specifically for that mark and will ignore any occurrences of the word without it (but only if you choose Accent Sensitive).

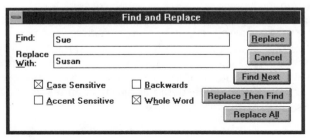

Figure 12-11:
The Find and
Replace
dialog box.

Backwards doesn't mean it's looking for euS. Normally the find or find and replace commands work forward from the cursor to the end of the document. If you want to search from the cursor to the beginning, use Backwards.

To be sure that you find all occurrences of a word, it's best to put the cursor at the beginning of a document before you start beating the bushes for that special word.

After you've made all your decisions, typed in the text that you want to find, and typed the text that you want to use as a replacement, it's time to get the whole process started. You can choose one of the following:

- *Replace* to begin at the cursor and go forward through the document, find the first occurrence of the search text, and replace it with the replacement text.

- *Cancel* to stop the whole process dead in its tracks.

- *Find Next* to find the first or next occurrence of the search text, but not do any replacing.

- *Replace Then Find* to replace the first occurrence and then find the second occurrence of the search text.

- *Replace All* to get it done quickly by replacing every occurrence of the search text with the replacement text without asking each time. Use this choice carefully, as strange and unpredictable things may happen. Imagine, for instance, if the word Sue starts a sentence — "Sue us at your peril" becomes "Susan us as your peril."

The clever little searcher may often find an occurrence of the search text behind the Find and Replace dialog box, which means you may sometimes have to move the dialog box out of the way to see the highlight. Also, remember that you can't use the find and replace feature unless you are in edit mode (Ctrl+E or Edit⇨Edit Document).

A simpler use of the Edit⇨Find & Replace feature is finding without replacing. Enter search text in the Find text box and then choose Find Next. As you search for text in different databases, you may notice that you see a different dialog box. If you find a query builder dialog box, don't panic. Remember two things: if you see the query builder, then the database has been indexed; and you can read about the query builder in Chapter 16.

If You're a Bad Spellar

Even if you are a good speller, you are bound to make a typographical error sometime in the next few years. You need to be ever vigilant for that occurrence — ready to pounce on it and correct it before it gets printed or replicated to thousands of recipients who will laugh quietly up their sleeves at you for an easily corrected oversight.

 In the dialog box in Figure 12-12 you see that the person who knocked out the memo didn't notice that *corporate* was spelled wrong. Then again, maybe he didn't know how to spell it. No matter — the spell checker found the mistake.

After you save (just to be safe) but before you print (to save paper), choose Tools⇨Spell Check or click the spell check icon. Regardless of where you last

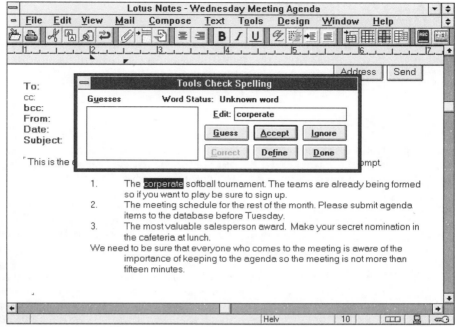

Figure 12-12:
It's always a
good idea to
use the spell
cheker.

saw your cursor, the spell checker starts at the beginning of the document. If it finds a word it doesn't recognize, it highlights the word (sometimes behind the dialog box) and waits for you to take some sort of action. Among the actions you could take are these:

- ✔ Go get a cup of coffee and let the spell checker wait until you are ready.

- ✔ Choose Accept the word if you want the spell checker to leave this spelling alone for the rest of the document.

- ✔ Choose Ignore the word if you want to accept the misspelling this time, but continue to watch for it in the rest of the document.

- ✔ Choose Define to add the word to the Notes dictionary so that it will never, ever be highlighted again. Use this carefully, because adding a misspelling to the dictionary can be very embarrassing. Forevermore, Notes will ignore that misspelling.

- ✔ Choose Guess to have Notes provide alternative spellings for the selected word.

- ✔ Type the correct spelling in the Edit text box.

- ✔ Choose Correct to replace the goof with a word that you highlighted with Guess or that you typed in the Edit text box.

- ✔ Choose Done anytime that you want to stop the spell check. Promise that you'll spell check it later?

Whistles and Bells

To round out our chapter, we present two neat little tricks that that you may find to be useful as you create the great American memo. They didn't fit neatly anywhere else in the chapter, so here they are at the end.

Doclinks

Cufflinks for your favorite doctor? Chains around a document? This is Notes, not a metalwork artist — your doctors have to get their own cufflinks. A *doclink* is a connection between the current document and another document.

Suppose that you are sending a memo to an associate about a report that is in another database. Rather than saying "Find the document for yourself, you lazy bum," you can put a symbol of the report in your memo. When the lazy bum receives the memo, a mere double click the symbol opens the document.

The recipient must have access to the database and the document that you are linking in your memo. An error message appears on-screen if someone clicks a doclink and he/she doesn't have rights to access the documents or the database itself or doesn't have physical access to the server that contains the database that contains the document that lives in the house that Jack built. One of the databases to which others do not have access is your own mail database. So don't doclink one of your mail messages into another message and send it off.

To create a doclink, you need to open the document that will contain the link and you need to be in edit mode. Switch to the document to be linked or highlight it in a view and then choose Edit⇨Make DocLink. Switch to the document that will contain the doclink and choose Edit⇨Paste. Figure 12-13 shows a quick memo with a doclink to a report.

When your recipients receive the memo, each can double-click the doclink. The document itself opens before their very eyes. It beats typing the whole report all over again, doesn't it? Just for the record, you need to be in edit mode to add a doclink to a document, but you don't need to be in edit mode to open a doclink.

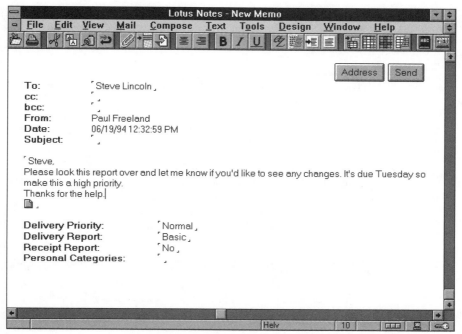

Figure 12-13: This memo contains a doclink to another document.

Hey, get your popups

Remember when you were in school and your teacher would say a new word and then would say, "Let's all say that together." Then the whole class would dutifully pronounce the word. (That's the same kind of teacher who says, "Put on your thinking caps.") There are times when you might include a word like that in something you write. You may need to define it, or you may need to add more information about the word. You may prefer not to include the information in the text itself because not everyone needs to see it or they only need to see it once.

In such times, a *popup* is useful. A simple example is a memo you may write to the department saying, among other things, "Call me anytime if you have questions." Most people know your extension, so you don't want it to be constantly visible in the memo. So you create a popup associated with the word "Call" so that if anyone forgot your number, clicking the word briefly shows your extension on the screen.

In Figure 12-14 is a memo with a popup inserted at the word "projects." Most of the workers know the projects for next month, but the popup reminds them if they need to be reminded.

Notice that there is a little box around "projects." That box is a subtle symbol that there is a popup associated with that word. The box is green on color monitors and black on monochrome monitors. Ugly, you say? Maybe, but if there is no box, how will the readers know that there is a popup associated with the word? However, if you insist, you can suppress display of the popup box in the Insert PopUp dialog box, as shown in Figure 12-15.

To create a popup, first type the text that will have a popup associated with it. Highlight the text and choose Edit⇨Insert⇨PopUp. In the "Enter the text of the PopUp" dialog box, type the text to be associated with the highlighted text. You can add a lot of text, but generally popups are used for small bits of information. That's not a rule; it's just the way that most people use them.

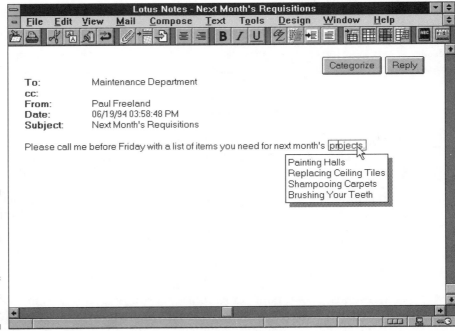

Figure 12-14:
By clicking the word "projects," anyone can see the list of next month's projects.

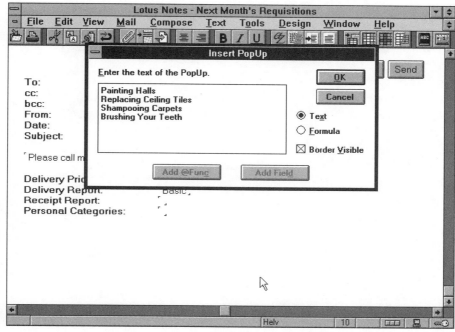

Figure 12-15:
In the Insert
PopUp dialog
box, you can
tailor popups
to your
specifications.

For those of you adamant about not showing the box, click the Border Visible box to remove the X and then wish your readers luck in finding the popup. You could elect to remove the border, but format words with popups differently — use blue italicized text, for instance — and inform your readers elsewhere in the document that blue italicized text is a popup.

If you double-click a popup when you are in edit mode, the dialog box appears so that you can change something about the popup. If you click the popup when you are not in edit mode, the box with text that you typed appears, but you can't edit it.

Chapter 13
Have It Your Way

In This Chapter

▶ Changing the appearance of mail memo forms

▶ Creating a new memo form

▶ Changing views

▶ Changing the icon for your mail database

▶ Adding certification to your ID

▶ Creating encryption keys

▶ Adding a password to your ID

▶ Using Tools⇨Setup

*W*hen you get a new office or desk (or place to stand if you're a real junior in the company), one of your first official acts is to make your new location seem familiar. Out come the pictures — your family, your significant other, your pet dog, cat, or cobra. You arrange the articles in the drawers so they are right where you need them and spread out your personal treasures across the expanse of your desk. There, now you feel at home. Well, you feel at work, anyway.

In similar fashion, as you snuggle into your use of Notes, you may find that you would like to change some things about the way the program looks and works. The reasons may be cosmetic, like changing the color of the background and text of your memos, or functional, like designating your server or choosing a password for your user ID. Speaking of pictures, if you're a bit artistic, you could even change the icon for your mail database so it looks like something especially meaningful to you, like someone you love, your car, or your favorite dessert.

Mail That Says, "ME"

Do you lie awake at night worrying that your memos look like everyone else's in your organization? Neither do we. But you never know; you may start. Well, roll over and go back to sleep. Rest assured that when you get to your computer, you'll have at your very fingertips the capability to completely change the appearance of every memo you send from that moment forward. Not only that, there are several other aspects of your mail database you can change. We'll cover them all in this section.

A form with fashion

When you choose Mail⇨Compose⇨Memo or Compose⇨Memo, you call to the screen a blank memo form into which you enter your message. That same form is like a lens through which you read the memos that others have sent you. The form is like the memo paper you keep in your desk drawer — it has your name or a logo on it and may even be a color other than white. Why not have the same qualities in your Notes memos?

Why not indeed? There are three kinds of reasons why you might want to change a memo form:

- ✔ You want to change the way memos look on your screen as you read or write them.

- ✔ You want people who receive your memos to see a different memo format than the one they normally see.

- ✔ You want some fields (for instance, the To: field) to always have a certain default value automatically.

If we wrote about every detail of redesigning your mail memo form, this book would be twice as thick as it is now and would cost twice as much. If your curiosity gets the best of you, use the help feature to figure out what to do when you find yourself in an unfamiliar dialog box.

To start the whole process of customizing your mail memos, your first step is to at least select the icon for your mail database. Then choose Design⇨Forms. In the dialog box that appears, select Memo and then choose Edit. Figure 13-1 shows you how a form looks when you are editing it.

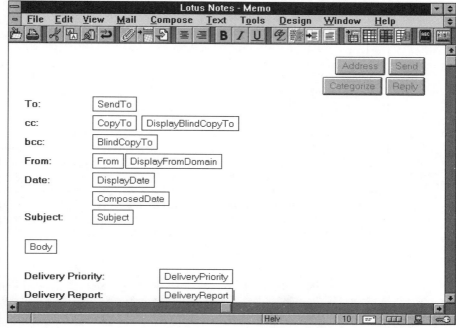

Among the quick changes you can make to your form are the following:

- ✓ Change any of the field titles like To:, From:, or Subject: by simply editing them.

- ✓ Change the font, font size, or color of the field titles by highlighting the text and using the Text menu.

- ✓ Change the font, font size, or color of any field itself by highlighting the field definition box and then choosing the changes you want. You could, for instance, make one of the fields bold or make it a different font from the rest.

- ✓ Add other text or objects to the form. For instance, you could place below the body of the memo a sincere, heartfelt, and original message such as "Have a nice day" to warm the cockles of the reader's heart.

The words in boxes are the fields themselves. Double-click any of them to see the actual field definition in a dialog box. Mess with the contents of those boxes at your own risk — changing field definitions is beyond the scope of this book. If you do start to make some changes and get panicky, press Esc and choose No when the prompt asks if you want to save the form.

One other change you might want to make to the memo is changing the background color. Figure 13-2 shows the dialog box that appears right there on your screen when you choose Design⇨Form Attributes. Notice that at the bottom is the word Color, beside which you see some boxes. If this book were in living color, you could see the rainbow of hues available for your memo form's background. To select a color, click the one you like or press Alt+L and then type the letter of the color you want. There are other options in this dialog box, but they are a bit too advanced for this book.

Keep in mind your text color as you pick a background color. (Of course, it'll be black unless you change the text color for the field definition and the field titles.) You can create some really hard-to-read combinations if you're not careful. Imagine black letters on a brown background. If you change text colors too, you can even get stuff like yellow letters on a pink background. It may sound springtime fresh and colorful, but the lack of contrast means you won't be able to read it! As a general rule, keep backgrounds light and letters dark. Light letters on a dark background are much harder to read.

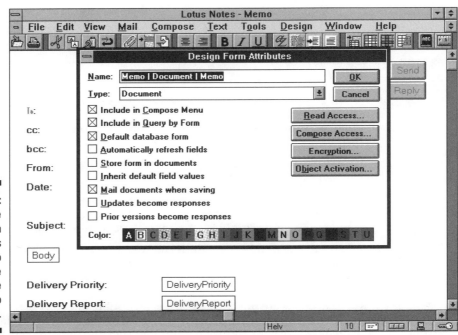

Figure 13-2:
Use the
Design⇨Form
Attributes
dialog box to
change the
color of the
memo
background.

One little point you ought to know — all these changes will only be visible at your end when *you* are looking at memos. So far, you have been changing forms for the first reason mentioned earlier: changing the way the memos you read and write look on your own screen. That is, when the recipients open their copy of your memo, they see the plain old memo form they are used to seeing because *their* form is the one used at *their* computer to read all the memos they've received.

Is there anything you can do for this sorry situation? Yes! Choose Design⇨Form Attributes and, in the dialog box, choose Store form in documents. Now, when recipients receive a copy of *your* messages, *your* form will be the one used to display *your* messages. However, there is a price to pay for including a form in a memo when you send it. The memo will be much bigger, byte-wise. That means e-mail databases fill up faster and transmission over networks and modems takes longer. But that's a small price to pay for your work of art, right? Well, perhaps in the interest of being a good citizen, you should only use this technique when you need to, rather than just on a whim. Or at least make sure it's not your boss's e-mail database that you're filling up! So now you have changed a form for the second reason: changing the way your memos look on others' screens.

After you have changed the memo form to your satisfaction, press Esc. At the prompt choose Yes; you do want to save the form. From now on, whenever you choose Compose⇨Memo, as you are writing the memo you will see your new form. If you store the form in the documents, your form will be the one that others see when reading your memos.

A form is born

The third reason for changing memos is to have some fields filled in for you automatically. You can create a new form for special occasions that does just that.

The dialog box you see when you choose Design⇨Forms certainly lets you *change* your forms, but it also gives you the power and the ability to *create* new forms. Assume for this illustration that you want to change the memo form slightly to create a form for use when you send memos to certain friends.

Choose Design⇨Form and highlight Memo, but this time choose New Copy in the Design Form dialog box you see in Figure 13-3. (If you choose New, you have to design a form from the ground up. Instead, you can just change an existing form — that's much easier.)

Figure 13-3:
The Design
Form dialog
box.

You probably don't send courtesy copies or blind courtesy copies of personal memos, so you might want to delete those field titles and the field definitions. Highlight them and press Delete to remove them.

Although it is OK to delete the cc: and bcc: fields, Notes uses many of the other fields behind the scenes (such as the To: and From: fields), so it's best to avoid deleting any other fields.

If this memo is always going to go to certain of your friends, you can add their names to the default formula of the To: field. If it is a departmental memo, you can put the name of the group in the To: field (assuming that the group name has been defined in either your or the company's name and address book).

After you're done designing your form, press Esc. You'll be prompted to give the new form a name; any name (even with spaces) is fine, but remember that only the first 32 characters of the name will be visible later. How about "Personal Memo | Memo"? You may use any name of up to 32 characters before the vertical line (the *pipe symbol*), but be sure you include the pipe symbol and the word *Memo*.

Now you have a new form to use. Choose Compose, and there, in the list of things you could compose, is your new form. Make personal memos short while you're on company time — the boss may be watching. But hey, won't the crowd be impressed! You're well on your way to becoming a true Notes nerd.

A custom view, designed by you

Views are ways of looking at a list of documents in a database. Each database has a bunch of views so that you can get at information in several different ways. However, you and I both know that nothing is etched in stone. You have the power to change these views. You're not a factory-made individual — you might not be satisfied with the factory-made views. Here's how to change them.

With columns and justice for all

Sometimes people who send memos choose Yes in the Receipt Report field so that they know when you open their memos. Maybe you're one of those people who just *hates* this. They're watching to be sure that you really read the message they sent? The nerve!

This change to a view tells you when a memo is waiting in your database that has *Yes* in the Receipt Report field. We'll even show you how to read it without a receipt report being sent — that will teach those busybodies a lesson!

First, be sure you're highlighting your mail database icon or that you've opened the database. Now, choose Design⇨Views and highlight the view you want to change. Might we suggest the *All by Category* view, since that's the one you probably use the most? It's probably already selected. If it isn't selected in the list of views, select it and then pick Edit.

You need a new column in the view to show when the Return Receipt field has Yes. Put that new column right after the date column. In the row of column titles, highlight the box to the right of Date and then choose Design⇨New column. Before you can sing the Russian National Anthem, the dialog box that you see in Figure 13-4 appears.

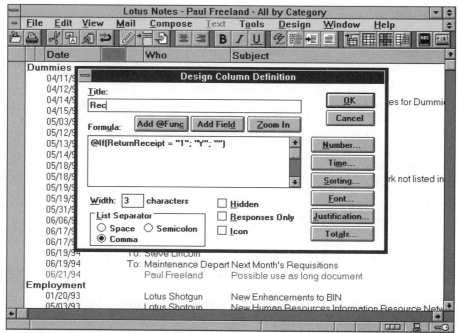

Figure 13-4:
The dialog box for defining a "return receipt has been requested" column.

In the Title text box, type **Rec.** It's going to be a narrow column, so there won't be space for more than that. Now for the formula — it's Notes nerd time. Just type this in the Formula box and don't ask any questions: `@if(ReturnReceipt= "1"; "Y"; "")`. This isn't the time for creativity; the formula has to be exact. Set the Width to be three characters. One other setting you should make, just for the experience more than anything else, is to choose Justification and then choose Center. Click OK to dismiss the dialog box, press Esc to finish designing the view, and choose Yes to save the new view.

Now, what does it all mean? Well, *Rec* is an abbreviation for Receipt. That will be the title of your column. The formula is cleverly crafted to put a Y in the new column if the Return Receipt field has a Yes. The Y will be centered in the column so it won't look like it's stuck on the end of the date in the column just to the left. Now, when you look at your mail database again using the All by Category view, you will see a Y in the Rec column if someone wants to know when you open that message.

While there is really nothing wrong with people wanting to know when a message they sent is opened, you might be one of those people who resents it. If so, here's the trick to read the message without actually opening it. Highlight the message in the view (don't open it though) and then choose Mail⇨Forward. The memo appears on the screen ready for you to address it to someone else, but as far as the original sender is concerned, you never opened the message. You needn't send it to anyone, of course, just read it and then dismiss it from the screen.

This little lesson in changing a view can be just the beginning. Armed with the skills we've shown you here, you can make far more sweeping changes. But you can't change everyone's view of the world — just your own views of your own databases. You don't have the authority to change view designs for databases on the network . . . yet. Once you become a Notes power user (read *nerd*), just march into the office of the Notes administrator and demand the right to mess with any and every database you see. In the meantime, check Chapter 10 for information about how you can create your own private views for any database.

By the way, if you decide that the column is not something you really need, you can get rid of it. Go back to Design⇨View and choose the All by Category view. Highlight the Rec column, press Del, and choose Yes when the dialog box asks `Permanently delete the selected column(s) from the view?`

My! View's changed

While you're in the business of changing views, a couple of other possible changes are lurking in the dialog box that you see when you choose Design⇨View Attributes. You can see it even sooner than that because the dialog box is in Figure 13-5.

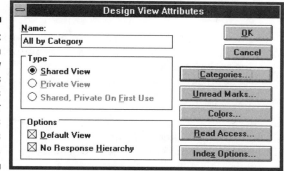

Figure 13-5:
The Design
View
Attributes
dialog box is
useful for
making lots
of changes
to a view.

Check out the buttons along the right side of the dialog box. Here are the changes you can make using three of them:

- ✔ Categories — Choose this and another little dialog box appears, in which you can choose whether categories should be expanded (you can see the documents that each category contains) or collapsed (only the category titles appear) when you open the database.

- ✔ Unread Marks — Choose this to specify whether unread documents will be distinguished by a star and a different color. Your choices are *None:* unread documents are displayed the same as other documents; *Unread Documents Only:* only main documents (not response documents) show unread marks; and *Compute and Display at All Levels of View:* all unread documents, even categories containing unread documents, show unread marks.

- ✔ Colors — Here you can pick from 15 stunning colors for Unread Documents, Column Totals, and Column Headings. You can also choose from over 20 delightful shades for the background color of the view. (We say "over 20" because there are 21.)

After you have chosen OK to dismiss the Design View Attributes dialog box, why not add a column to tell the number of documents in each category in this All by Category view? Select the left-most column in the row of column titles and choose Design⇨New column. In the Design Column Definition dialog box, make the width 3 and click OK, enter a # in the Title text box and this formula in the formula text box:.

```
@IsCategory(@DocChildren)
```

Press Esc and save the redesigned view. When your documents reappear in the view, you can see how many are in each category.

Icons customized while u wait

Actually, you have to do more than just wait. You have to do the work here. Your desktop has a box with an icon for each database you've added. Your e-mail database icon, which looks like everyone else's, is yours to change if you want — here's your chance to strut your stuff, be an individual, leave the pack behind, show off your creative genius . . . and waste a little time.

Start by selecting your e-mail database and then choose Design⇨Icon. A palette appears with the tools and colors you need to create an eye-catching crowd-pleaser. Of course, the normal crowd seeing this icon will be just one (you), but don't let that dampen your enthusiasm.

Figure 13-6 shows the dialog box with an icon nearing artistic completion. To the untutored eye, it may only be a G with a crooked line under it and a white border. To the true connoisseur, however, it's an artistic whole, proclaiming to the world this vital message: "e-mail Database for someone whose last name begins with G."

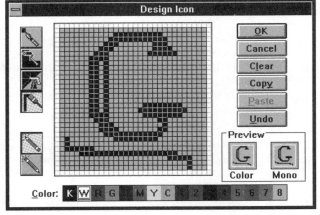

Figure 13-6: This dialog box is a complete artist's studio with everything you need to create an icon.

The boxes to the left, the tools, allow you to color whole areas at once, individual squares, or straight lines with the color you chose. The pencils at the bottom are for drawing and erasing (should you spill a little paint in the wrong place in your creation).

If, *sacre bleu*, you've made a series of mistakes and want to start all over again, choose Clear, and the entire palette is emptied of color — you may start again. When you make a simple mistake, choose Undo and it's as though the most recent action never took place.

As you work, you can check the Preview window to see how the icon will look on a color or monochrome monitor. Once you're satisfied, click OK and, voilà, your database has a new icon.

Using Copy, you can place the icon from another database on the Clipboard and then Paste it into the current palette, thereby copying another master's work. Or why not get into PaintBrush, create an original drawing, and then copy and paste it into the icon palette?

Certify Me, Quick

When you go out of the country, you usually need a passport, unless you're at the beach and simply swim out too far. Sometimes you need to have your passport stamped with special permission to visit specific places. Notes uses a kind of passport and visa, too. In Notes, your passport is your Notes ID and the visa is a certificate. Your ID says you are a Notes user, and the certificates tell which organization(s) will allow you to access their servers.

Normally, you just use Notes in your own organization. Sometimes people leave an organization — and not always for the right reasons, if you get our drift. Some of those people may become bad guys. Of course, every organization should keep an eye on comings and goings to be sure that only current members have access to Notes. But just in case someone slips through the cracks, everyone's certification expires after a couple of years.

When your certification is about to expire, you need to get recertified — or on some dark day in the not-too-distant future that you will find you simply can't access any Notes servers. You will usually receive a notice from the Notes administrator telling you that your number is up and you need to get recertified soon.

To see when your certificate expires, choose Tools➪User ID➪Certificates. Highlight each certificate (assuming you have more than one — most people don't) and the information in the dialog box will tell you when it expires. You can see a sample certificate information box in Figure 13-7.

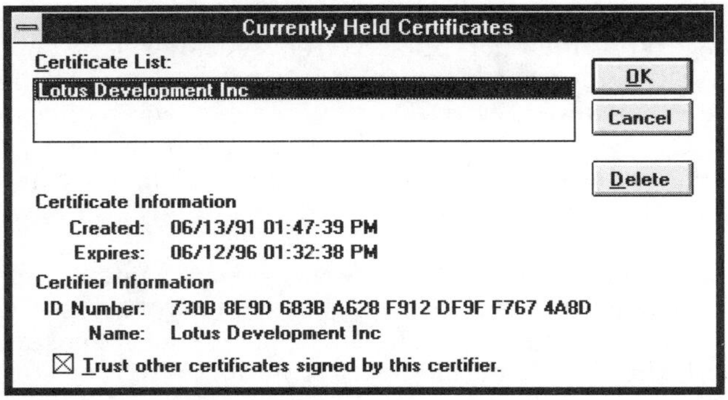

Figure 13-7:
This is the
Currently
Held
Certificates
information
box.

Currently Held Certificates

Certificate List:

Lotus Development Inc

OK

Cancel

Delete

Certificate Information
  Created: 06/13/91 01:47:39 PM
  Expires: 06/12/96 01:32:38 PM

Certifier Information
  ID Number: 730B 8E9D 683B A628 F912 DF9F F767 4A8D
  Name: Lotus Development Inc

☒ Trust other certificates signed by this certifier.

There is another reason to get certified — you may need to communicate with a Notes user in another company. Because that organization uses a different certificate, you can't just send a message and assume it's going to get there.

The good news (not that there was really any bad news) is that it's easy to get certified — and it's free — and it doesn't happen very often (usually only once every a couple of years) — and the sun'll come out tomorrow. Here's what you do. Use Mail⇨Send User ID⇨Request Certificate. In the dialog box that appears in Figure 13-8 and on your screen, you'll notice that you need to enter the name of the person to send it To. You'll need to ask around your organization or call the other organization to find the name of the person who is the *certifier,* who issues certificates.

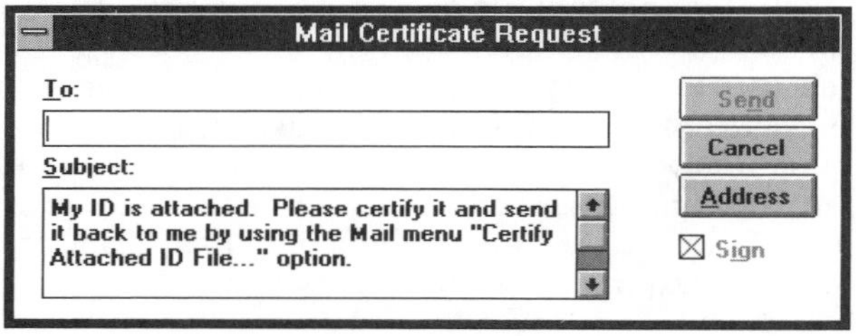

Figure 13-8:
This is the dialog box you use when you need a new or renewed certificate.

Mail Certificate Request

To:

Subject:

My ID is attached. Please certify it and send it back to me by using the Mail menu "Certify Attached ID File..." option.

Send
Cancel
Address
☒ Sign

Once the certifier receives the request, you can expect a return memo with the new certification attached. When this joyous event occurs, use Tools⇨User ID⇨Merge Copy to merge the new certification into your user ID. It's like adding a visa to your passport.

Honey, Where Are My Encryption Keys?

Cloak and dagger stuff, this encryption. You encrypt information when you want to be absolutely sure information is not going to be seen by the wrong eyes or even a wrong whole person. Encrypting means scrambling the information in a field. It takes place behind the scenes, and the only teeny little hint that something is encrypted is that sending or opening a document containing an encrypted field takes a little longer.

There are two instances in which you may encrypt information: your mail messages and specified fields in other databases. Encryption uses *keys* to scramble and rearrange the data so that it doesn't make any sense during transmission. In the case of mail messages you want to encrypt, you don't have to do anything about keys. Encrypted mail scrambles only the *body* field and uses the public and private encryption keys associated with the user ID for each recipient. It's all automatic.

However, if you are using a database that has an encryptable field, you may choose to encrypt the data in that field. In that case, you have to supply legitimate readers of the data with a special encryption key that you create. No key means no reading; the field will appear empty. Remember, if a field is encryptable, the field markers (the little corners showing the beginning and end of the field) are red.

Suppose you are entering data in a personnel database in which one section is for performance evaluations. Other sections are for information everyone in the company might need, like phone number, location, or favorite fingernail polish color. That information doesn't need to be secret, but the evaluation information does. So you decide to encrypt the field.

First, you have to create the encryption key. Use Tools⇨User ID⇨Encryption Keys⇨New. In the dialog box like the one in Figure 13-9, give the new key a name, preferably something you'll associate with its purpose. Note the cleverly chosen name for the key you'll use to encrypt the Evaluations field in personnel records.

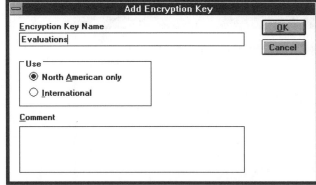

Figure 13-9:
This simple
dialog box is
where
encryption
keys are
created.

Normally you can leave *North American only* checked — but this assumes that the database will only be seen in North American installations of Notes. If you have offices around the world that might use the database, then you should choose International. There is a different way of encrypting information outside North America. (The U.S. government requires this distinction. We could tell you why, but then you'd have the CIA following you around, too.)

Now that you have created the key, you need to use it in the document you are writing. If you haven't already done so, use Compose to start a document and then choose Edit⇨Security⇨Encryption Keys in the dialog box like the one in Figure 13-10. Choose the key you want to add and choose Add. The encryption key is now added to the document so that you can encrypt the field, but who can decrypt it? You? Yes, but no one else yet.

Figure 13-10:
With this
dialog box,
you can
assign an
encryption
key to the
form.

We need to send the key to anyone who needs to see the field. Choose
Mail⇨Send User ID⇨Encryption Key, select the key you want to send (as we did
in Figure 13-11), and type a cheery little note to accompany your gift of an
encryption key.

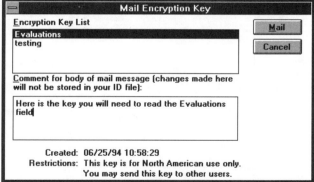

Figure 13-11:
Use this
dialog box to
send the
encryption
key to
everyone
needing to
see the
Evaluations
field.

Choose Mail and, in the next dialog box, type in the name, names, or group to
whom you are sending the key. You can send courtesy copies (cc:) to people
who ought to know you've sent the key, but those folks will not receive the key
itself. The Subject: line of the memo will contain the text in the Subject box, but
you may change it if you want it to say something else. Happy with everything
in the dialog box? Fine; choose Send.

One more question from Notes and the key's on its way. A question box appears, asking, Should the recipients be allowed to send this key to other users? This is your call. If the information is terribly sensitive and you want control over who sees it, choose No. People can ask you to send the key to others if necessary. If you don't want people to bother you by requesting the key all the time, then choose Yes.

You're done with your part, but the recipients will have a small chore when they receive the key. They need to highlight the memo containing the key and then choose Mail⇨Accept Encryption Key.

Just in case it ever comes up, remember that you do *not* use this procedure to encrypt your mail memos.

Hammering on Notes with Some Tools

The little Notes engine is throbbing quietly and efficiently somewhere inside your computer: messages are moving, secrets in encrypted fields are being kept, and you've even succeeded in customizing the look of some of your forms. However, once in a while you may feel that things are not quite perfect — that a few things are still not quite right. The Tools menu is definitely a place where you should look when you are interested in tinkering away at Notes to make it behave the way you want.

Some ID ideas

Your User ID is the file that allows you to use Notes. If someone gets hold of your ID, that person now can use Notes pretending to be you — sending off messages, reading your mail, and peeking into encrypted fields that only a small group of the inner circle of the chosen few are supposed to see. Where is your ID? Only you know that for sure, but it's probably in several places: in the Notes directory (folder) of your computer, on a floppy disk for backup storage in case something happens to your computer, and, if you have a laptop, in the Notes directory there, too. So there may be three separate Notes ID files which some ruthless person could use to his or her own advantage. Even somebody with a few ruths may take your ID and use it for nefarious purposes. Anyone with access to your computer has access to your ID.

The solution is to protect your ID with a password *right now*. Choose Tools⇨User ID⇨Password⇨Set. Figure 13-12 shows the relatively simple dialog box into which you type your password.

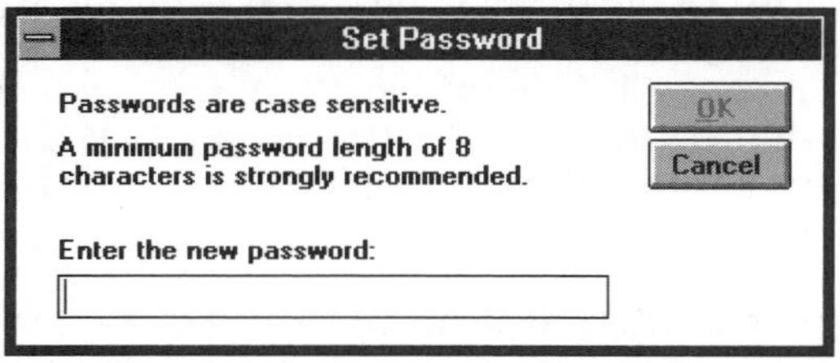

Figure 13-12:
This is the
dialog box
where you
protect your
ID file with a
password.

```
┌─────────────────────────────────────────────────────┐
│ ─ │              Set Password                         │
├─────────────────────────────────────────────────────┤
│ Passwords are case sensitive.             ┌────────┐ │
│                                           │   OK   │ │
│ A minimum password length of 8            └────────┘ │
│ characters is strongly recommended.       ┌────────┐ │
│                                           │ Cancel │ │
│ Enter the new password:                   └────────┘ │
│ ┌─────────────────────────────────────┐             │
│ │                                     │             │
│ └─────────────────────────────────────┘             │
└─────────────────────────────────────────────────────┘
```

Keep the following facts in mind as you decide on a password:

- ✔ You may use a password of any length.

- ✔ Notes recommends a minimum of eight characters, simply because it's many times harder to figure out a long password than it is to figure out a short one.

- ✔ This may be obvious, but . . . be sure it's something you're going to remember. We all have to remember PIN numbers, credit card codes, login names, network login passwords, gym locker combination, in-laws' birthdays, and the date of our tetanus booster. Anytime we forget one of these, somebody treats us as though we're wearing a clown suit. If you set a Notes password and forget it, you are out of luck. No one will look at you disapprovingly, but you'll have to get a new ID and start all over, and all your old messages will be unreadable.

- ✔ This, too, may be obvious, but make sure the password isn't something that someone else will figure out. Using your own first name is not the most secure password.

- ✔ Passwords are case sensitive, so GOOBER is different from Goober is different from goober is different from gOober is . . . well, you get the point.

- ✔ As you type in your password, only Xs appear to protect your password. Notes takes passwords VERY seriously.

- ✔ You will be prompted a second time to be sure you didn't make a mistake.

- ✔ The password protects this ID only. In other words, if you protect the ID file on your main computer, it will have no effect on your laptop's copy of the ID.

- ✔ The best way to handle the above issue is to password protect the ID on your main computer, then copy it to a floppy disk, and then copy it from the floppy disk to your laptop. Delete any copies of the ID file that are not password protected, or keep them under lock. (Usually, people say *lock and key*, but if the key were around, why bother with the lock? And what if it's a combination lock?)

Each of your ID files may have different certificates associated with it. You can see what certificates are associated with an ID file by choosing Tools⇨User ID⇨Certificates. Add a password to the ID with the largest number of certificates and copy that ID to the floppy and your other computers. If each ID has different certificates, add the password to each separately.

If you leave your computer, you ought to take steps so that if any ruthless bad guys walk by, they can't gain access to Notes on your computer. Press F5 or choose Tools⇨User Logoff. That immediately disables your access to Notes until you enter your password again. There is even a way to get Notes to press the F5 key automatically if it notices that you've been away for a while.

Of course, Notes doesn't know if you have physically left the computer, but it does know how long it has been since you used Notes. After a certain amount of time, Notes starts missing you and disables your access until you enter your password.

To enable this time-out procedure, again use Tools⇨User ID⇨Password⇨Set. A different dialog box appears this time. You can see in Figure 13-13 that there is a place in this box to enter the number of minutes of inactivity Notes will allow to pass before disabling your personal access.

Figure 13-13:
This dialog box appears the second time you use Tools⇨User ID⇨Password⇨Set.

Enter Password
Enter the password for Paul Freeland:　　　OK　Cancel
✕✕✕✕✕✕✕✕✕✕✕✕✕✕
Automatically log off after [15] minutes of inactivity

If the specified time goes by or if you press F5, a screen prompting you for your password will appear the next time you try to do something with Notes. Type in your password, press Enter, and off you go.

If you decide to remove the password protection from your ID file, use Tools⇨User ID⇨Password⇨Clear. Type your password and choose OK, and the password is no more.

Perhaps you just got married and have a new name, or you're in the witness protection plan and need a new name, or the name you have been using in Notes isn't quite right. You can see a bunch of information about your User ID by choosing Tools⇨User ID⇨Information, but don't try to change your User Name by choosing Change User Name. If you do, you won't be able to use Notes anymore. First, use Mail⇨Send User ID⇨Request New Name. Mail this request off to the proper authority and wait for a response. When the response arrives, open it, choose Mail⇨Accept Certificate, and then choose OK in the Accept New ID Information dialog box.

Tools that set up the user

When you start your car, you may fasten your seat belt, adjust the mirror, and set the volume on the radio before you head out into traffic. When you start Notes, there may be things you do or things you would like Notes to do. Some of those can be set in the Tools⇨Setup⇨User menu. Figure 13-14 shows the User Setup dialog box.

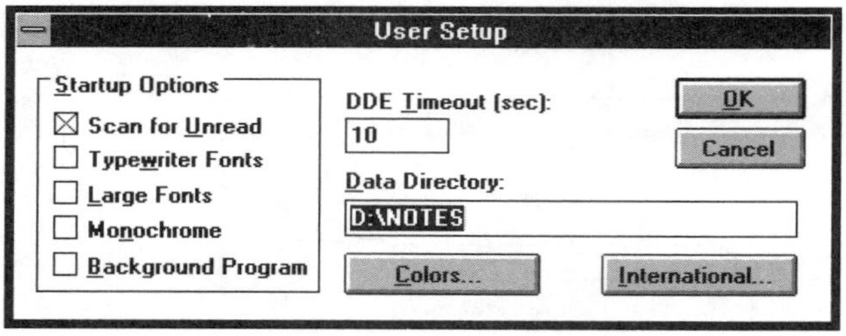

Figure 13-14:
The Tools
User dialog
box for
making
changes to
the way
Notes starts
and works.

User Setup
Startup Options
☒ Scan for Unread
☐ Typewriter Fonts
☐ Large Fonts
☐ Monochrome
☐ Background Program
DDE Timeout (sec): `10`
Data Directory: `D:\NOTES`
OK
Cancel
Colors...
International...

If you select Scan for Unread the next time you start Notes, you will see a dialog box like the one in Figure 13-15 telling you how many unread messages or documents you have. Tell Notes which databases you are interested in having it check. It's doubtful you want to know about all the unread documents in all the databases you may have on your desktop.

To specify which databases are checked, use Tools⇨Scan Unread⇨Choose Preferred. Select a single database and then use the Enter key (or Shift plus the mouse) to select more than one. Finally, select OK. This change will take effect the next time you start Notes.

Figure 13-15:
You can
customize
Notes to
display a
count of
your unread
messages
when you
start Notes.

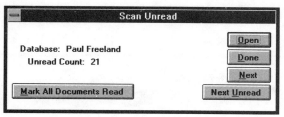

For those for whom colors make the world go 'round, click the Colors button and then choose new default colors for Background, Text, Database Icons, and Pictures (graphics displayed in documents). Remember that this selection of colors is for your own display only.

Click the International button, and, among other things, you'll be able to change the collation sequence (the way Notes sorts documents in views), the measurement units from Imperial (gallons, inches, miles, six packs) to Metric (meters, liters, tweeters), and the dictionary (so that when the spell checker finds errors, it will present the right alternative spellings for your context).

Chapter 14
Notes on the Road

In This Chapter

▶ Getting ready to take Notes on a trip
▶ Replicating your mail
▶ Making your modem manipulate your messages
▶ Saving on your phone bill

*J*ust because you have to travel away from the office doesn't mean that you can't read your mail, use your databases, and generally stay plugged in to what's going on back at the office. In this chapter, we'll explore what you have to do to use Notes on the road.

Replicating Is Where It's At

Let's say your company has one Notes server in Boston, one in New York, and one in London, and on each of these servers your administrator has placed a copy of some database that your company uses to discuss marketing strategy for the coming year. Obviously, you need the documents that have been added to the database by your English colleagues to be show up in the databases in New York and Boston. And if someone in New York edits a document, you would want the changes to be distributed to Boston and London. And what if someone in Beantown deletes a document? You'd want that document to be deleted in both New York and London, too.

Beantown is a nickname for Boston, in case you didn't know. It has something to do with Boston Baked Beans, which are candy-covered peanuts sold at great expense to tourists. They're usually sold by street vendors near a place called Faneuil Hall, where all the tourists congregate. They have pretty good food there and usually a bunch of street musicians and mimes, if you're into that kind of thing.

What were we talking about? Oh, yes — replication. Replication is the process that Notes uses to keep the three databases synchronized with one another. Your administrator schedules calls between the servers; the Boston server may call up the New York server at 8 a.m. and then call the English server at 9 a.m. Then it would place another call to New York at 11 a.m., call England again at 1 p.m., and so on, and so on.

That's nice, but why do you care? Because whenever you need to use Notes away from the office, you use the same process.

You have your laptop all set up and ready to go. Grab a cab to the airport, check your bags, and get on the plane. You're trapped in that seat for the next three hours, so why not use the time to catch up on some of your e-mail? By the end of the trip, you have 11 new e-mail messages to send, and you've composed a few documents in the databases that you brought with you, too.

Now fast forward to your arrival at the hotel. You're all checked in: you've hung your suits in the closet, checked out the treats in the honorbar, and paid off the bellman (two bucks just to turn on the TV, what a rip off). So now how are you going to send off that e-mail, post those documents you composed on the plane, and see if any mail has been sent to you while you were cruising at 35,000 feet? You guessed it, you're going to replicate the databases on your laptop with the server back at the office.

Getting Your Computer Ready to Go

Needless to say, you must get prepared for your new-found career as a replicator before you even leave the office; you don't want to be stuck in the hotel room without the proper setup. Here's a checklist of the stuff you have to bring with you:

- Your computer
- Notes
- A modem
- A phone cable to connect the modem to the phone jack
- Your USER.ID file
- Your Personal N&A Book
- Some databases
- Some phone numbers
- A clean pair of socks and maybe a couple of shirts, depending on the length of your stay

Taking a computer on a trip

Personal computers are certainly a great deal smaller than the computers of yesteryear. (We're resisting the temptation to launch into a story about how, when we first started in the computer business, computers were as big as a refrigerator and took three days to add up a list of numbers.) If you're lucky, you have a laptop computer. It's nice and small and may even have a color screen. Many laptops have modems built right in, so that's one less thing to pack for your trip.

If you don't have a fancy little laptop, you should read this part of the book anyway, even if you won't be going anywhere. If you need to set up Notes on your computer at home, the steps are almost exactly the same.

Practice setting up and using Notes from your laptop *before* you leave for your trip. That way the administrator can hear you scream (and come to help) if you can't figure out how to hook up the @#*^#$ modem.

Telling Notes about your modem

Ever wonder what a *modem* is? The short answer is that it's a piece of hardware that lets your computer (in the hotel room) and another computer (the server back at the office) talk to one another over the telephone. The long answer is boring and technical, so we'll keep the nitty-gritty details to a minimum.

A couple of words about modems

Modems are rated by their speed. Your modem may be called 14.4BPS (if you're lucky) or 2400BPS (if you're not so lucky). *BPS* stands for Bits Per Second, and it represents how fast your computer can send information over the phone. 2400BPS (sometimes they say 2400 *baud*, which means the same thing) means 2,400 bits per second, which is pretty slow. 9600BPS is four times faster, and 14.4BPS actually stands for 14,400 bits per second, and that's about the fastest modem that's commercially available right now. You don't even have to know what a *bit* is to realize that the faster you can send them, the better!

The speed of your modem is especially important when you are dialing in to the server to replicate. The faster the modem, the faster you can replicate, and the shorter the phone call, the smaller the phone bill. (That's really important if you're calling from a hotel room, because many hotels add a *huge* surcharge to outgoing calls. A 25-minute call to the home office can end up costing a lot of money.)

Most people find that a 2400BPS modem is so slow as to be impractical to use with Notes. A modem that's 9600BPS is pretty decent (it's what one of the authors of this book uses). A modem that can go 14.4BPS is *really* fast and the best you can have. (It's the kind the other author of this book has, and that makes the first author pretty jealous.)

Telling Notes about your modem

To get Notes ready to use your modem, you have to do two things:

> ✔ Tell Notes that you have a modem.
> ✔ Tell Notes what kind of modem you have.

Of course, you don't just say, "Notes, I have a modem." What you really have to do is *enable a serial port,* which sounds much worse than it really is.

Enabling your serial port

To enable a serial port, choose Tools⇨Setup⇨Ports and watch for the dialog box shown in Figure 14-1.

This one is pretty easy because all you have to do is select the name of the port to which your modem is connected from the list box and click the Enable Port check box.

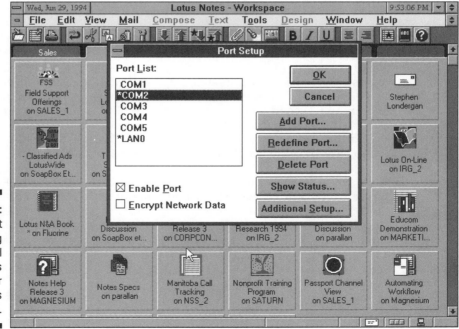

Figure 14-1:
Use the Port Setup dialog box to tell Notes where your modem is plugged in.

What isn't so easy is knowing which port your modem is connected to unless you use a Macintosh. If you *don't* use a Mac, the port names listed will be COM1, COM2, COM3, and so on. Your modem will almost certainly be connected to either COM1 or COM2. If you're not sure which one you use, call your administrator to find out. (Some computers have their mouse plugged in to COM1, so the modem is connected to COM2.)

If you have a Mac, the port name will either be MODEM or PRINTER. The correct answer is probably obvious, unless you have some compelling reason to plug your modem into your printer port.

So anyway, after you have selected the correct port name and clicked the Enable Port box, you're almost done. Hold off on clicking <u>O</u>K until you read the next section, because you have to tell Notes what kind of modem you have.

Configuring your modem

While you're in the T<u>o</u>ols⇨<u>S</u>etup⇨<u>P</u>orts dialog box, you should check out the Additional <u>S</u>etup button. When you click it, Notes presents you with the dialog box shown in Figure 14-2.

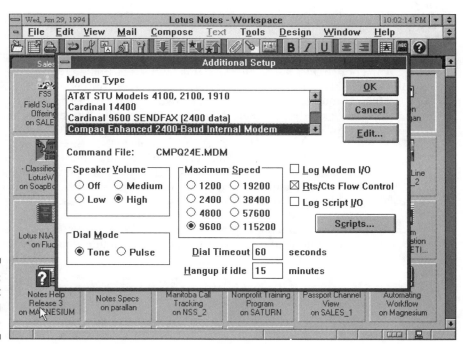

Figure 14-2:
The Port Setup dialog box.

The dialog box has a bunch of options, but you only have to worry about two things. OK, maybe three things.

The first thing you need to do is select the brand of modem you own from the list. This is important, because different modems work differently, and Notes needs to know exactly which you have.

If your modem doesn't appear in the list, choose Auto Configure (it's near the bottom of the list). And if that doesn't work out, try one of the Hayes modems, because many modems can pretend they are Hayes modems. If that doesn't work, call your administrator and ask which you should choose.

The list of modems actually represents a bunch of *modem command files*. When you install Notes, you automatically get one of these command files for just about every modem under the sun. (They are really just ASCII files with the extension *.MDM*.) If you are short on disk space, you could delete the ones you don't need from your Notes data directory.

The other things you need to worry about are the Maximum Speed buttons. All you have to do is click the speed of your modem.

Don't get your hopes up; if you only have a 2400BPS modem, clicking the 9600BPS button is *not* going to speed it up. (Nice try, though.)

The last thing you *may* want to worry about is the Speaker Volume, where you can choose Off, Low, Medium, or High. When you make a call from your computer to a Notes server, you briefly hear some high-pitched whistles and squeals and pops and squeaks as the two modems figure out how fast they can talk to one another (the server's wicked-fast 14.4BPS modem may have to slow down to talk to your crummy 2400BPS modem). You can decide to turn off the volume altogether, but then you won't be able to listen in to the beginning of their conversation. You just might want to listen in sometimes — especially if you are having trouble connecting — so that you can hear what's going on. On the other hand, if your modem works A-O-K, you could decide to turn the speaker off so that you don't have to listen to all that noise.

After you have selected your modem's name from the list, set the speed at which it communicates, and (perhaps) set the volume, you can click OK and be done with it.

Setting up your Personal N&A Book

If you've been using Notes at the office, you have probably already used your Personal N&A Book to compose a couple of group documents so that you can easily send mail to your friends. (If you haven't and you want to, refer to Chapter 6.)

Your Personal N&A Book is an important thing to take with you when you'll be using Notes from afar, because in it you store the phone numbers for the servers you'll be calling.

Adding a connection document

Notes needs to know the telephone numbers of the servers you intend to call. It stores them in *remote connection documents* that are in turn stored in your Personal N&A Book. You compose the documents yourself, as we'll explain in the next couple of paragraphs.

First things first. You have to find out the server telephone numbers; this is another pearl of knowledge that you'll have to solicit from your Administrator. In fact, you may need more than one number, because you'll probably be calling more than one server. Call your administrator, explain that you are getting ready to use Notes away from the office, and ask for the appropriate numbers.

At the very least, you'll need the phone number of your Home Server.

After you have the numbers you need, open your Personal N&A Book — the icon looks like Figure 14-3. If you can't find the icon on your desktop, use File⇨Open Database to get it. It will be on your local hard disk.

Figure 14-3:
Your
Personal
N&A Book.

After you have the database open, choose Compose⇨Connection⇨Remote, and you'll get a document like you see pictured in Figure 14-4. This will be one of the remote connection documents that stores the phone number of the server you'll be calling.

Now it's just a matter of filling in the blanks, and you only have to worry about the fields at the top — for now.

Notes automatically fills in your name as the name of the computer that will be making the call, but you have to enter the name of the server you'll be calling. You also have to enter the port name that the modem should use in the Use port(s) field — pick the same port that you enabled earlier in this chapter. Enter the phone number of the server in the Dial phone number field and then save the document as you would save any other (by pressing Esc and clicking Yes).

If you're calling more than one server, you have to compose an additional Remote Connection document for each.

Reviewing the connection documents

To see the remote connection documents that you have composed, open your Personal N&A Book and choose View⇨Connections. You see a view like the one in Figure 14-5. You can double-click any one of the documents to review it.

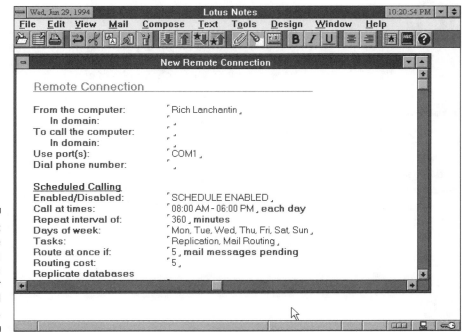

Figure 14-4:
A remote connection document in your Personal N&A Book.

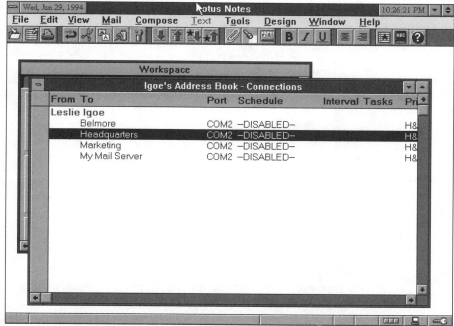

Figure 14-5:
The
Connections
view in your
Personal
N&A Book
shows your
remote
connection
documents.

Making a copy of the database to bring with you

To make a copy of the database that you'll be replicating, select the database and choose File⇨New Replica. When you do, you get the dialog box shown in Figure 14-6.

Notes knows which database you're copying because you selected it before you chose File⇨New Replica, and it makes a pretty good guess about what the filename will be on your computer.

Most people name the local copy the same as the database on the server, but you can, if you want, give the copy of the database a name that's different from the original.

In most cases, you should leave the Replicate Access Control List button selected, assuming that the Access Control List on the server is also the one you want for your local copy. (If that sounds confusing, just leave the button selected, and we'll explain it in a minute.)

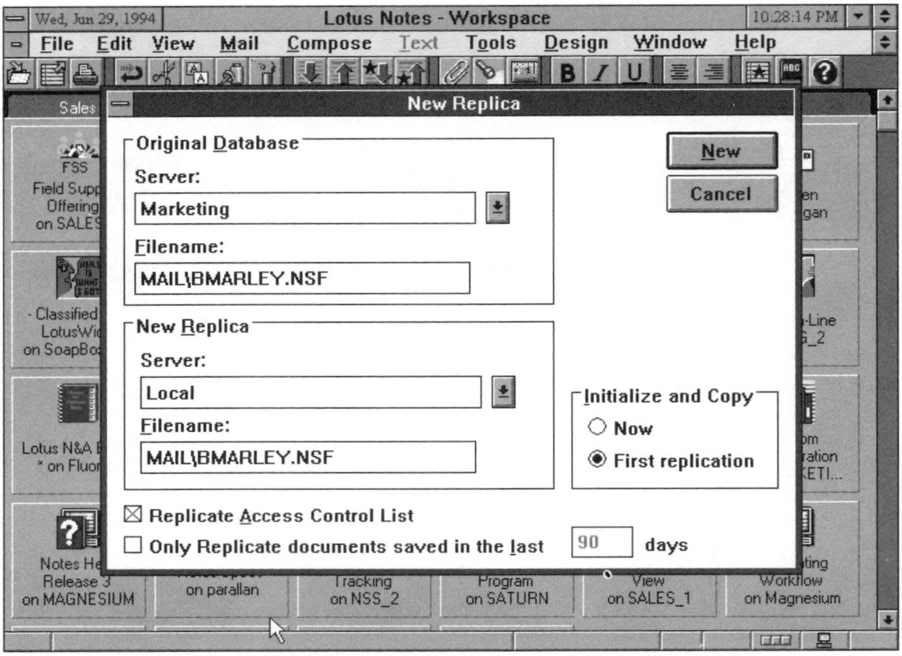

Figure 14-6:
Use the
New Replica
dialog box to
make a copy
of a
database to
take with
you.

Notes databases (even your mail database) are usually pretty big; they can be several hundred megabytes in size. So you may be in for a rude surprise when you try to replicate one of these monsters onto your laptop, because you probably don't have room for all those documents. Then again, you probably don't really need to have them all. Use the Replicate Only Documents Saved in the last 90 days button to only get documents that have been added to the database recently. For example, if you are making a copy of your mail database to take with you on a trip, you can click the button and change the 90 to a 10. Now the copy of the database that you bring with you will be a great deal smaller than the copy that's on the server. Travel light, we always say!

Your last decision in the File⇨New Replica dialog box is when to Initialize and Copy the database — in other words, when are you going to perform your first replication? You can do it right *Now* or at your *First replication*. (That means "later.") We recommend that you choose First replication so that you can check a couple of things before you try to replicate for the first time. So if you're following our advice, leave the Initialize and Copy option set to First replication, and click New to create a new database.

When you click New, Notes creates a *replica stub* copy of the database, as you can see in Figure 14-7. A replica stub is a database that's totally, completely, we're not kidding around here, empty. It has no forms, no views, no documents, no nuthin'. The database won't get filled up until you perform your first replication.

One more thing to check before you replicate for the first time

You won't be surprised to hear that you can screw up replication, and for once we're going to advise against blind optimism. Before you try to replicate a database for the first time you should make sure that your database's Access Control List is set appropriately.

Select your database and choose File⇨Database⇨Access Control List. When you do, you get the dialog box that's shown in Figure 14-8.

Many of the entries in the list may not make any sense, but that's OK. You're checking to make sure that the name of the server with which you'll be replicating is listed and that its Access Level is set to *Manager*. If your server isn't listed, or if it's listed at anything other than Manager, you can use the Add or Update buttons to rectify that problem.

Figure 14-7:
When you create a New Replica copy of a database, you get a replica stub.

Marketing
MAIL\BMARLEY.
NSF

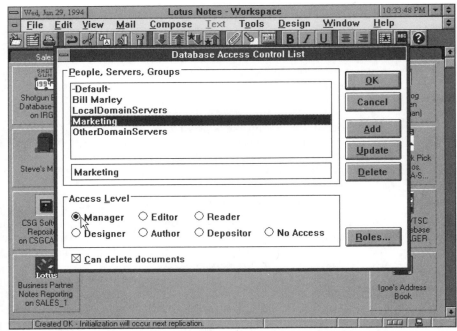

Figure 14-8:
Check your
database's
Access
Control List
before trying
to replicate.

In most cases, you'll want to list the server as Manager in the (local) database's Access Control List, but it may not be a bad idea to check with your all-knowing administrator — he or she may have a good reason to list the server differently. The right answer depends very much on the way your administrator has set up Notes at your company, so it can't hurt to ask.

Replicating for the first time ever

Now we'll have a short quiz. Please select the one and only correct answer for the following question.

You have a database on your computer that you're going to replicate with a database on a server. This will be the first time you've ever replicated the database, and you know that a whole bunch of documents have to get replicated into your copy of the database — several megabytes worth. Do you:

1. Perform the first replication over the phone from your hotel room, where long-distance phone calls cost about $1.00 per minute? Total time spent to replicate: 2.75 hours. Total cost of this one phone call: $237.50.

2. Perform the first replication while you're still at work, over the LAN, where it will be extremely fast and won't cost anything? Total time spent to replicate: 11 minutes. Total cost: $0.00.

3. Quit your job and start selling candy-covered peanuts outside a well-known tourist trap in Boston? Total time spent: The rest of your life. Total cost: $1.79/lb. for the peanuts.

We hope you chose answer 2.

To have Notes replicate a database, select the database in question, choose Tools⇨Replicate, and look for the dialog box that you see in Figure 14-9.

As usual, there are many more options here than you need to concern yourself with, especially this first time. We'll explain the intricacies of the Tools⇨Replicate dialog box a little later in this chapter, so for now just choose the name of the server with which you'll be replicating. If you're replicating your mail database, your home server's name will already be there. Make sure that the *Selected database(s)* check box, the *Receive documents from server* check box, and the *Send documents to server* check box are all selected (they will be by default), and, if you have one, you should turn *off* the check box that says Run In Background for reasons we'll explain later. Click OK and then sit back and watch the lower left-hand corner of the screen. You'll see messages down there about how things are proceeding, in the same place you see those *New Mail has been delivered to you* messages.

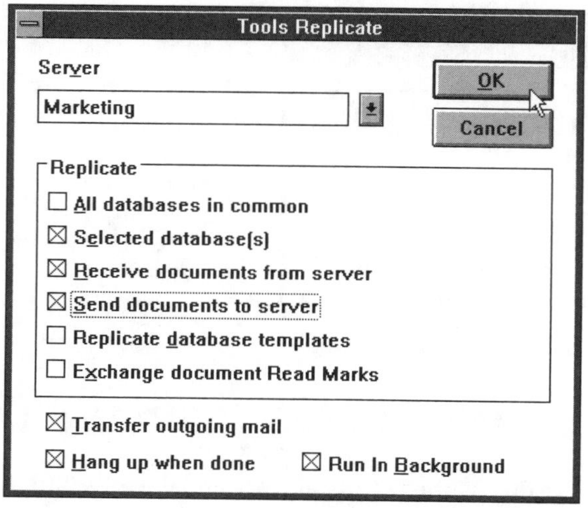

Figure 14-9:
The Tools⇨
Replicate
dialog box.

When Notes is finished, you see something along the lines of the dialog box pictured in Figure 14-10.

Well, five or six pages after you started, you're finally ready to take your computer on the road. The whole process took so long (both to do and to read about) because you were setting up for the very first time. From here on out, replicating will be a breeze — we promise.

In case you need to refer to the steps someday, here's a short-and-sweet list of what you do to prep your computer for a trip:

- ✔ Use Tools➪Setup➪Ports to enable your communications port.
- ✔ Use Tools➪Setup➪Ports➪Additional Setup to tell Notes what kind of modem you have.
- ✔ Open your Personal N&A Book and use Compose➪Connection➪Remote to compose remote connection documents for the servers you'll be calling.
- ✔ Select your database and use File➪Database➪Access Control List to make sure that your server's Access Level is set to *Manager*.
- ✔ Use File➪New Replica to make the first copies of the databases you'll need.
- ✔ Use Tools➪Replicate to refresh your databases.

Do all the setup tasks while you're still at work, including replicating the databases for the first time.

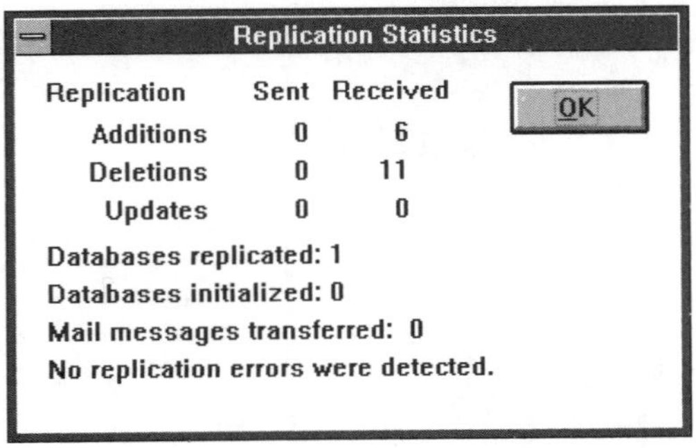

Figure 14-10:
After it finishes replicating a database, Notes tells you how things went.

Replication Statistics		
Replication	Sent	Received
Additions	0	6
Deletions	0	11
Updates	0	0

OK

Databases replicated: 1
Databases initialized: 0
Mail messages transferred: 0
No replication errors were detected.

Using Your Computer away from the Office

Most times, you use Notes while you are at work and plugged into the LAN. Notes knows you're connected to the network, so when you dash off an e-mail, Notes knows to whisk it off to the server through that wire snaking out of the back of your computer and into the wall.

But what if you're *not* connected to the network? What if you're working at home, or you've taken your computer on a trip and you're in a hotel room? Notes has to know that when you send a mail message, it *shouldn't* try to send it through the network, 'cause you ain't got one. Instead, Notes needs to let the mail messages you compose at home pile up so that later, when you call into the server, it can send the messages then.

Location setup

Tell Notes where you are by choosing Tools⇨Setup⇨Location. Using the dialog box shown in Figure 14-11, tell Notes what to do by selecting from the first two buttons. If you are working from home, the road, or anywhere that you are *not* connected to the network, choose Workstation based mail. If you are connected to a network, choose Server-based mail.

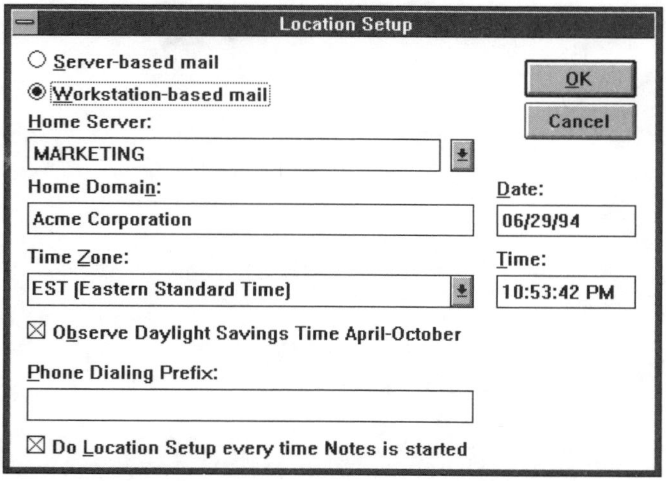

Figure 14-11:
Use Tools⇨
Setup⇨
Location to
tell Notes
whether
you are
connected
to the
network.

Location Setup

○ Server-based mail

◉ Workstation-based mail

Home Server:

MARKETING ±

OK

Cancel

Home Domain: | Date:

Acme Corporation | 06/29/94

Time Zone: | Time:

EST [Eastern Standard Time] ± | 10:53:42 PM

☒ Observe Daylight Savings Time April-October

Phone Dialing Prefix:

☒ Do Location Setup every time Notes is started

If you travel often and are constantly switching back and forth (one day you're using computer on the road, then you're back at the office, then the road for two days, then the office for a couple of days), check the *Do Location Setup every time Notes is started* box. That way, each time you start the program, Notes will present you with the Location Setup dialog box so that you won't forget to tell Notes where you are.

If you have been on a trip and turned on Workstation-based mail, don't forget to set it back to Server-based mail when you get return to the home office (and plug your computer back into the LAN). If you forget and leave Workstation-based e-mail turned on even after you're back on the network, Notes will never send off any of your outgoing e-mail because *it* thinks you're still using your computer at home.

When you turn on Workstation-based e-mail, you are really telling Notes to hold any outgoing e-mail you've composed until the next time you make a phone call to the server. This pending e-mail gets collected in a special database on your workstation called *MAIL.BOX*. The icon for your mailbox database will look like the one pictured in Figure 14-12.

Don't confuse your mail*box* with your mail *database*. Your e-mail *database* is the one you use to read e-mail that's been sent to you, compose your own messages, and so on. Your mail*box* database is only used to queue up e-mail when you're working away from home. In fact, if you find the icon on your desktop, there's no good reason for you to ever mess with it; just leave it alone!

Figure 14-12:
Notes holds pending e-mail in your mailbox when you turn on Workstation-based e-mail.

Sending mail from afar

With two small differences, composing and sending e-mail when you're remote is no different than composing and sending mail when you're on the network.

Difference #1: E-mail is delivered "later," when you call into the server. This can take some getting used to. When you're connected to the LAN, e-mail gets delivered more or less instantaneously to the recipients. If you're working remotely, though, you won't actually dispatch the messages until you make a phone call to the server.

Difference #2: If you're a fan of the Mail⇨Address feature, you're in for a big letdown. Using Mail⇨Address at the office lets you easily peruse your company's Public N&A Book, which is located on your home server. If you're using Mail⇨Address at home, you can't see the company's Public N&A Book; you can only see your Personal N&A Book. Bummer.

Reading your e-mail from afar

Reading your e-mail remotely isn't all that different, either. You just have to be careful that, when you go to open your e-mail database, you double-click the icon for the copy of your e-mail database that's on your workstation and *not* the icon for the copy of the database that's on the server. Choose View⇨Show Server Names if you're not sure which is which; the icons look like the ones in Figure 14-13. Choose View⇨Show Server Names if you're not sure which icon is for the server and which is for the local copy. In the figure, the database on the right is the local copy.

Move all of the icons that represent the local databases to a different workpage and then name the page something like *At Home* so you'll be able to quickly tell the difference.

Figure 14-13:
When traveling, read your e-mail in your local database (the icon on the right), not in the server one.

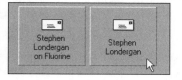

Reading documents while on the road

If you bring a copy of a database other than your e-mail database with you on the road, you just have to be careful that you use the correct (meaning *local*) icon, as we discussed with your e-mail database.

Other than that consideration, you can read the documents in a local database the same way you read the documents when you're using the server's database back at the office.

Composing documents from afar

More good news: composing a document in a local database isn't any different, either. Of course, when you compose a document in a database on a Notes server, other people can see it and read it the minute you save it. But if you're composing documents in the bush, those documents won't be accessible by your co-workers back in the office until you replicate your database with the server's database.

OK! Enough talk! Let's call the server and replicate!

When you are ready to replicate a database — because you have added some documents to your database, or because you want to see if any new documents have been added to the database back at the office, or perhaps because you want to dispatch the fifteen e-mail messages you just composed — choose Tools➪Replicate. You use this command, along with a couple of the options in the dialog box, to synchronize the databases on your computer with the databases on the server. When you choose Tools➪Replicate, you get the dialog box shown in Figure 14-14.

The Server drop-down box is where you choose the name of the server you want to call; you only see the servers for which you have already composed a remote connection document in your Personal N&A Book.

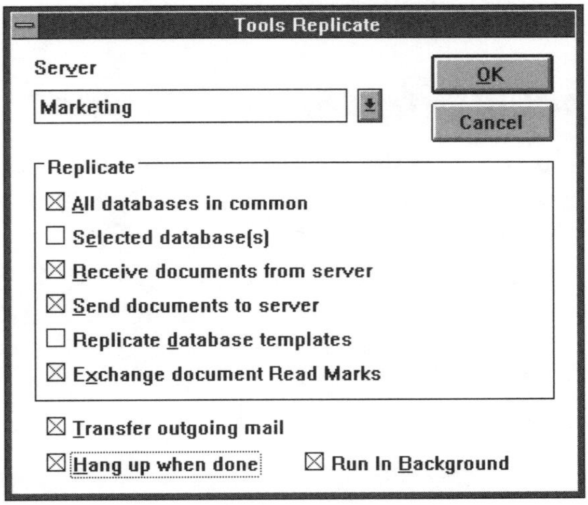

Figure 14-14:
The Tools➪
Replicate
dialog box.

```
┌─────────────────────────────────────────────────────────┐
│ ▬                    Tools Replicate                     │
│                                                          │
│  Server                             ┌──────────────┐     │
│                                     │      OK      │     │
│  ┌────────────────────────────┐ ▼  ├──────────────┤     │
│  │ Marketing                  │    │    Cancel    │     │
│  └────────────────────────────┘    └──────────────┘     │
│                                                          │
│ ┌─Replicate──────────────────────────────────────────┐  │
│ │  ☒ All databases in common                          │  │
│ │  ☐ Selected database(s)                             │  │
│ │  ☒ Receive documents from server                    │  │
│ │  ☒ Send documents to server                         │  │
│ │  ☐ Replicate database templates                     │  │
│ │  ☒ Exchange document Read Marks                      │  │
│ └────────────────────────────────────────────────────┘  │
│                                                          │
│   ☒ Transfer outgoing mail                              │
│   ☒ Hang up when done      ☒ Run In Background          │
│                                                          │
└─────────────────────────────────────────────────────────┘
```

You have to decide which databases you will replicate during this call. Select the Select All databases in common box if you want Notes to replicate every database that's on both your workstation and the server you'll be calling. On the other hand, if you want to replicate just one (or two, or three, or anything other than *all*), you have to back up a bit. You have to shift-click all the ones you want to replicate, and *then* choose Tools⇨Replicate, and *then* choose *Selected database(s)*.

The Receive documents from server box and the Send documents to server box do exactly what they sound like they do: they let you choose whether or not documents will be sent from the server to your workstation and whether or not documents will be sent from your workstation to the server.

Most people leave both the Receive documents from server and the Send documents to server boxes checked every time they replicate — and you probably should, too.

Choosing the Replicate database templates box replicates the templates on your workstation with the templates on the server — choose this only if you're really, really, really sure you want to, and not just because someone at your company told you that you are supposed to. Most people do *not* need to replicate database templates.

You also have to decide if you want to click the Exchange document Read Marks box. Why? When you read a document in the database that's on your computer, Notes is very good about marking it as read so it doesn't show up in red in the view and so it doesn't have the star next to it. That's old news, right? We discuss Read marks in Chapter 8.

When you read a document on your computer, Notes does not mark the copy of the document that's in the database back on the server as having been read. So when you return to the office next week and open the database on the server, all those documents that you read locally while you were on your trip are still marked as *unread* in the database on the server.

Choose the Exchange document Read Marks box to rectify the problem. Now when you replicate, your computer will also tell the server which documents you have read. And when you get back to the office next week, there won't be all that confusion. The only argument against Exchange document Read Marks is that it makes the phone call take longer. So if you're in a hurry or you want to save a couple of bucks on the phone call, leave the box unchecked — but just be prepared for a bunch of documents that you've read on the road to appear as unread in the database back at the office.

At the bottom of the Tools⇨Replicate dialog box, there's a check box that says Transfer outgoing mail. This is the option you use to have Notes send any outgoing mail (that's being held in your MAIL.BOX database) during the phone call. For most calls, you leave this option selected.

Last but not least, check the box Hang up when done. Usually, you use Tools⇨Replicate to dial in to a server and replicate the databases and use this check box to tell Notes to hang up as soon as replication finishes. Occasionally, though, you may deselect the Hang up when done box so that the server stays on the line after it replicates. You may do this if you know you're going to send the responses right away to any new messages you find in your updated e-mail database. Staying on the line (by *not* choosing Hang-up when done) means that when you do the *next* Tools⇨Replicate in a few minutes, you won't have to place another phone call. You'll still have the server on the line from the last phone call.

Of course, all the while, you're probably paying long-distance phone rates for the phone call and you're also tying up the server's modem so that everyone else who tries to call in is getting a busy signal. But hey — you're an important person, right?

Now that we've dragged you through every last option in the dialog box, the bottom line is that you choose Tools⇨Replicate, pick the server you want to call, and leave all the boxes checked.

Background or foreground?

Skip this next couple of paragraphs if you're a Mac user, because Macintoshes can't do background replication.

If you use Windows or OS/2, you also have the option of asking Notes to use *background replication*.

If you choose to use background replication, Notes actually starts another mini-program (guess what's it's called — Lotus Notes Background) that has a sole purpose in life of calling the server and replicating the database(s) in question. This separate program is good, because if you don't use background replication, your whole computer will be tied up when Notes makes the call — you'll just have to sit there and look at it while it replicates. You won't even be able to play Solitaire!

If, on the other hand, you choose to use background replication, you can press Ctrl+Esc to switch back to Notes and continue to read your mail, check your databases, and all that fun stuff, all the while knowing that your faithful Lotus Notes Background program is taking care of calling the server and replicating the databases.

You should *always* use background replication.

When replicating in the background, you see a window like the one shown in Figure 14-15.

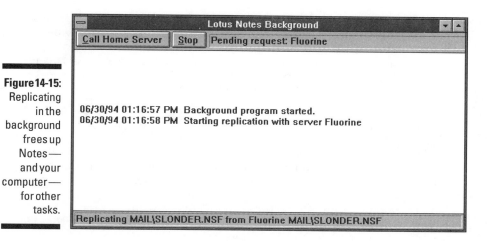

As you can see, the background program has buttons to Call (your) Home Server and to Stop the current call. Most times, though, you don't really even have to look at this window unless you need to hang up the phone in a hurry or check the results of the last call.

Enough already!

When you finally click OK in the Tools⇨Replicate dialog box, Notes starts to replicate. If you decided to replicate in the background, Notes starts the Background Progam and makes the call. If you are *not* replicating in the background, Notes is smart enough to figure out that it has to make a phone call to replicate the databases you've chosen. You have to confirm this call when it shows you the dialog box you see in Figure 14-16. Unless you want to bail out, click Yes.

Foreground or background, you hear the modem clear its throat and dial the server. You can watch the progress by either watching the background program or by watching the lower-left corner of the screen (if you're not replicating in the background).

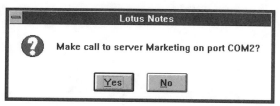

When Notes is finished replicating, it tells you what happened during the call. If you replicated in the background, look at the background program window to see the statistics. If you replicated in the foreground, you get a dialog box that tells you what went on. One place or the other, you'll see exactly how many documents you sent, how many you received, how many databases were replicated, and how many mail messages were sent.

Scheduling

So far, we've been replicating on demand — in other words, every time you want to replicate, you (manually) choose Tools⇨Replicate to place a call. If you use Windows or OS/2 (but not Macintosh), you can instead schedule calls between your workstation and the server. That way, you don't have to call the workstation manually. Your workstation is automatically calling in all day long according to a schedule that you define.

To schedule automatic calls to a server, you have to edit the remote connection document for that server. Open your Personal N&A Book and choose View⇨Connections. Select the document for the server to which you want to schedule calls and press Ctrl+E to edit it. You get a document like the one you see in Figure 14-17.

First, move the cursor to the Enabled/Disabled field, and then press the spacebar to choose Schedule Enabled.

Next, you have to set the *Call at times* field. You can either enter a range of times, like 8:00 AM – 10:00 PM, or a series of separate times, like 8:00 AM, 8:30 AM, 1:00 PM, 2:45 PM.

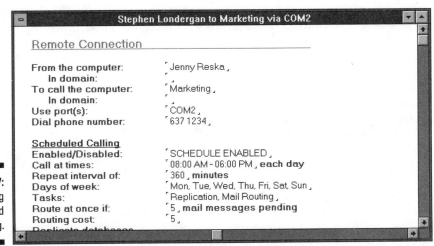

Figure 14-17: Enabling scheduled calling.

The exact times when Notes will call is determined both by the Call at times field and by what you enter in the Repeat interval of field. The Repeat interval of field expects a number of minutes; you enter a number like 30, 60, 120, or 360.

Let's say you enter **8:00 AM – 6:00 PM** in the Call at times field, and you enter **360** in the Repeat interval of field. That actually means that you want your workstation to make four calls to the server: the first call at 8:00 a.m., the second call three hours later at 11:00 a.m., the third call three hours after that at 2:00 p.m., and so on until 6:00 p.m. If you wanted to make calls more often, you reduce the Repeat interval of field. For example, entering 60 would make eleven calls to the server.

If, on the other hand, you enter a series of times in the Call at times field, the Repeat interval of value tells Notes how long it should keep trying to call back if the scheduled call doesn't work out because of a busy signal or something. If you enter **8:30 AM, 1:00 PM, 2:45 PM** in the Call at times field and **60** in the Repeat interval of field, Notes makes its first call to the server at 8:30 a.m. Assuming that call was successful, it won't call again until 1:00 p.m. If at 1:00 p.m the call doesn't go through — maybe the server's phone is busy — Notes keeps trying to call back for one hour. If after an hour it still hasn't gotten through, Notes gives up on that call and won't try again until the schedule says so. In this case, that would be at 2:45 p.m.

After you've figured out your schedule (8:00 AM – 6:00 PM with a 360-minute repeat interval is pretty common), you have to set the Days of week field, where you just enter the days of the week when you want to call, separating each with a comma. (Do you get paid overtime for working on the weekend? We hope so.)

Last is the Tasks field. In most cases, you want Notes to do two things when it calls: replicate all your databases and deliver all your pending e-mail. If, on the other hand, you want a certain call to only deliver e-mail or only replicate databases, you would use Space to change the contents of the Tasks field.

You can ignore the rest of the fields in the remote connection document; they are only used by your administrators for scheduling connections between servers. When you're finished filling out your remote connection document, press Esc and choose <u>Y</u>es to save the document.

Remember that you can set up your workstation to call more than one server by composing more than one remote connection document in your Personal N&A Book? You have to be especially careful not to schedule more than one call at the same time if you'll be calling more than one server. A common type of mistake is to schedule one set of calls between 8:00 a.m. and 10:00 p.m. with a repeat interval of 60 minutes and then schedule another round of calls to a different server between 11:30 a.m. and 11:30 p.m. with a repeat interval of 90 minutes. What happens at 1:00 p.m. when you have two calls scheduled? You guessed it, Notes only makes one of the calls and ignores the other call altogether.

If you're scheduling calls to more than one server, make sure that you choose ranges and intervals that don't overlap with one another. Maybe you could have one set of calls starting at 8:00 a.m. with a 60-minute repeat interval and the other set of calls set to kick off at 8:15 AM, calling back at 60-minute intervals. Or start the second set at 8:30, or 9:30, or 8:45. Just pick a time and interval that won't end up asking Notes to make two calls *at the same time*.

Of course, not everybody who replicates bothers with scheduled calls; you can always just use the Tools⇨Replicate dialog box to replicate whatever and whenever you want. Scheduled calls can be a nice way to save time, though — when you get back to the hotel after a busy day, your e-mail and documents will already be waiting for you.

Saving on Phone Bills

Now that you're an expert on the basics of replication, we're ready to delve into some of the fancy options available for you to fine-tune exactly what happens when a database is replicated.

Selective replication

Selective replication is a way for you to pick and choose exactly which documents you want to replicate. Let's say that, when you travel, you don't want to replicate all your e-mail, you only want to replicate messages from a certain list of people — your boss, your boss's boss, and that guy down the hall who's always sending you jokes. Selective replication is just the answer. Or maybe you replicate a sales activity database, but you want to replicate only the hot leads.

We hope the benefits of selective replication are obvious: fewer messages to replicate equals less time on the phone equals smaller phone bills.

To write one of these money-saving formulas, select the database in question and choose File⇨Database⇨Information⇨Replication⇨Selective (phew!). You get the dialog box shown in Figure 14-18.

Unless you've already modified the formula, the Copy documents selected by box will have the formula *Select @All*. Enter the formula you want in the field and click OK when you're done. As usual, you don't have to worry about the rest of the options in the dialog box. If your administrator tells you that you have to mess around with the other settings, your administrator will also tell you exactly what to do.

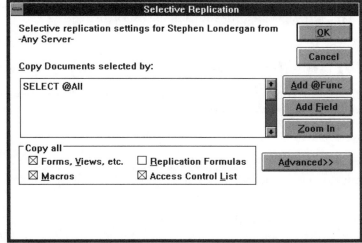

The
Selective
Replication
dialog box.

The formulas used for selective replication can get pretty fancy, but in most cases they're easy. The basic idea is the word *select,* followed by a field name, followed by a comparison operator (usually an equals sign), followed by a value.

In the following example of a selective replication formula, we're asking Notes to replicate only documents from a couple of people.

```
SELECT FROM = "Leslie Igoe" : "Liz Bedell" : "Bill Clinton"
```

The next example formula only replicates documents that are both "Leads" and marked as "Hot."

```
SELECT FORM = "Lead" & STATUS = "Hot"
```

This example replicates all the documents in the database, *except* those for the Garden State.

```
SELECT STATE != "New Jersey"
```

As you might expect, it's hard to predict exactly what formula is the right one for you. We *can* tell you that if you want to replicate only e-mail from certain people, you use a formula very much like the first example, substituting the appropriate names for the ones used above — unless you happen to know Leslie, Liz, and Bill.

If you need a formula to replicate only certain documents from a database, ask the database designer and/or your administrator for help.

Truncate and remove

Another option you can use to make your replication calls short and sweet is the second-to-last button on the File⇨Database⇨Information⇨Replication dialog box, as shown in Figure 14-19, called Truncate large documents and remove attachments.

If you choose to Truncate large documents and remove attachments, Notes will trim any document that's more than 40,000 bytes long and will not replicate any attachments at all.

Although the big documents and attachments will not get replicated to your workstation, the whole document, and any attachments, *will* still be in the server's database.

Figure 14-19:
You can also tell Notes to grab only a piece of every document when you replicate.

```
┌─────────────────────────────────────────────────────────┐
│ ─              Replication Settings                      │
│                                                          │
│  Replica ID:   85255CFF:00718E26        ┌──────────┐    │
│                                         │    OK    │    │
│                                         └──────────┘    │
│                                         ┌──────────┐    │
│                                         │  Cancel  │    │
│                                         └──────────┘    │
│  ┌─Priority────────────────────┐        ┌────────────┐  │
│  │ ● High  ○ Medium  ○ Low     │        │ Selective..│  │
│  │                             │        └────────────┘  │
│  └─────────────────────────────┘        ┌────────────┐  │
│                                          │View history│  │
│                                          └────────────┘  │
│  □ Do not replicate deletions to replicas of this database│
│  □ Disable replication of this database                  │
│  □ Remove documents saved more than  [ 90 ] days ago     │
│  ⊠ Truncate large documents and remove attachments       │
│  □ Replicate database Title, Categories, and Template Names│
└─────────────────────────────────────────────────────────┘
```

Dialing in to a Server "Live"

If you have a relatively fast modem — 9600BPS or better — you may not have to replicate at all. (Now they tell us, right?) You can use the Tools⇨Call menu and dial in to the server directly. If you do, you'll be able to use the server databases in exactly the same way that you do when you're accessing them over the network — it'll just be slower. If you only have a 2400BPS modem, it'll be a great deal slower.

When you choose Tools⇨Call, you'll get the Call Server dialog box, as shown in Figure 14-20.

All you need do is select the name of the Server you want to call and, in most cases, click Auto Dial. Use the Manual Dial button if you have to dial the number yourself — maybe you have to enter a long calling card number or you have to ask an operator to be transferred to the server's extension.

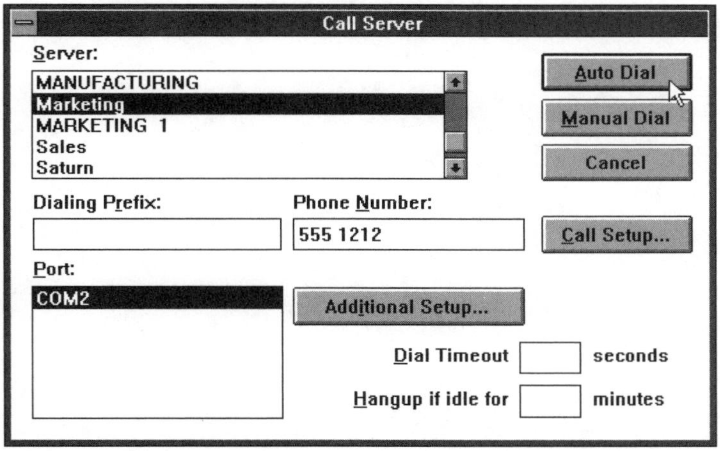

Figure 14-20:
The Call
Server
dialog box.

Shooting Troubles

If you've made it this far in the chapter — and we've got to admit that this is probably the toughest chapter in the whole book — you've probably realized that setting up and using Notes remotely is a relatively complicated thing to do. And the more complicated something is, the greater the chance of screwing it up, right?

Fear not! Your administrator is your ally. Call on him or her to help you before you leave on your trip and even while you're gone.

The good news is that if you're going to have any problems with replication, it'll be the first couple of times you try. Once you get it all figured out, it'll be smooth sailing. *And* it's worth the effort — we promise.

Chapter 15

Working Together: Notes and Other Computer Programs

● ●

In This Chapter

▶ Moving data into Notes

▶ Moving data out of Notes

▶ How to speak OLÉ without learning Spanish

● ●

*T*here are many advantages to using Notes; you're probably aware of many of them already unless this is the first section of the book you're reading. If you are just joining us, you will be interested to know that Notes works in Windows, OS/2, Macintosh, and Unix. In all these environments, you can take information of all sorts from another application (Microsoft Word, for instance) and use it in Notes.

The business of getting the information from one application into another varies from the relatively simple to the relatively complex. Your choices are the Clipboard, File⇨Import, File⇨Export, attachments, dynamic data exchange (DDE), and object linking and embedding (OLÉ).

Scissors 'n Glue

Back in the good old days, when you wanted to include a picture, a hunk of text, a graph, or a table of data in something you were typing, you pulled the paper out of the typewriter before you filled it with text. Then you used scissors to cut out the picture/text/graph/table and found a bottle of glue to paste it into the blank space in the typed copy. This system is not very high tech, could be pretty messy, and made it pretty hard to jam that piece of paper back into the typewriter if you needed to type some more.

Nowadays, with the advent of the personal computer, you do exactly the same thing except without the scissors and paste. You can add objects to Notes documents, like a graph in 1-2-3 for Windows, a paragraph in Word, or a graphic in Freelance. While you're in the object's home program, highlight the object and copy it. In most programs, you would do this with Edit⇨Copy. Then switch into Notes, position the cursor, and choose Edit⇨Paste. Unless the object was too big to fit in the Clipboard (like if you tried to copy 3,000 cells from a Lotus 1-2-3 worksheet), you see a copy of the original data in the Notes document.

If for no other reason, this system is preferable to the scissors-and-glue system because the page with the glued thing doesn't stick to all the other pages. It's also faster, it's seamless, and it gives you the ability to move the pasted object around or delete it completely if you change your mind. Besides that, you can edit the pasted object after you've pasted it into Notes.

This copy-and-paste system works fine if the source application supports the use of the Clipboard and if you are able to open the source application to get at the information you want to copy. Keep in mind that if the data in the source application changes, Notes will not update its copy of the data — with this method, Notes has no way to know what goes on in the source application. Unlike most of the other techniques, you can use copy and paste within Notes to copy data from one Notes document into another. Most of the other techniques only work with data and files created outside of Notes.

Got a Paper Clip?

What if you can't use the Clipboard? Your next weapon in the arsenal of using non-Notes data is *attaching* files to documents, which is covered in more detail in Chapter 6. It doesn't matter whether Notes supports the file format, whether the original application has ever even heard of the Clipboard, or what kind of laundry detergent you are using — in a rich text field, you can attach any file to any Notes document.

 Place the cursor where you want a symbol of the attached file to be, and then choose File⇨Attach. All the reader will see is a symbol of the file; if possible, it will be an icon of the original program. An Ami Pro icon, for instance, will represent an Ami Pro file. Because you can attach any kind of file, sometimes the icon will not match the source application. For instance, if you attached a batch file or an executable file (one with the EXE extension), the file would be represented by what looks like a piece of paper with the corner folded over.

You can't see or edit the data from an attached file in a Notes document. The purpose of attaching a file is simply to give that file to others, not to use the data in your Notes document.

Importing a File into a Document

Let's say that you are composing a Notes document, and you need to include a bunch of pages that you've already typed in WordPerfect 4.1. This is a case where you can't use the Clipboard to include the document, because WordPerfect 4.1 isn't even a Windows program and doesn't know anything about the Clipboard. You could attach the file, but you want the people who will be reading your document to see the actual text of the WordPerfect document, not that crummy little icon.

What do you do? You *import* the WordPerfect file. Importing is how you convert a file from WordPerfect right into the Notes document you are composing, and right into the rich text field in which you are typing. You could also convert files from lots of other programs, like Lotus 1-2-3 or WordStar.

How do you do it? First, get the cursor to the spot in the rich text field where you want to insert the file. By the way, don't even think about importing a document into any other kind of field besides rich text. Then choose File⇨Import, and watch for the dialog box that's so prominently displayed in Figure 15-1.

Use the Directories, Drives, and File Name boxes to find the file you're importing, and use the List Files of Type drop-down box to tell Notes what kind of file you're importing. After you've found the file, click Import, and voilà, the file appears inside your Notes document.

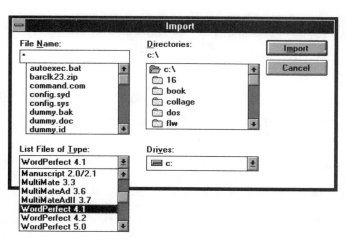

Figure 15-1:
Use
File⇨Import
to include
the contents
of a file in a
rich text
field.

When you do import a file, Notes converts it to regular text, so feel free to liven it up by changing the fonts, making some of the words bold, or whatever.

Using File⇨Import to include a foreign file in a rich text field is your technique of choice if the file's source application either isn't installed on your workstation (maybe someone else gave you the WordPerfect file, but you don't have WordPerfect on your computer) or can't be copied and pasted via the Clipboard. Although File⇨Import does convert foreign documents, try the Clipboard first when incorporating information from other programs.

Here's a (long) list of the kinds of files that you can import into a rich text field:

- ✔ ASCII
- ✔ Microsoft Word RTF
- ✔ Lotus 1-2-3 Worksheet
- ✔ Lotus PIC
- ✔ ANSI Metafile
- ✔ TIFF 5.0 image
- ✔ BMP image
- ✔ Ami Pro
- ✔ DisplayWrite DCA
- ✔ Manuscript, version 2.0 and 2.1
- ✔ MultiMate, versions 3.3, 3.6, and 3.7
- ✔ WordPerfect, versions 4.1, 4.2, 5.0, and 5.1
- ✔ WordStar, versions 3.3, 3.31, 3.45, 4.0, 5.0, and 5.5
- ✔ PCX image
- ✔ Microsoft Excel, versions 2.1, 3.0, and 4.0
- ✔ Microsoft Word for Windows, versions 1.0 and 2.0
- ✔ Binary
- ✔ Interleaf ASCII

If you need to import a file that is not in the list, see if the originating program can save the file in one of the formats that Notes supports. For example, if you needed to import a Quattro Pro spreadsheet, you could use Quattro Pro to save the file as a Lotus 1-2-3 worksheet and then File⇨Import the converted Lotus 1-2-3 worksheet.

Converting a Document to Something Else Altogether

You can probably guess that you can also convert a Notes document into a file that can be used by a different program. Perhaps you have found a Notes document that you want to give to a colleague, but they don't have access to Notes (do they know what they are missing?!). You can convert the Notes document to, say, a Microsoft Word document and then deliver the file to your friend on a floppy disk.

In the information age of the nineties, copying a file onto a floppy disk and then walking down the hall to hand-deliver it is euphemistically known as using Sneaker Net.

To convert a Notes file into another format, first find and open the Notes document that you want to export and then choose File⇨Export. You come face-to-face with the dialog box shown in Figure 15-2.

Use the Directories, Drives, and File Name boxes to specify the name and location of the file to create, and use the Save File as Type drop-down box to tell Notes what kind of file you want it to be. Click Export, and you're done. Now you (or your friend) can open the new file in the appropriate program.

Figure 15-2:
Use the
Export
dialog box
to convert a
Notes
document
into a
different file
format.

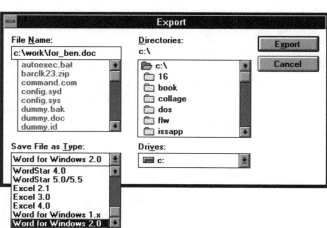

Here's the list of the file types to which you can export a Notes document:

- ASCII
- Microsoft Word RTF
- ANSI Metafile
- TIFF 5.0 image
- Ami Pro
- DisplayWrite DCA
- Manuscript, versions 2.0 and 2.1
- MultiMate, versions 3.3, 3.6, and 3.7
- WordPerfect, versions 4.1, 4.2, 5.0, and 5.1
- WordStar, versions 3.3, 3.31, 3.45, 4.0, 5.0, and 5.5
- Microsoft Excel, versions 2.1, 3.0, and 4.0
- Microsoft Word for Windows, versions 1.0 and 2.0

Just like File⇨Import, only use File⇨Export if you can't transfer the Notes document to the other program via the Clipboard.

View-Level Imports

Another way to bring information into Notes is to import not an individual document, but rather lots of documents at the same time. This method would be the appropriate choice if, for example, you have a Lotus 1-2-3 worksheet and you want to import it such that each row in the spreadsheet becomes a separate document in a Notes database. If your worksheet has 4,362 rows worth of information, you'll get 4,362 new documents in your Notes database.

What to do first . . .

First things first: you have to use 1-2-3 to set up the spreadsheet in a very particular fashion. You have to remove all the fancy formatting, blank rows, and so on that are typically included in a worksheet. In fact, there are a couple of very specific rules for preparing a spreadsheet to import into Notes.

➤ The column headings for the worksheet must be in row one of the worksheet and they must be the same as the field names in the Notes database. This is important, so call the person who created the database if you're not sure what the *exact* field names are in the Notes database.

➤ The rows of spreadsheet information must begin in row two of the worksheet and must be in a solid block. There can't be any blank rows in the middle of the spreadsheet, or else you'll get empty documents in your database.

So it probably makes sense to take the worksheet you intend to import and rearrange it to conform to the aforementioned rules, but then save it with a different name so as to not replace the original worksheet.

If you need to import any other kind of file, such as a big text file or an Excel worksheet, you're best off converting *that* file into a Lotus 1-2-3 worksheet and then importing the Lotus 1-2-3 worksheet into Notes. No surprise that the easiest kind of file to import into (Lotus) Notes is from (Lotus) 1-2-3, right?

What to do second...

After you've gotten the worksheet all ship-shape, open the database into which you'll be importing the worksheet and choose File⇨Import. Make sure that you just open the database without opening one of the documents or trying to compose a new document. That would make Notes think that you want to put the worksheet into just one document. Make sure that you have a view on the screen when you choose File⇨Import.

Use the dialog box to indicate the file that you want to import and (by using the List Files of Type drop-down box) to tell Notes that it's a 1-2-3 worksheet, as you see in Figure 15-3.

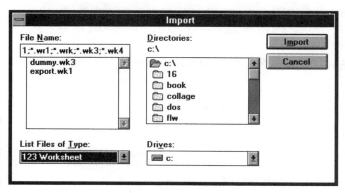

Figure 15-3:
The Import
dialog box.

When you click Import, Notes presents you with yet another dialog box, as you can see in Figure 15-4. Here you can tell Notes how to import the rows of the spreadsheet.

You have five decisions to make:

- ✔ Which form will be used to display the new documents
- ✔ Whether the new documents will be main documents or responses
- ✔ Which range in the spreadsheet to import; you can enter either the cell coordinates (like A1 .. D341) or a range name
- ✔ How the fields will be named; because you followed advice and were careful to make the spreadsheet column heading match the field name, choose WKS Title Defined
- ✔ Whether Notes should calculate any field formulas that have been defined on the form for each document as it is created

    If that's what you want, click the Calculate fields on form during document import box; if you're not sure whether you should check this box, check with the person who created the database. When in doubt, go ahead and click the box.

Click OK and you're in business. Notes will import the worksheet and convert each row into a brand new document for your database.

As you've probably guessed by now, there are actually a couple of ways to import documents. Even so, we've only discussed importing a Lotus 1-2-3 worksheet because it's the most common kind of import and because the other kinds of view-level import are pretty complicated. If you are convinced that you have to import a file that's not a 1-2-3 worksheet, you'll need help from the person who created the database or from your local Notes guru.

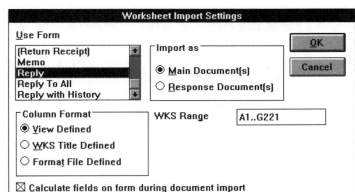

Figure 15-4:
The
Worksheet
Import
Settings
dialog box.

Converting a View into a Spreadsheet

Exporting from a view is even easier than importing into a view. The idea behind a view-level export is that you want to create a worksheet based on the columns in a view.

Although exporting a view to a spreadsheet is the most common kind of view-level export, you can actually export a view to any of the following four file types:

- ✔ A 1-2-3 worksheet, compatible with any version of Lotus 1-2-3 and also accessible by most other spreadsheet and database programs, such as Excel, dBASE, and Paradox

- ✔ An Agenda STF file, which is a file format used by a (discontinued) program from Lotus, so you can probably forget about this one

- ✔ A structured text file, which is an ASCII file that would then be imported into some other program

- ✔ A tabular text file, which is easy to import into other spreadsheet and database programs

To make a new spreadsheet file out of a view, first open the database in question and switch to the view that will be the basis of the spreadsheet that you are creating. When you export a view, you will only export the fields that are in the view, so if you need to export fields that are *not* in the view, you'll have to negotiate with the person who designed your database.

After you have the appropriate view open, choose File⇨Export and watch for the dialog box shown in Figure 15-5.

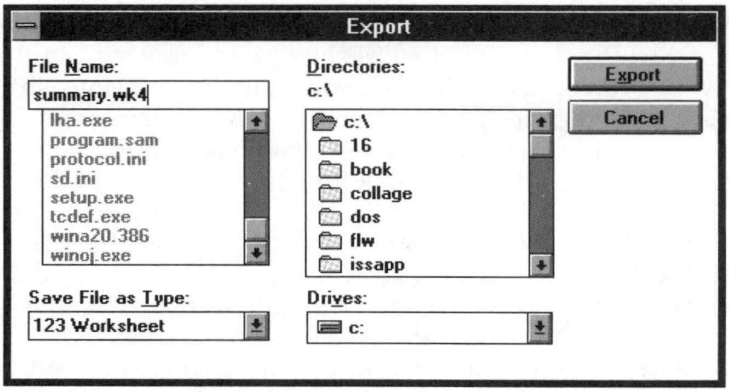

Figure 15-5:
You can also use the Export dialog box to convert a database view into a spreadsheet.

Export

File **N**ame:
summary.wk4

lha.exe
program.sam
protocol.ini
sd.ini
setup.exe
tcdef.exe
wina20.386
winoj.exe

Save File as **T**ype:
123 Worksheet

Directories:
c:\

c:\
16
book
collage
dos
flw
issapp

Dri**v**es:
c:

Export
Cancel

After you have indicated the name, location, and type of file to create, click Export. You'll see another dialog box where you tell Notes whether you want to export all the documents in the view or just those that you selected. If you only want some of the documents, use the mouse or spacebar to check them off before you even choose File⇨Export in the first place. You will also see a check box to Include View Titles, which will make each column heading in the worksheet match the database's field names. If you do not choose this option, the spreadsheet will not have any column headings. Click OK, and Notes creates a Lotus 1-2-3 worksheet for you based on the view that's open — and that's all there is to it.

If you intend to export data from a Notes view to a program other than Lotus 1-2-3, you should still export the view to a Lotus 1-2-3 worksheet and then use that other program to further convert the worksheet. Take it from us, using Lotus 1-2-3 is a lot (and we mean a *lot*) easier than using the structured or tabular text formats.

DDE

Both DDE (dynamic data exchange) and OLÉ (object linking and embedding) add data to your Notes document, but the data retains its identity as data of the original application. The data does not become native Notes data as it does when you choose any of the File⇨Import options we discussed in the previous sections.

DDE adds information to your Notes document but keeps an eye on the original data so that if you or anyone else changes it, the copy in the Notes documents will change too. However, you can't use DDE and OLÉ within Notes to link two Notes databases. Check Chapter 10 to find out how to create fields that use data from other fields or databases.

What makes DDE a bit confusing is the terminology; some words used in DDE are also used in other Notes contexts. For instance, the program in which the original data was created is called the *server*. The program into which the data is placed is called the *client* (a term sometimes also used for *workstation*). Keep in mind as you read this section that we are not talking about Notes servers and Notes clients, but DDE servers and DDE clients.

To create a DDE link, open the server application and create or open a file containing the data to which you'll be forging a link. If it's a new file, be sure to save it before trying to create the link. Highlight the data to link and choose Edit⇨Copy. Switch to the Notes document, place the cursor where you want to place the data, and choose Edit⇨Paste Special. The dialog box that appears is in Figure 15-6. Choose the format for the data to be linked. In the Display As list box, you may choose Rich Text Format (text arrives with all formatting), Picture (usually used for graphics objects), or Text (text arrives without formatting). After a few seconds the data appears in the Notes document. If the original selection contains multiple text formats, you may see an icon rather than the actual text.

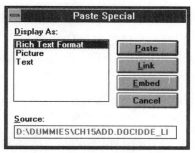

Figure 15-6:
Use the Paste Special dialog box to link data into Notes documents.

By creating a DDE link, you have created a compound document. Notes doesn't allow you to edit the linked data in Notes, though; to edit the data, you need to double-click the linked data or the icon. Notes opens or switches to the server application and file, where you may edit the data. As you do the editing, the changes are reflected immediately in the Notes document.

Not only can you edit the data, you can also edit the link itself. In the Notes document, choose Edit⇨Links. Watch for the dialog box you see in Figure 15-7.

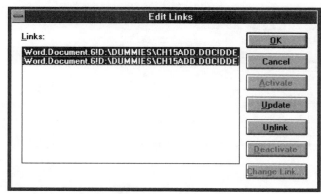

Figure 15-7:
The Edit Links dialog box.

In the Edit Links dialog box, you may choose to use any of the following:

- ✔ Activate a link if it has been deactivated earlier.
- ✔ Update a link if the link needs to be updated; for instance, if you choose to make updating of links manual rather than automatic.
- ✔ Unlink (permanently sever) the link between server and client.
- ✔ Deactivate the link temporarily between server and client.
- ✔ Change Link to make any changes (listed in the following paragraph) to the link. The Change Link dialog box is shown in Figure 15-8.

In the Change Link dialog box, you can change the link from automatic (DDE will make changes immediately in the client when the server file changes) to manual (you have to choose Edit⇨Links and click Update to update links). You usually choose manual if editing the server file slows down your computer's perfor-mance. You can also change the Application to a different server program, the File Name to a different file, or Item to edit another link to that file.

DDE requires that you have a saved file and the server application available to Notes. Often the server file itself will be on a Notes server (there are both uses of the word *server* in one sentence) so that the same file is available to all users. If all users of the Notes document don't have the same directory structure for the server application, Notes will not be able to open the application to allow updating. Also, if the file is moved or renamed, everyone loses the link between the original information and the information in the Notes document.

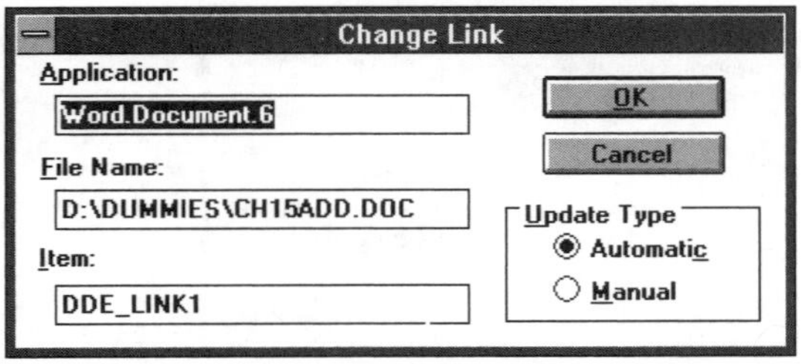

Figure 15-8:
The Change
Link dialog
box allows
you to alter
the link
between
client and
server.

Change Link

Application:
Word.Document.6

File Name:
D:\DUMMIES\CH15ADD.DOC

Item:
DDE_LINK1

OK

Cancel

Update Type
◉ Automatic
○ Manual

OLÉ

To the user, the appearance of a DDE (linked) object and an OLÉ (embedded) object will be the same. It may be an icon or it may be data, depending on the complexity of the data in the server file.

The difference between the two is that OLÉ embeds into the Notes document the file itself, not a link — so changes to the original file are *not* reflected in the embedded file.

Both DDE and OLÉ allow you to search for text as long as you follow two rules: you must link or embed the data as text or rich text, and the data must be visible (it can't be represented by an icon).

To embed OLÉ information in a Notes document, first open the original file in its original program and then copy the information to the Clipboard. In the Notes document, position the cursor in a rich text field and choose one of the following:

- Edit⇨Paste Special, pick a Clipboard format, and choose Embed.
- Edit⇨Insert⇨Object and, if it's a new embedded object, select an Object Type. Notes starts the program for the type you picked, and you enter data, which becomes part of the Notes document.
- Edit⇨Insert⇨Object and, if it's an existing file, select an Object Type and Choose File. Select the correct Drive and Directory and then highlight a file and choose OK.

OLÉ doesn't require that the readers of the Notes document have access to the original file because they have their own copy of the file. However, they do have to have the server application so that they can use it to edit the original data. To edit the original data, double-click the embedded data. The server application and the file will open. Any changes to the embedded file on one user's version of a document may not be reflected in other users' copies of the document, depending upon whether the documents are replicated to all other users.

Chapter 16

Full Text Search: Important Stuff that Got Shoved Towards the End of the Book

In This Chapter

▶ What is Full Text Search?

▶ Using the Search Bar

▶ Using the Query Builder

▶ Advanced searching

▶ Doing a Query by Form

▶ Building your own index

*I*f you've made it this far in the book, you're starting to realize what a powerful tool Notes is. Notes tends to catch on like wildfire; most companies using Notes end up with *a lot* of databases. They start using Notes to keep track of everything under the sun.

So how do you stay sane when presented with these electronic mountains of information? How do you avoid a diagnosis of Information Overload? Choose one of the following:

▶ Take a vacation

▶ Sell your computer so that you never have to use it again

▶ Consider Full Text Search

We can't help you if you opt for either of the first two choices, but we can help you use Full Text Search.

Just What Is Full Text Search, Anyway?

You just got a new job, and you're going to be taking business trips once or twice a month. The first thing you need to do is find out your company's policies for travel — what airline should you use, what hotels can you stay in, and, most important, do *you* get to keep your Frequent Flyer Miles? So you open up that trusty Human Resources Policies database, but there must be at least 700 documents in it. How are you going to find all the documents that have the word "travel" in them?

It's *Full Text Search* to the rescue. Full Text Search is a way for you to find all of the occurrences of a word (or of a couple of words) very, very quickly. You can search a huge database in no time at all. Most searches don't take more than two or three *seconds*. And when you ask Notes to search for the word "travel," it finds *all* the documents for you, no matter where (or how many times) the documents contain the word "travel."

Performing a Search

Notes has three ways for you to enter the criteria for your search:

- ✔ By entering the criteria directly in the Search Bar
- ✔ By using the Query Builder
- ✔ By performing a Query by Form

The method you choose is up to you; if you are just searching for a single word, it's probably easiest and fastest to use the Search Bar. If, on the other hand, you have a query that's a little more complex, check out the Query Builder and Queries by Form. We'll explore the intricacies of each in a minute.

Not all databases are created equal

You can't search all databases so quickly. Before you can try one of these lightning-fast queries, your administrator has to create a *Full Text Index* for the database.

If it turns out that the database that you want to search hasn't been indexed, you can either ask your administrator to set it up for you or you can read the section at the end of this chapter called (appropriately enough) "Creating Your Own Index."

Show me the Search Bar

The easiest way to see if a database has an index is to choose <u>V</u>iew⯑Show
Search Ba<u>r</u>. The Search Bar is what you use to enter the criteria for Full Text
Search. If the database hasn't been indexed, you see the dialog box shown in
Figure 16-1.

Figure 16-1:
This
database
has not
been
indexed for
Full Text
Searches.

If, on the other hand, the database has been indexed, the Search Bar appears at the
top of the View window, as shown in Figure 16-2.

Figure 16-2:
Use the
Search Bar
to enter
criteria for
Full Text
Searches.

Using the Search Bar

There are actually a bunch of ways to perform a Full Text Search. The most
common, and perhaps the easiest, is by using the Search Bar, as shown in
Figure 16-3. A lot of fancy buttons are on the bar, but, in most cases, you only
have to worry about two things: the Criteria Text box and the Search button.

The Criteria Text box   The Search button

Which view?

When you perform a search, Notes only searches the documents that are in the current, open view. So you have to be careful to choose the right view before you start your search. If the view you have open only shows documents from the first half of the year, your search will not look through the documents from the second half of the year.

The bottom line: make sure you open the right view before you do a search.

Just do it!

To perform a search, do the following:

1. **Enter the word or words you want Notes to find.**

2. **Click the Search button.**

In Figure 16-4, we're asking Notes to search for any document that has the word "bank" in it. Click the Search button, and presto! Notes presents a list of all the documents that have that word in them.

The results of a search

After you perform a search, Notes displays for you the documents that match the criteria you entered, and it lists them for you by *weight*. In other words, it first lists the documents that have the most occurrences of your criteria and then the documents that have fewer occurrences of the criteria. The vertical bar at the left-hand side of the view represents the relative frequency of your criteria in each document. The darker the bar, the more occurrences in that particular document. Take a look at Figure 16-5.

The "Hit" bar

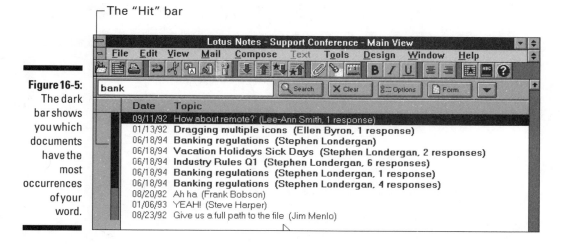

Figure 16-5:
The dark
bar shows
you which
documents
have the
most
occurrences
of your
word.

Reading the resulting documents

Read a document that was produced by a search the same way that you read any other document: double-click it or highlight it with the cursor keys and press Enter. When you do, Notes shows you the document and highlights (in little red boxes) the words you asked it to find, as you see in Figure 16-6.

When reading a document after performing a Full Text Search, press Ctrl and the + key to jump quickly to the next occurrence of the word in the document you are reading. You can also use Ctrl and the – key to jump quickly to the preceding occurrence of the word.

Make it easy for me: using the Query Builder

Although it's easy and fast to use the Search Bar when you're searching for relatively simple criteria, it's probably not worth the trouble to learn the intricacies of the Query Language that is used for more complex criteria. That's because Notes has a built-in *Query Builder*. When you choose Edit⇨Find and you are in an indexed database, Notes presents you with the dialog box displayed in Figure 16-7.

Let Notes do the work! By filling in the blanks in the dialog box, you can have Notes construct the relatively complex query statements that are needed for fancy searches. For example, let's say you want to find the documents that include the word "Funds" and also have the word "Banking" near the word "Insurance." At the same time, you want to exclude the documents that contain the word "April." Oh, yeah, and you only want the documents from before June 6.

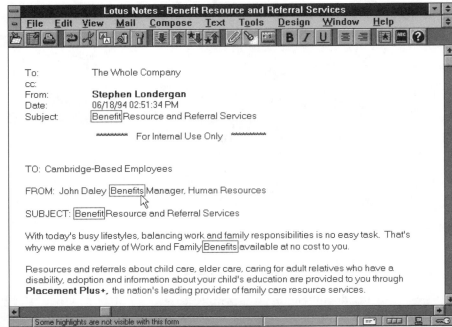

Figure 16-6:
Notes
highlights
the words
for which
you
searched.

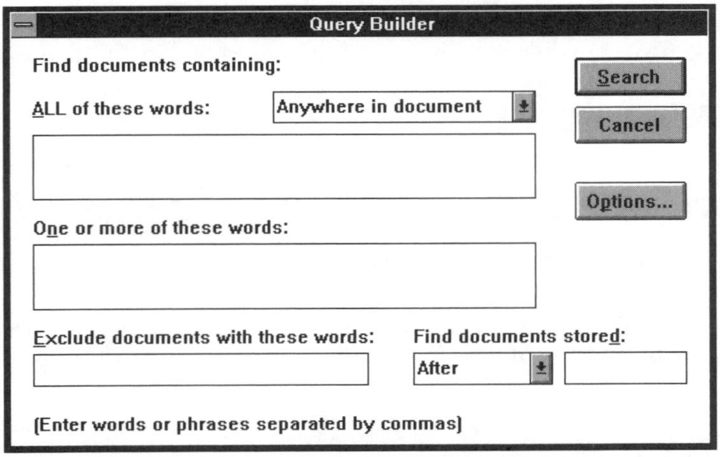

Figure 16-7:
The Query
Builder
dialog box
makes
executing
complex
searches
much
easier.

If you were to study up on the query language, you would find that the query statement to perform the aforementioned search looks like this:

```
(Funds) AND (Banking Insurance) AND NOT (April) AND
          ([_RevisionDate] < 06/06/94]
```

Pretty terrible, huh? Well, the whole point is that *you* don't have to understand that query language; you can get exactly what you want by filling in the Query Builder dialog box as depicted in Figure 16-8. When you click the Search button, Notes automatically figures out the correct criteria and performs the search for you. Trust us — you *don't* want to learn that query language.

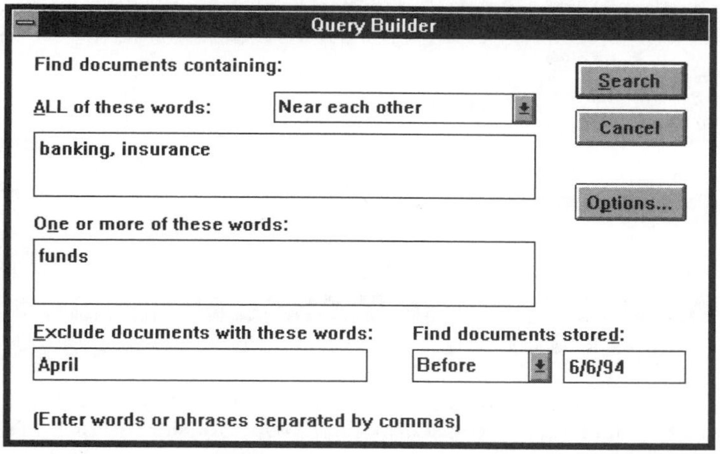

Figure 16-8:
Fill in the blanks in the Query Builder dialog box to perform complex queries.

Query Builder

Find documents containing:

ALL of these words: [Near each other   ▼]   [**Search**]
                                                            [Cancel]
```
banking, insurance
```
                                                            [Options...]

One or more of these words:
```
funds
```

Exclude documents with these words: Find documents stored:
```
April
```
                              [Before ▼] [6/6/94]

[Enter words or phrases separated by commas]

How about a Query by Form?

Another way to make your life easier is to do a *Query by Form*. That means that you use one of the forms in the database to tell Notes which words you're looking for and in which fields you're looking for them.

To do a Query by Form, click the Form button in the Search Bar. When you do, Notes gives you a drop-down box that lists the name of the forms in the database, as shown in Figure 16-9.

Figure 16-9:
Use the Form button in the Search Bar to perform a Query by Form.

Form
| Memo |
| Reply |
| Reply To All |
| Reply with History |

After you pick the form you want to use, Notes gives you an empty version of the form (as you see in Figure 16-10), into which you can enter the words for which you want to search. After you have entered the criteria in the appropriate fields, click the Search button to find the documents. Query by Form is like using the Query Builder; you fill in the blanks and let Notes do the work to figure out the syntax of the query statement.

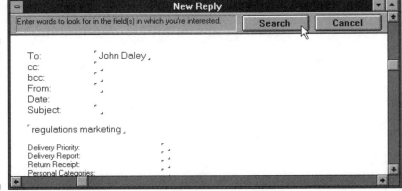

Figure 16-10: Enter the words you want to find in the appropriate fields and then click Search.

"So," you ask, "what's the difference between doing a Query by Form and just entering your criteria in the Search Bar?" With Queries by Form, it's easier to do complicated searches, because you don't have to study up on the fancy query statements that it would take to get Notes to search only certain fields.

Searching more than one database at a time

If you need to search more than one database, you first have to open all the databases involved. There's a little trick to getting more than one open at the same time: click the first database's icon *once*, and then hold down Shift as you click the other databases that you want to open. Finally, hold down Shift key and *double*-click the last database you want to search. In other words, you click the first database, Shift-click the second, third, fourth (and so on.) databases, and last of all, Shift-double-click the last database. When you do, you get a view that looks like Figure 16-11.

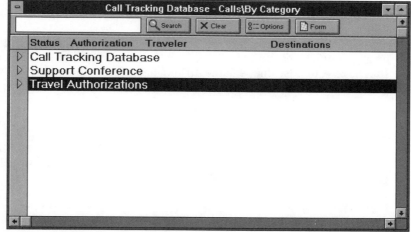

Figure 16-11:
You may
open more
than one
database at
a time.

After you have the databases open, you search them just as you would search a single database — either by using the Search Bar, using the Query Builder, or doing a Query by Form. After you have searched the multiple databases, the view displays the name of the database and tells you how many documents were found in that database. To actually see the documents from each database, click that little triangle that appears in the left-most column of the view — like Figure 16-12.

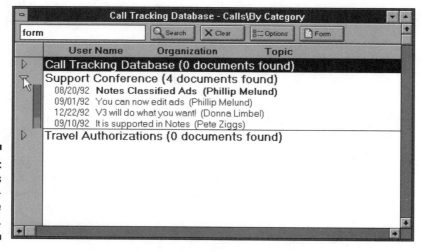

Figure 16-12:
The results
of a multi-
database
search.

Creating Your Own Index

You can create your own indexes, too. How about indexing your mail database? That way, it'll be easy and fast when you need to find all those old messages that have your customer's name in them or to quickly put your hands on all the messages that are about a certain project.

Maybe not...

As the great Robert Heinlein once said in *The Moon Is a Harsh Mistress*, "There ain't no such thing as a free lunch."

Literary allusions aside, there are a couple of issues to consider before indexing every database in sight.

Issue #1: Indexing a database takes up more disk space — maybe an additional 50 percent (or more) of the database's size. In other words, if your mail database takes up, say, ten megabytes of disk space, indexing could increase the size to 15 megabytes. It's hard to predict exactly how big the index is going to be because it depends very much on the type of database you are indexing. If you have a database that has a lot of pictures in it and a relatively small amount of text, that database's index won't be as big (percentage-wise) as it would be for a database that's almost all text.

Of course, if the database you're going to index is on a Notes server, you won't be as conscious of the disk space requirements because you're not going to use any of *your* computer's hard disk space — the index is stored with the database on the server.

(Don't let your administrator read that last paragraph, because administrators are *extremely* concerned about disk space on the server. That's their job.)

Issue #2: Like a beautiful lawn or a good haircut, indexes have to be maintained. As documents are added to and removed from the database, the index has to be periodically updated to be kept abreast of the new and deleted documents. Who's going to do the work to keep up the index?

Here again, if the indexed database is on the server, maintaining the index is more your administrator's concern than it is yours. In fact, the indexes are automatically kept up-to-date if the databases are on the server.

On the other hand, if the indexed database is on your computer's hard disk, *you* have to be responsible for keeping it up to date — that means periodically choosing File⇨Full Text Search⇨Update Index. (More about maintaining the local indexes in a minute.) It doesn't sound like much, but this maintenance takes time — how much time depends on how many documents have been added to the database since the last time you updated the index.

The bottom line is that if you index a database that's on your computer (as opposed to one that's on the server), you have to be prepared to sacrifice some disk space and remember to keep the index up-to-date.

Issue #3: Almost forgot — you cannot index a database that's on your own computer if you have a Macintosh. Mac users can create indexes for databases that are on the server, and Mac users can certainly use the indexes for the databases on the servers. You just can't create an index for a database that's local.

Creating the index

To create a new Full Text Index for a database, click the database's icon and then choose File⇨Full Text Search⇨Create Index. When you do, Notes presents you with the dialog box shown in Figure 16-13.

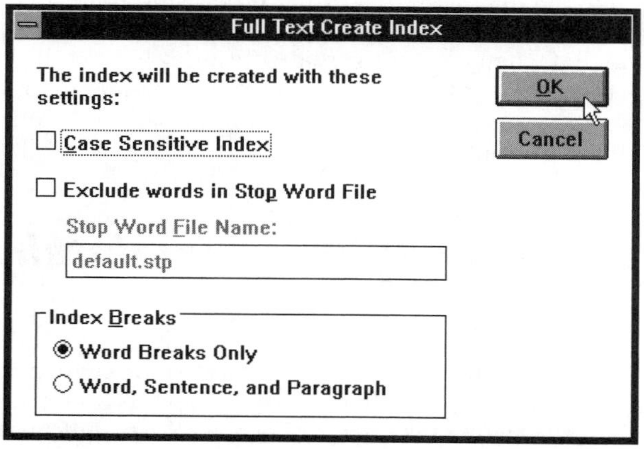

Figure 16-13: Choose File⇨Full Text Search⇨ Create Index to index a database.

```
┌─────────────────────────────────────────────────────┐
│ ▭           Full Text Create Index                   │
├─────────────────────────────────────────────────────┤
│ The index will be created with these      ┌────────┐ │
│ settings:                                 │   OK   │ │
│                                           └────────┘ │
│ ☐ Case Sensitive Index                    ┌────────┐ │
│                                           │ Cancel │ │
│ ☐ Exclude words in Stop Word File         └────────┘ │
│    Stop Word File Name:                              │
│    ┌──────────────────────────────┐                 │
│    │ default.stp                  │                 │
│    └──────────────────────────────┘                 │
│  ┌─Index Breaks──────────────────────┐               │
│  │ ◉ Word Breaks Only                │               │
│  │ ○ Word, Sentence, and Paragraph   │               │
│  └───────────────────────────────────┘               │
└─────────────────────────────────────────────────────┘
```

What happens when you click OK depends on the location of the database that's being indexed. If the database is on the Notes server, the server takes care of creating the index. You'll be able to do a search in a little while — how long depends on how big the database is and how busy the server is. Most times it won't take more than 10 or 15 minutes to create the index on the server.

If, on the other hand, the database you're indexing is on your computer, you'll see the dialog box shown in Figure 16-14. You have to create local indexes manually, so you have to click Yes and then go get a cup of coffee. How long it takes to create the index depends on the size of the database, but it won't take more than five or ten minutes.

The real difference here is that if you index a database on the server, you're free to go about your business while the index is completed. If, on the other hand, you index a database "locally," you'll have to sit there like a chump until it finishes because it ties up your workstation.

Figure 16-14:
Local
indexes
have to be
manually
created.

Don't feel as though the weight of the world is on you shoulders; it's usually not your responsibility to create an index for a database that's on a Notes server. In fact, you may find that when you try to create the index Notes tells you that you aren't allowed. If this happens to you, just call 1-800-YourAdministrator. The good news is that your administrator has probably already indexed all the databases that are important — so you don't have to worry about it.

Add this to your daily chores: maintaining the index

Creating the index takes a while because Notes has to index every single document in the database that first time. The good news is that updating the index after that first time won't take so long because Notes only has to update the index to reflect the changes (new, deleted, and edited documents) that have been made since the last time you updated the index.

If the indexed database is on a Notes server, maintaining the index is a job for your administrator. That's one less thing you have to worry about! Your administrator controls the frequency with which the index is updated — whether it's instantly, hourly, or daily. The more often the update, the slower the server will be, so you might have to do some negotiating (or resort to bribery) to get your administrator to agree to an index that updates the instant that the database changes.

You can probably skip reading the next six paragraphs

When you create an index, you can fine-tune exactly how the index works with some of the options in the File⇔Full Text Search⇔Create Index dialog box. They're not for the faint of heart, and most people don't need to use them. So you should only read the next five paragraphs if you're especially curious.

If you click Case Sensitive Index, Notes tracks the word "travel" separately from the word "Travel." (Small "t" vs. big "T.") A case-sensitive index takes up more disk space than one that's not case-sensitive (approximately 10% more), and it will take longer to update — so you probably won't want to bother. Of course, if you really do need to distinguish between words based on whether or not they are capitalized, it's nice to have the option.

You can also tell Notes not to index certain words by clicking Exclude words in Stop Word File. This is a trick to make the index smaller by telling Notes to skip some words altogether. For example, if you were indexing your mail database, it's a safe bet that you'll never need to search for "Londergan" (assuming your name is Londergan), or the word "Acme" (assuming you work at Acme Foods), or the word "Marketing" (assuming you work in the Marketing Department). If you're convinced that you need a Stop File, and you don't know how to edit one, ask your administrator for help.

The Stop File is just an ASCII file, so you can edit it with any text editor, such as the Windows Notepad. Unless you tell Notes differently, the file is called DEFAULT.STP and is located in your Notes data directory.

The last item in the dialog box is the Index Breaks field. Use this only if you need to fine-tune how Notes handles proximity operators in advanced queries. We could take the next three pages of this book explaining what Index Breaks are all about, but in the end, you'll conclude that they're not worth the trouble. (Trust us — we've never led you astray before, right?) If you're bent on learning more about Index Breaks, take a look in the Notes Help database and/or your trusty manual.

You are more involved in the upkeep of indexes for databases that are on your own computer. Every so often — maybe once a day, maybe once a week — you have to choose File⇔Full Text Search⇔Update Index.

Why is it so important to update the index? Well, if you don't, your searches will produce incomplete results. Say you update the index for your database on Tuesday. On Wednesday, you add a bunch of documents to the database. On Thursday, you perform a search for the words "travel AND hotel." The results of your search will not include the documents that you added to the database on Wednesday because you haven't updated the index. Get the picture?

At the very least, update the index every time you get ready to do a new search — unless you know that none of the documents have been added (or edited) since the last time you updated the index. If you are not sure when you last updated the index, check out File⇔Full Text Search⇔Information.

No More Searches — Not Today, Not Tomorrow, Not Ever

If you decide that you don't need a database to be indexed after all, choose File⇨Full Text Search⇨Delete Index.

Part V
The Part of Tens

The 5th Wave   By Rich Tennant

©RICH TENNANT

"IT'S NO USE, CAPTAIN. THE ONLY WAY WE'LL CRACK THIS CASE IS TO GET INTO PROF. FLINK'S PERSONAL MAIL FILE, BUT NO ONE KNOWS THE PASSWORD. KILROY'S GOT A HUNCH IT STARTS WITH AN 'S,' BUT HECK, THAT COULD BE ANYTHING."

In this part...

*L*ists are short, fun (maybe), and easy to read. So why not have a bunch of lists to make this book go out with a bang? (If you've managed to get this far, you certainly deserve a break.) Not all the lists have *exactly* ten items, but we don't want you to think that you've been cheated!

And so, in that inimitable *...For Dummies* style, we present you with The Part of Tens. Grab a cold drink, curl up in front of the fire, and get ready for a a bunch of lists that we hope will clear up a few common misconceptions, reiterate a few key points, and make for an easy read.

We could give you a list of ten reasons why you should read The Part of Tens, but that'd be silly, wouldn't it?!

Chapter 17

Ten SmartIcons
You're Sure to Use a Lot

In This Chapter
▶ The top ten SmartIcons
▶ What they do

*Y*ou remember SmartIcons, don't you? In this chapter we discuss the ten that you'll use most often. You can check out Chapter 13 for more information about SmartIcons, too.

Print

 To print the open document or view, click this SmartIcon.

The Print SmartIcon prints whichever document or view is open — it's a shortcut for choosing File⇨Print.

Spell Check

 To check the spelling of the document you're composing or editing, click this SmartIcon.

The Spell Check SmartIcon checks the open document for spelling errors — it's a shortcut for choosing Tools⇨Spell Check.

Cut

 To delete the currently selected text or document, click this SmartIcon.

The Cut SmartIcon deletes the selected text or document — just like Edit⇨Clear.

Attachment

 Click this SmartIcon to insert an attachment.

 The Attachment SmartIcon opens the Insert Attachment(s) dialog box and allows you to insert a file in the document you are composing.

You can only attach a file when the cursor is in a rich text field.

Copy

 Copy the selected text or document to the clipboard by clicking this SmartIcon.

The Copy SmartIcon is a shortcut for choosing Edit⇨Copy.

Paste

 Use this SmartIcon to paste the contents of the clipboard.

Clicking this SmartIcon is the same as choosing Edit⇨Paste.

Navigate Next Unread

 To go to the next unread document in a database, click this SmartIcon.

This SmartIcon is especially helpful when you are reading your mail.

Categorize

 Categorize the selected (or open) document by clicking this SmartIcon.

 This SmartIcon is the same as choosing Tools⟶Categorize and is especially useful when you are reading your mail.

The Categorize SmartIcon is in the Mail palette. (See Chapter 13 for more information on the Mail palette.)

Mail Address

 Clicking this SmartIcon address the message you are composing.

 Clicking this SmartIcon is the same as choosing Mail⟶Address.

The Mail Address SmartIcon is in the Mail palette.

Forward

 To forward the document you are reading to someone else, click this SmartIcon.

This one's a shortcut for choosing Mail⟶Forward.

Chapter 18

Ten Cool Tricks You Can Use to Impress Your Friends

In This Chapter
▶ The chapter title says it all

1 f you *really* want people to think you know what you're doing, you gotta read this chapter to learn the ten best, secret tricks Notes has up its sleeve. Learn 'em, live 'em, love 'em!

Double-Click the Right Mouse Button

Whenever you want to close a document or view, you can double-click the *right* mouse button instead of choosing File⇨Close Window. It takes a little getting used to if you're not familar with using the right mouse button, but it's a fast way to close the open document.

Mac users don't have a right mouse button, so this impressive trick is unavailable to them. Sorry.

Press Tab to Check for New Documents

If you are at the workspace (in other words, if you don't have any windows open), you can press Tab to start checking each database on your workspace for new documents. Pressing Tab at the workspace is really just a shortcut for choosing Tools⇨Scan Unread⇨Preferred Databases.

Press F9 to Update Databases

Another trick to use at the workspace is to press F9. Doing so tells Notes to check each database on the current workspace page for new documents and display the number of new documents right there in the database's icon. Whenever you want an up-to-the-minute report of new documents, press F9.

Hold Down Control while Changing Views

To switch to a view and keep the same document highlighted, select the document in question and hold Ctrl key while you choose the new view from the View menu.

Make a Document Private

If you are composing a document in a database in a server, you can decide that you only want certain people to see the document. By creating a *Read Access List*, you can be very specific about the names of the people who get to read your contribution. Your fellow users who open the database but whose names are *not* in your Read Access List will not be able to see your document at all. In fact, they won't even find the document in the view!

To make a document available to only a subset of the people who can use the database, choose Edit⇨Security⇨Read Access while you are composing the document. Using the dialog box shown in Figure 18-1, you determine who gets to read your document.

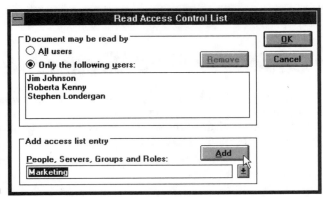

Figure 18-1:
The Read
Access
Control List
dialog box.

First, choose Only the following <u>u</u>sers and then type each of the names in the Add access list entry box. You have to choose <u>A</u>dd after you type each name. If you know there's a group of people defined in the Public Name and Address Book and you want to give that entire group access to your document, you can enter a group name (as we have in the example). When you're done listing the names of the people, choose <u>O</u>K.

Make sure you include your own name in the Read Access Control list, or you will not be able to read the document yourself.

If you know your document will be replicating to another Notes server, you have to include the name of the server in the list of "people" who can read the document, too.

Change the Music That You Hear When You Get New E-Mail

If you use Windows, you can have Notes play a WAV file to tell you when new e-mail has been delivered, instead of the boring old "beep beep beep" message. To tell Notes to play your special tune, add the line

```
NewMailTune=c:\windows\tada.wav
```

to your NOTES.INI file, substituting the appropriate filename and path for the WAV file that you want to hear.

To hear this change, you have to have a speaker on your computer that can play music. Assuming that you do, prepare for a real symphonic delight!

NOTES.INI is an ASCII file full of configuration information, and it's (usually) in your Windows subdirectory. You can edit it using either the Windows Notepad or SysEdit program.

The bad news: if you don't use Windows, you can't do this. Sorry!

Automatically Reply to Incoming Messages while You're on Vacation

If you expect to be out of the office for a while and you won't be checking your mail by modem, you can write a special macro that automatically sends a form letter to people who send you messages, telling them that you're on vacation, won't be back for a couple of weeks, will respond to their message then and so on, and so on.

Macros can be pretty complicated, so be careful to follow these steps exactly:

1. **With your mail database open, choose Design⇨Macros and then choose New.**

   You can name the macro anything you want, but the rest of the options must be set exactly as you see them in Figure 18-2. (Of course, you should enter the name of the server that has your mail database in the list box that says Server/workstation on which to run.)

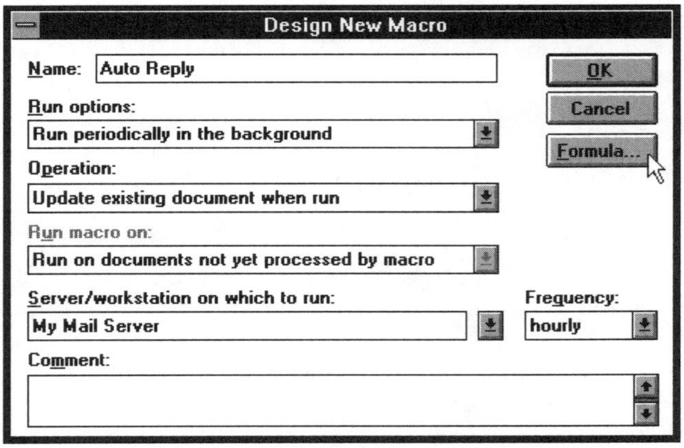

Figure 18-2: Designing a macro to automatically reply to e-mail received while you're on vacation.

2. **Choose Formula and enter a formula very much like the following:**

```
SELECT Form = "Memo" : "Reply" & ComposedDate >
    @Date(1994;8;1;17;30;0);
@MailSend(From +
    @If(@IsAvailable(FromDomain);FromDomain;"");"";"";
```

```
"RE: The message you sent to Stephen Londergan";
"Hi " + @Left(From;" ") + "-" +
@NewLine+
"Steverino is out soaking up the rays until Sept. 1, and
        will be unable to reply to your message until
        then. If you need a reply sooner, please contact
        Rich at x217.")
```

Your formula should be *exactly* like the one above, with only two changes:

- ✔ You can include any message in the last line, but make sure you enclose the whole thing in quotes. Also, substitute your name in the third line.
- ✔ You must modify the @Date formula in the first line to tell the macro when it should start replying for you.

The @Date formula uses the following syntax:

```
@Date(Year;Month;Day;Hour;Minute;Second)
```

In our example, the macro will automatically reply to any messages that are received *after* 5:30 PM on August 1, 1994. Let's say you are going to sneak out early for your vacation, and you want the macro to reply to messages received after 3:00 p.m. on April 5, 1994. You substitute

```
@Date(1994;4;5;15;0;0)
```

in the @Date part of the formula.

Because the server will automatically send the messages in your absence, make sure that you include your name in the message. Otherwise, the people who get the automatic replies won't know who's on vacation — the messages will be from "Your Mail Server."

When you get back to work after your vacation, use the Design➪Macros dialog box to change the frequency of the macro to Never so that the macro stops replying for you.

If you wrote a macro using the example formula, the message the server sends will look like Figure 18-3.

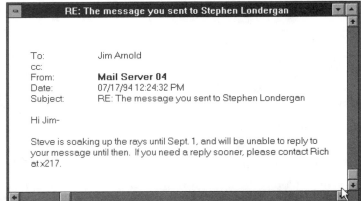

Figure 18-3:
An auto-
reply e-mail
message
from the
server.

Automatically Categorize Your Incoming E-Mail

Another relatively simple macro you can use is one that will try to automatically categorize e-mail as it is delivered to you. Based on certain rules that you establish, you might decide that any incoming message that has the word *Meeting* in the Subject field should automatically go into your *Schedule* category. If the Subject contains the word *Baseball*, perhaps you'll want to categorize it as *Personal*. And if the message came from your boss, you want to categorize it as *Read right away*.

To automatically categorize your incoming e-mail, follow these steps:

1. **With your e-mail database open, choose D̲esign➪M̲acros and then choose N̲ew.**

   You can name the macro anything you want, but the rest of the options must be set *exactly* as you see them in Figure 18-4.

2. **Choose F̲ormula and enter a formula very much like the following:**

```
SELECT @All;
FIELD Categories :=
@If(
@Contains(Subject;"Meeting");"Schedule";
@Contains(Subject;"Baseball");"Personal";
@Contains(Subject;"Status");"Reports";
@Contains(From;"Mary Kuppens");"Read right away";
@Contains(Subject;"Urgent");"Hot Issues";
@Contains(Subject;"Weekend");"Personal";
;"")
```

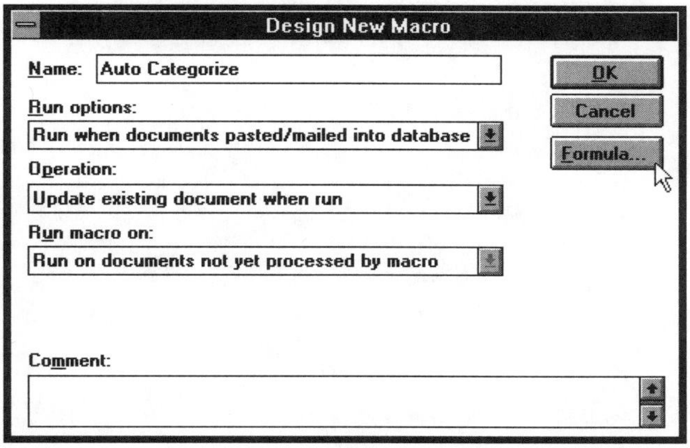

Figure 18-4:
Writing a
macro that
automatically
categorizes
incoming
e-mail.

For your formula, the first, second, third, and last lines must be *exactly* as you see them in the preceding code, but you are going to have to modify the other lines to suit your taste.

Although you can add more @Contains formulas to establish more rules, you can't predict every word that someone might send you in the Subject field, so you're still going to end up with some documents that arrive uncategorized.

Press the Right Mouse Button to Preview What a SmartIcon Does

Unless you use Macintosh (in which case you don't have a right mouse button), you can click any SmartIcon with the *right* mouse button to see a hint about what the SmartIcon does.

Turn Off New E-Mail Notifications

If you are annoyed by the constant "beep beep beep" signal that Notes uses to say that new e-mail has been delivered, you can disable it. Choose Tools⇨Setup⇨Mail and turn *off* Check for New Mail Every *nn* Minutes. You can always change your mind later and turn this option on again if you decide that you miss those "beep beep beep" alerts.

Chapter 19
Ten Time Savers

In This Chapter

▶ Using the Status Bar to check for mail
▶ Creating addressee groups
▶ Simplifying a complex address
▶ Truncating documents during replication
▶ Replicating selectively
▶ Replying with history
▶ Replicating in the background
▶ Replicating on a schedule

Don't waste time. Time is money. Money is the root of all evil.

Be that as it may, only a few weirdos would argue that it is bad to find ways to save time. This chapter contains a bunch of hints, tricks, and procedures to do your work in Notes faster, thereby freeing you for more important pursuits like going to meetings, making the coffee, cleaning your desk, or taking a nap.

Using the Status Bar to Check for E-Mail

Down at the bottom of the Notes window is the Status Bar. You may remember from Chapter 11 that you can use the Status Bar to set the font style and font size (which is also a time saver) and to select a different SmartIcon palette (Chapter 2). You can also use it to check for new mail. Figure 19-1 shows the Status Bar.

Figure 19-1:
The Status
Bar.

Whenever someone sends you a message, it arrives in your e-mail database marked unread, waiting for your attention. You may hear the catchy little tune Notes plays, or you may see the message New mail has been delivered to you, but you will also see an envelope in the Status Bar. If there is no envelope in the Status Bar, you have no unread mail. Click the envelope and your mail database is opened or brought to the front with the last view you used.

There, marked with stars and colored red, are your new messages. Don't forget the tricks for reading your mail: use the SmartIcons or Tab and Shift+Tab to see the next or preceding unread message. See Chapter 3 for more complete information about reading mail.

Deliver de Letter — de Sooner, de Better

Why waste your time entering long lists of addressees or typing confusing addresses when you could be quickly sending the memo on its way? These two tricks allow you to type a minimum of information about individuals or groups and then force Notes to supply all the gory details.

Grappling with groups

If you regularly send memos to groups of people — certain friends, selected coworkers, all managers, or the cafeteria staff, you will get tired of typing everyone's name separately into the memos every time you want to fire off a note to the group. The more names involved, the more quickly you'll start to avoid sending memos so that you won't have to do all that typing.

Of course, you could open a previous memo you sent to that group and paste the addresses into a new memo, but a faster technique is to use a group name. Sometimes a higher authority has already defined the group you want to send a memo to; you can check by opening the Public Name and Address Book and choosing <u>V</u>iew⇨<u>G</u>roups. Double-click a group name to see who is included. If everyone or almost everyone that you want to send a memo to is there, simply address your memo to the group name, and it will go to everyone on the list. If there are some people who should get the memo but whose names are not in the group, you need to type their names separately.

You can't exclude a person in a group; you can't type *Managers, but not Keeble Mortimer* for instance.

If the group doesn't already exist, you can create one of your own. With your Personal Name and Address Book open, choose <u>C</u>ompose⇨<u>G</u>roup. Figure 19-2 shows a form in which we are creating a group. In the Group name field, type a succinct name that will remind you of the nature of the group. *Friends* or *Sales Managers* are good examples. Names like *My Very Special Friends* or *Sales Managers — East —* may be a bit more of a problem simply because you may forget to include the word *Very* or the second dash when you type the address. Notes can't send the memo until you get the address right.

In the Members field, type the correct mailing address of all people and groups you want to include in the group.

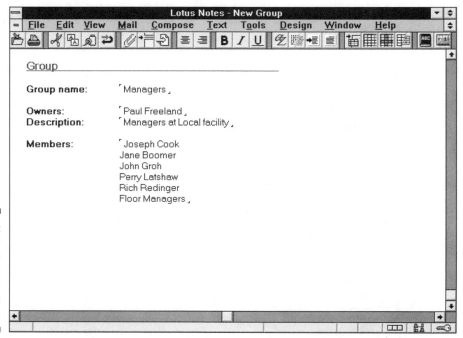

Figure 19-2: Creating a group in the Personal Name and Address Book.

You can have up to six nested levels of groups. In other words, a group can be included in another group, that group can be included in yet another group, and so on until the original group is buried six levels within the last group. For instance, you could create a mammoth group called Worldwide Sales Force. Within that group you could include Western Hemisphere Sales; within that group could be North American Sales; within that, Eastern Region; within that, Northeastern Sales; and within that, Pennsylvania Sales Force. But if you try to include a seventh group (Eastern Pennsylvania Sales) in that group, when you try to mail a memo that includes Worldwide Sales Force as an addressee, you see an error message on the screen saying `Groups cannot be nested more than 6 levels deep when mailing.`

Managing mammoth monikers

Sometimes a person's name is more than just first and last name. CompuServe or Internet addresses, or even official names of people within your organization, may cause carpal tunnel syndrome every time you type them. Rather than typing the entire mess, create a Person document for that one long name. As in the preceding section, open your Personal Name and Address Book and choose Compose⇨Person. Type the person's first name in the First Name field, last name in the Last Name field, and type the complete address in the Full Name field.

In Figure 19-3, we have created a person document for Dwight Babcock. When sending a memo to Dwight, you can just type his name; Notes automatically supplies Dwight's complete address: UNIXML::"babcock@cleona.ingress.COM" @ CORPVAX.

Figure 19-3:
Use a person document to save yourself having to type confusing addresses.

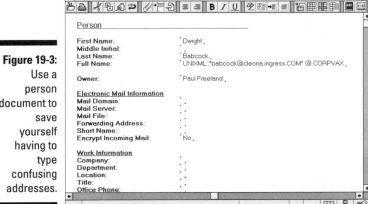

Replication for Those on the Run

When you're on the road, you need to call your Home Server to replicate your e-mail database and catch up on all the latest from the office. Sometimes you get messages from long-winded folks. You might also get a holiday greeting with a cute, festive, appropriately heartwarming graphic and a tune attached, swelling the whole thing to more than a million bytes. So while Frosty the Snowman and all eight reindeer are replicated along the phone lines, your phone line and computer are tied up, leaving you sitting there watching the process. Fa la la!

Is there a way to prevent the replication of long messages, attachments, and time-consuming graphics? Yes! Use File➪Database➪Information➪Replication. Notice in the dialog box in Figure 19-4 that the Truncate large documents and remove attachments box is checked. Now Notes replicates only the first 40K bytes of each memo and does not replicate attachments (but does replicate the documents themselves). Any document that has been truncated is marked with the word *Truncated* in views in your e-mail database.

This option does not affect the original document in your e-mail database on the server. So when you get back to the office and read messages right from the server, all attachments and all large memos will be intact. This command only affects replication to remote workstations.

Figure 19-4:
Use the
Replication
Settings
dialog box
to prevent
replication
of large
documents.

```
┌─────────────────────────────────────────────────────────────┐
│ ▬              Replication Settings                          │
├─────────────────────────────────────────────────────────────┤
│  Replica ID:   85255CC4:00605237          ┌─────────────┐   │
│                                           │     OK      │   │
│                                           └─────────────┘   │
│                                           ┌─────────────┐   │
│                                           │   Cancel    │   │
│  ┌─ Priority ──────────────────────┐      └─────────────┘   │
│  │                                 │      ┌─────────────┐   │
│  │ ○ High   ◉ Medium   ○ Low       │      │ Selective...│   │
│  │                                 │      └─────────────┘   │
│  └─────────────────────────────────┘      ┌─────────────┐   │
│                                           │View history..│  │
│  □ Do not replicate deletions to replicas of this database  │
│  □ Disable replication of this database                     │
│  □ Remove documents saved more than  [90]  days ago         │
│  ⊠ Truncate large documents and remove attachments          │
│  □ Replicate database Title, Categories, and Template Names  │
└─────────────────────────────────────────────────────────────┘
```

If, after you replicate, you realize that you really need the attachment that got lopped off during replication, highlight the memo and press F9 or choose View➪Refresh Truncated Document. A prompt asking if you want to call your server appears, and then the normal replication process continues from there. After the process is finished, the complete document with attachments, graphics, all text, house guests, and dirty laundry will be in your remote workstation's e-mail database.

Eclectic Replication

There are several reasons why you may want to select only certain documents to be replicated to a remote workstation:

- ✔ You elected to truncate documents, but now you see that you need the complete version of one or two of the truncated messages.

- ✔ You know that lots of messages are waiting and don't want to take the time to replicate them all.

- ✔ You only want to see messages from certain people.

- ✔ You only want to see the most recent messages.

- ✔ You want to prevent some messages from replicating because they contain more work and you want to sleep in tomorrow.

When you want to replicate only certain messages, you need to write a *selection formula*. Choose File⇨Database⇨Information⇨Replication⇨Selective. Figure 19-5 shows the Selective Replication dialog box. In the Copy Documents selected by box, enter a formula to select the types of messages that you want to receive. Replace the SELECT @All that is already there.

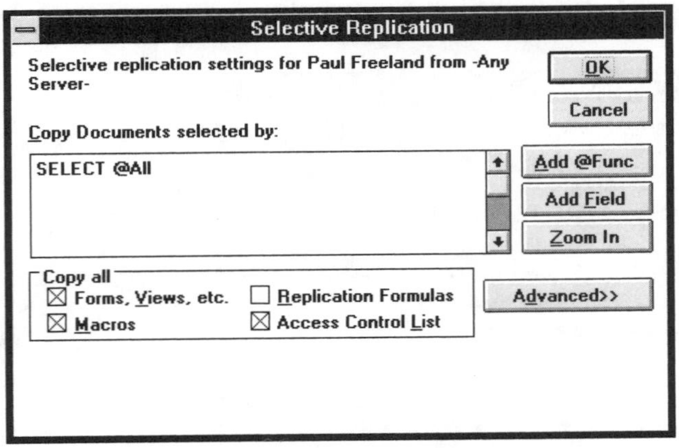

Figure 19-5: To restrict replication, replace the SELECT @All formula with a more selective one.

Here are three examples of formulas you can write:

- ✔ To replicate memos only from specific people, use the following:

```
SELECT FROM = "Jimmy Stewart" : "Lana Turner"
```

- ✔ To exclude memos from someone, such as the boss, use this:

```
SELECT FROM != "Thurston Howell"
```

- ✔ To replicate only memos created after September 11, 1994, use the following:

```
SELECT @CREATED > [9/11/94]
```

Those Who Ignore History

Imagine getting a memo like this:

```
Here are the answers to the questions in your previous memo:
Yes
Maybe
No
Tomorrow sometime.
She can't until after the convention.
You do and I find out, I don't care, that's all I hope!
```

Like many of us here in the mainstream of corporate America, you may be wondering what the original questions were — even if it was you who asked them in an earlier memo. Someone who uses Compose⇨Reply to answer your questions gets a blank memo form with only your name (you sent the original memo) and the original subject line. It's their job to make their memo make sense.

Wouldn't it be easier if the reply included the original memo so that you could see what the heck the questions were? Of course it would. Use Mail⇨Compose⇨Custom Forms and choose Reply with History. The memo form that appears includes any and all previous memos so that you can see the history of the contents of the current memo.

Replicating and Chewing Gum at the Same Time

If you need all documents complete and unaltered, then replication may take a long time. While replication is in progress, do you have to sit and twiddle your thumbs, watch a sitcom on TV, or even take a nap? Yes, if you are using a Macintosh. On other platforms, you can elect to have replication occur as a background process so that you can go on using your computer while replication is taking place. Unfortunately, background replication is not possible on the Macintosh.

Choose Tools⇨Replicate⇨Run in Background. When you launch the actual replication, it runs as a separate process from any other work you want to do. To see how replication is coming along, use Alt+Tab to switch to the background replication.

Your phone line is usurped during replication, but not your computer. Depending upon the type of computer you are using, you may find that its performance is somewhat slower.

Replicating and Sleeping at the Same Time

Need your computer *and* your phone line *and* an up-to-date mail database? Then you need to tell Notes to replicate while you're sleeping or playing golf. Even if you don't play golf, you can tell Notes to replicate your database on a regular schedule during times that don't interfere with your computing or your phone conversations.

To schedule regular replications, you need to do several things:

1. **Create a remote connection document.**

   Open your Personal Name and Address Book and choose Compose⇨Connection⇨Remote. Figure 19-6 shows a remote connection document in the making. You can leave most of the default information in the form as it is and only change the few bits of data to suit your needs.

   The information provided in the figure will cause Notes to call the server named Wotan starting 3:00 a.m. and keep trying until 6:00 a.m. each weekday. We changed the repeat interval from 360 minutes to 0 minutes, because we want Notes to contact the home server just once, replicate, and then take the rest of the day off until 3:00 a.m. tomorrow. The number that appears in the Repeat interval of: field tells Notes how often to call and replicate during the hours that you specify in the Call at times: field.

After you have made any and all necessary changes, save the remote connection document.

2. **Alert Notes that there will be a background process taking place.**

   Choose Tools⇨Setup⇨User and check Background Program. Figure 19-7 shows the User Setup dialog box with the item you have to check.

3. **If you are using Notes within Windows, be sure SHARE.EXE is loaded.**

   Edit your AUTOEXEC.BAT file and add a line that loads Share. Consult your Notes administrator, your DOS manual, or the closest techie to find out the exact syntax for the command on your computer.

4. **Restart Notes.**

   Because you changed a startup option, you need to restart Notes so that the startup option can take effect. Of course, your computer must be on and have Notes running for the replication to occur on schedule. Notes is a great program, but it can't start your computer and then start itself.

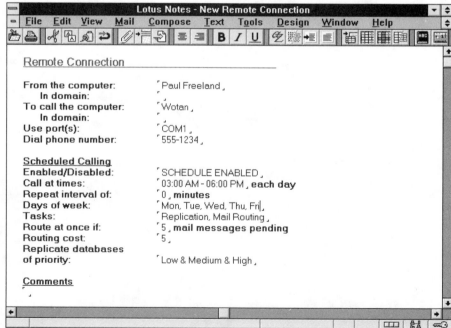

Figure 19-6:
A remote connection document tells Notes how to replicate on a schedule.

Figure 19-7:
Check
Background
Program if
you want
Notes to
replicate on
schedule.

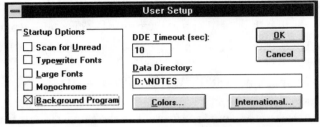

Chapter 20

Ten Things You Should Never Do

- -

In This Chapter

▶ The ten worst things you can do when using Notes

▶ The reasons why you should never, ever do them

▶ What to do if it's too late — because you've already blown it

- -

Generally, we encourage you to be adventurous, try new things, check out menus that you've never used before, and generally live on the edge. But, just as the nascent mycologist has to learn to eschew certain dangerous and poisonous mushrooms in favor of the edible ones, you need to know about the ten things in Notes that you should never, ever do.

Don't Change Your Notes Name

Maybe you just changed your name. Maybe you just got married and you're going to start hyphenating your name with your spouse's — from now on, it's "Bill Rodham-Clinton." Or maybe you have to change your name because you got a new job at your company — instead of "Lisa Kolb/Marketing/Acme," now it's "Lisa Kolb/Sales/Acme."

Of course, you want your name in Notes to change, too so that the new messages you send and the new documents you compose have your new name.

As tempting as it may be, you should never, ever choose Tools⇨User ID⇨Information⇨Change User Name. If you do (and you won't, because we warned you not to, right?), you will be able to change your name, but in the process you'll lose all your certificates.

If you've never even heard of a certificate before, you will learn all about them real quick if you change your name, because you will no longer be able to access any of your company's Notes servers.

If you really want to change your Notes name, you should use Mail⇨Send User ID⇨Request New Name. This way, your administrator can change your name but make sure that you don't lose your certificates.

If it's too late, because you already did Tools⇨User ID⇨Information⇨Change User Name, your only recourse is to call your administrator. There isn't anything *you* can do to fix the problem.

Don't Delete Your E-Mail Database

You probably have Manager access to your e-mail database. That's good, because you want to be able to customize your e-mail forms, change the way your views look, and generally do anything you want to your e-mail database.

That can also be bad — if you're not careful — because as Manager, you can use the File⇨Database⇨Delete command to completely, totally, irreversibly, forever, we're not kidding here, delete your *entire* e-mail database. And when we say entire database, we mean it; this command will delete every last e-mail message!

So *don't delete your e-mail database!*

If it's too late and you've already deleted your e-mail database, call your administrator. Be prepared to grovel, and hope that your administrator has a backup copy.

Don't Save or Send a Message Without Spell-Checking It First

As the olde saying goze, yOu onley have one chanse to maik a good furst impresssion — so don't blow it by e-mailing or posting documents that are full of typos. What excuse do you have for sending e-mail with spelling errors when you can always use Tools⇨Spell Check to correct your errors? Shame on you!

Don't Remove Your Password

Passwords are important in Notes for two reasons.

First, you don't want anyone to read your e-mail, and you don't want the casual passerby to sit down at your desk and compose a few messages (full of four-letter words) under your name, right?

Second, you have an obligation to your company not to let anyone use your USER.ID; if someone from your company's competition gets their hands on your USER.ID, that person can act as you — in fact, as far as Notes is concerned, they *are* you. So that nasty person can read all the company's confidential databases that only you are supposed to be able to access.

So don't, and we mean *don't*, even consider removing your USER.ID's password. As long as your USER.ID has a password, someone could steal your computer, but you (and the rest of your company) wouldn't have to worry about the thief getting any unauthorized access.

If it's too late and your (un-password-protected) USER.ID has been compromised, you should contact your administrator *immediately*.

If your USER.ID came without a password, you should set one *right now* by choosing Tools⇨User ID⇨Password⇨Set.

Don't Forget to Press F5 When You Go to Lunch

Did you read the previous section? The same security concerns apply to an unattended Notes workstation, even when your USER.ID does have a password. So, before you leave your workstation unattended, remember to always press F5. That way, anyone trying to use your computer will be prompted for your password, and they'll be locked out when they can't give it.

Don't Let Temp Files Pile Up

Notes has a *design limitation* (that's a *bug* to you and me) that causes it to fill up your hard disk with temporary files.

Every once in a while — maybe once a month — you should look in your Windows program directory, your Notes data directory, and your TEMP directory for files whose filename begins with a tilde (which looks like this: ~), or whose extension is TMP. If you find 'em, you can delete 'em.

Notes puts these temporary files on your hard disk whenever you launch an attached file.

Don't Forget to Consult the Manuals

Sure, we know, everybody hates to read computer manuals, but the Notes manuals really aren't as bad as some. They're not exactly the most exciting things you'll ever read, but they do contain useful, even vital, information about how to use the program.

So, when you're stumped, consider a perusal of your nearest set of Notes documentation. As they say in the computer business, when all else fails, RTFM. That stands for **R**ead The **F**lippin' **M**anual.

Don't Forget to Save Early and Often

Notes is like any computer program; unexpected power interruptions can be tragic. It's important to get into the habit of saving your work early and often. You can choose File⇨Save or press Ctrl+S.

Don't Forget to Turn on Server-Based Mail When You Get Back to the Office

If you use the same computer when you travel as you do in the office, you know to use Tools⇨Setup⇨Location⇨Workstation-based mail to have Notes accumulate your outgoing mail until you make a phone call to your home server.

Don't forget to use Tools⇨Setup⇨Location⇨Server-based mail when you plug your computer back into the LAN upon your return to the office. Otherwise your outgoing e-mail will never leave your workstation; it'll just keep piling up in your workstation's MAIL.BOX.

Refer to Chapter 14 for more information about using Notes while traveling.

Don't Talk to Strangers

And don't believe everything you read, either.

Chapter 21

Ten Neat Things You Can Buy for Notes

▶ Some Notes "extras" that are fun and can make your life easier

▶ Where you can get them

*I*n addition to the "core" product, a number of Notes add-ons exist — some are called "Companion Products" — that you or your administrator can purchase for Notes.

InFax

Lotus Development sells a product called InFax. This item is a program that your administrator installs on your Notes server that allows you to get faxes delivered to you as e-mail. When someone wants to send you a fax, the person uses their regular fax machine to call your Notes server (instead of your fax machine), and the server converts the incoming fax to an e-mail message that you receive right along with your regular messages in your mail database.

Pretty cool, but a document that has a fax embedded in it can be quite big, so be prepared!

OutFax

Lotus also sells OutFax, which is just the opposite of InFax. It's a program that lets you *send* faxes through Notes mail; you compose an e-mail message as you normally would, but the special address that you use tells Notes to convert the message to a fax and call your friend's fax machine to deliver it.

Just think of it — you can send faxes without ever printing them on a piece of paper and without having to walk down the hall to the fax machine!

Beeper Gateway

If you carry a SkyTel alpha-numeric beeper, your administrator can buy and install a gateway from Lotus that sends your (specially-addressed) e-mail messages right to your beeper.

If you have the gateway installed at your company, you can also use macros to have the server automatically forward your e-mail to your beeper or forward messages from a news database to your beeper.

CompuServe

CompuServe has been providing dial-in services for years and has also started to make Notes servers available, too. For a fee, you can use your Notes workstation to call into these servers, where CompuServe has set up some public discussion databases — and it's also a great way to send e-mail to other companies.

Additionally, CompuServe hosts a Lotus Notes-related forum where you can ask questions, get information, download databases, and generally talk to a bunch of Notes "geeks." (The authors of this book have been known to put in an appearance there, too, but they're not geeks.)

If you subscribe to CompuServe, use GO LOTUSCOMM to access the forum.

WorldCom

WorldCom is a company that lets you use their Notes servers while paying for the amount of time you're dialed in to them. WorldCom offers lots of public discussion databases, Internet groups, and some news services (databases that get daily feeds from wire services), and is also a good way to send Notes mail to users who don't work at your company. WorldCom is a great place to ask people any questions that you have about using Notes, too.

If you want to really see what's going on with other Notes users around the world, consider subscribing. You can reach WorldCom at 800-774-2220.

A Mail Gateway

A mail gateway is a program that your administrator can buy and install that allows you to send e-mail to people who use other systems for their e-mail — cc:Mail, DaVinci, or even the Internet.

Carthage Today

Carthage Today is a Notes-based news subscription service that's available for a yearly fee. You tell the service what kind of stories you are interested — maybe you want information about certain products or business, your competitors, the World Wrestling Association, and so on — and it scours a ton of news services from all around the globe and then sends you the results every day via Notes. Real state-of-the-art Information Superhighway stuff.

The service can be reached at 800-748-3737.

Memory

Like any program, Notes is happiest when it has lots of memory, so it can never hurt to install some more RAM — especially if you own a Macintosh!

PhoneNotes

PhoneNotes is a program that does two things: it embeds a phone message in a Notes document, and it reads a Notes document to you over the telephone, using one of those cheesy computer-generated voices. It's still pretty neat, though; imagine getting your phonemail messages sent to you as e-mail!

More Copies of This Book

We're sure you would agree that no Notes workstation is complete without at least one copy of *Lotus Notes For Dummies*, right?

The 5th Wave   By Rich Tennant

"OH YEAH, AND TRY NOT TO ENTER THE WRONG PASSWORD."

Chapter 22
The Ten Most Common Problems

● ●

In This Chapter

▶ The ten most common problems you (might) encounter when using Notes

▶ The ten easy ways to avoid the ten common problems

● ●

*H*ey, you can't expect everything to work perfectly all the time, and Notes is no exception. In this chapter, we discuss the ten most common problems — and their ten matching solutions.

Your Laptop Won't Connect to Your Server

Problem: You're trying to use Notes remotely, but every time you try to make a call, you get an error message that says `Modem could not connect dial tone`.

Solution: Did you know that there are two kinds of telephone lines? One is called *analog*, and the other is *digital*. You don't need to know what the difference is between them — you do need to know, however, that Notes (and any computer program, for that matter) can only use analog lines with its modem. If you get the aforementioned error message when you try to call in, the problem may be that the phone line you've plugged into the modem is digital, instead of analog. Most offices (and many hotel rooms) are equipped with digital lines, and that causes all kinds of problems for Notes.

The bottom line is that you have to find an analog line to use your modem with Notes. It figures that there's no way to tell the difference between an analog line and a digital one by just looking at the jack in the wall, so you'll probably have to ask someone if you need help. Good luck explaining this to most hotel operators!

If all else fails, you can plug your modem into the phone line that's being used for the closest fax machine, because they need analog lines, too.

You Can't Edit a Field

Problem: You're trying to compose (or perhaps edit) a document, and you can't edit a particular field. You've tried the arrow keys, the Tab key, and even the mouse, but you can't even get the cursor into the field.

Solution: This is one for your administrator (less likely) or the database designer (more likely) to solve. Notes has many security features, and they're all under the control of the designer and administrator. Call one or the other of them and explain the problem. They'll offer a solution.

You Can't Use a Doclink

Problem: You double-click a doclink icon, but you can't open the target document.

Solution: Tell the person who composed the document in the first place. Most likely, they've created a doclink to a database that you don't have access to or to a document that's in a database on a server that you don't have access to.

Your Server Isn't Responding

Problem: You double-click a database icon, but get either `Server servername is not responding`, **the error** `Network operation did not complete in a reasonable amount of time`, **or perhaps** `Remote system is no longer responding`.

Solution: Each of the above error messages indicates a network problem, over which you have no control. (It's not *your* job to keep the servers in good working order!) As is often the case, the solution to this problem begins with a call to your administrator.

You Don't Have the Right Certificate

Problem: Whenever you try to access a server, you get the error message `Your ID has not been certified to access the server`.

Solution: Call your administrator and explain the problem.

You Can't Open a Database

Problem: Whenever you try to use a particular database, you get the error message `You are not authorized to access that database.`

Solution: Once again, call your administrator and report that the Access Control List is incorrect for the database in question.

Call the Access Control List the "ACL" when you talk to your administrator to look like you know what you're talking about.

You Can't Use Full Text Search

Problem: You are trying (unsuccessfully) to create a new Full Text Index.

Solution: If the database that you're trying to index is on a Notes server, the problem is usually that your administrator has set up the server to not allow Full Text Indexes. Indexes take up lots of disk space, so sometimes administrators get stingy.

If you are trying to create an index for a database that's on your Macintosh workstation, save the dime and don't bother calling your administrator, because Macs just don't support local Full Text Indexes (although you can use an index if the database is on a Notes server).

You Can't Delete a Document You Composed

Problem: You composed a document in a database, and now you want to delete it — but you can't, no matter how many times you press Delete.

Solution: Call your administrator and/or the database designer, and ask them to check that the database is properly recording author names in the documents and that the Access Control List allows you to delete documents.

You Can't Launch an Object

Problem: You double-click an embedded object's icon, but you can't get the other program to load.

Solution: To open an embedded object, you have to have the program that was used to create the object in the first place installed on your computer. If the object is an embedded Lotus 1-2-3 worksheet, but you don't have 1-2-3 installed on your computer, you will *not* be able to launch or edit that object. (You may also have to install a newer version of Notes; contact your administrator, who'll know what to do.)

You Don't Know Who Your Administrator Is

Problem: You've read this book, and it seems that every time there's a potential problem, we use the "Call your administrator" cop out. The problem is that you don't know who that is!

Solution: Ask somebody else, or consider changing jobs so that *you're* the administrator and then call yourself.

Part VI
Appendixes

The 5th Wave   By Rich Tennant

"I'll tell you this-retraining for client/server isn't going to be easy. Do you know how old some of these dogs are?"

In this part...

The rest of this book is full of appendixes (or appendices, if you prefer). In the human body, the appendix is a forgotten, useless little part of you that suddenly calls attention to itself by becoming inflamed and threatening to kill you. Nothing will ever happen to draw your attention to this book's appendixes, but you may want to take the time to look at them, even if ignoring them won't kill you.

You've got six appendixes to browse through. Appendix A tells you how to install a Notes Workstation, Appendix B lists all the SmartIcons and tells you what they do, Appendix C lists all the major commands and function keys, Appendix D describes the database templates you get with Notes, Appendix E gives you valuable insights into using Notes in a remote workstation, and Appendix F includes Macintosh tips (not to be confused with steak tips) and hints for using Notes on a Mac. And don't forget Appendix G — the glossary.

Appendix A

Installing Notes as a Workstation

● ●

*I*f you don't have Notes installed on your computer, then this appendix had better be one of the first things you read, even though it's near the end of the book. The information here is for installing Notes as a workstation, or *client*. (If you are a Notes administrator planning to install Notes as a server, there are large tomes full of complicated technical information for you to use, which you get when you buy Notes.) The purpose of this appendix is to hold your hand and guide you as you sit blinking before flashing screens and bewildering options, afraid that making the wrong choice will cause your computer to burst into flames.

So, How Do I Do It?

Installing Notes as a workstation is no more complicated than installing any other software; the trick is understanding the choices you have to make.

1. **The first thing to do is to find the disks labeled Lotus Notes Client Install.**

   Be sure the disk is appropriate for the platform into which you are installing Notes: Macintosh, Windows, UNIX, or OS/2. If you don't have the disks, ask your Notes administrator. You may find that, instead of needing disks, you'll be installing directly from the network because your crafty administrator has stored the files where everyone can get at them. In that case, get instructions from your crafty administrator about how to get started, because each network setup is a bit different from the others and we don't want to give you a bum steer.

2. **Insert the Lotus Notes Client Install disk in the disk drive and start the install program.**

   To install in Windows, start Windows, open Program Manager, and select File⇨Run. Type **A:\INSTWIN.EXE**. Don't select Run Minimized.

   To install in OS/2, start Presentation Manager, open an OS/2 window, and type **A:\INSTPM.** You can also open File Manager, choose File⇨Run, type **A:\INSTPM,** and choose Run.

To install in Macintosh close all open applications, insert the Notes Install disks and then double-click the Install Lotus Notes icon. When you see the easy install screen (see Figure A-1), choose Install.

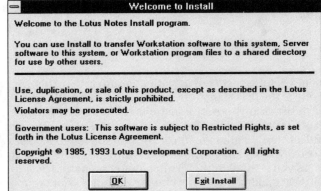

Figure A-1:
The friendly introductory screen for Notes installation.

3. **The next step, shown in Figure A-2, is easy: you are going to Install Workstation software on this system**.

Click the box next to that choice and wait awhile so that the install program can go sniffing around your hard disk drives looking for possible locations to place the program.

Although we hope this appendix contains everything you need to know about installing Notes, anytime you want more information about a choice, click the Help box to get specific, helpful, warm, friendly advice.

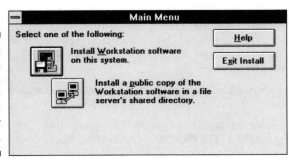

Figure A-2:
Choose to install on your system by clicking the upper box.

4. Decide how you will be running Notes.

Figure A-3 shows you deciding how you will be running Notes. You can run the whole program on your very own local personal computer, or you can use a public copy of Notes stored somewhere on the network. If you choose the latter option, only certain files will be placed on your local hard drive. If you are going to run Notes from the network, your administrator will tell you how you are to run Notes and where the program files are stored.

In this book, we are proceeding on the assumption that you are going to run your own copy of Notes on your own computer. Therefore, on that assumption, choose Install your own copy of Notes on this system by clicking the box next to that choice.

Figure A-3:
We assume here that you will be installing and running Notes from your own local copy.

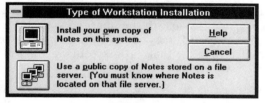

5. Decide what to install and where to install it.

The next blizzard of options you have to deal with is the Specifying Directories for the Notes Files dialog box, like the one in Figure A-4. Having sniffed around your computer in all the possible places where it could place Notes, the install program asks you to decide what to install and where to put it.

In the Drive/Available Space section of the dialog box, you see all hard disks and the amount of space available on each. This is a very important dialog box, so take the time to choose carefully among the options so that you don't have to do it all again.

Specifying Directories for the Notes Files

Files to Install:	Size:	Install Here:	
☒ Program files	7,144 K	C:\NOTES	Browse Disk
☒ Personal data files	2,376 K	C:\NOTES	Browse Disk
☒ Template application files	1,152 K		
☒ Example files	3,584 K		
☐ Documentation databases	3,728 K		
☐ Help	6,544 K		
☐ Tutorial databases	960 K		

Available
Drive   Space:
C: 22,024 K
D: 6,624 K
E: 0 K
I: 2,052 K

Total size of selected files: 14,256 K

[OK]   [Main Menu]   [Help]

Figure A-4:
Choose
where
Notes
should be
installed.

You should choose to install Notes on the drive with the largest amount of space available. Don't try to tuck Notes into a disk that seems to have just the right amount of space, because the numbers you see in this dialog box are approximate. You may find that you run out of disk space before installation is complete. Besides that, as the size of the Notes directory grows — and it will — you may run out of disk space.

Before you're done with this dialog box, you also need to specify what files you want to install to your hard disk. The groups of files are listed in the column headed Files to Install, and next to each is the approximate size of the group. The following list is a brief description of each group:

- *Program Files* — Selected by default. You need these files to run Notes — that says it all. Without this group of files you do not have Notes on your computer. Don't deselect this choice unless you like doing install several times, you have already installed the files in an earlier install, or you are using a public network copy of Notes.

- *Personal Data Files* — Selected by default. These files are the ones that tailor Notes to your own personal use. Regardless of where you are installing Notes, you need these files. Deselect this group only if you are reinstalling Notes and know that the files already exist on your computer.

- *Template Application Files* — Selected by default. These are empty database shells that you can use as templates for databases you may choose to create later. Included are Customer Tracking, Correspondence, Discussion, Document Library, Mail, News, Service Request Tracking, Status Reports, Meeting Tracking, Reservation Scheduler, and Things To Do database templates. They are all described in Appendix D. You may want to deselect this group if you are sure that you don't intend to create your own databases and you want to save about 1MB of disk space.

- *Example Files* — Selected by default. This group of files is related to the Template Application Files. They are databases created with the templates to show you how the templates can be used. You might consider installing them if you install the templates. You can study them and delete them later.

- *Documentation Databases* — Not selected by default. These are databases containing information about the following rather technical aspects of Notes. You can probably do without these files:

    Dial-Up Notes

    Internals: Security

    Internals: Databases

    Internals: Data Exchange Facilities

    Running Lotus Notes on Banyan VINES

    Running Lotus Notes on Pathworks

    Running Lotus Notes on TCP/IP

    Running Lotus Notes on Novell NetWare

- *Help* — Not selected by default. If you are new to Notes, you ought to install this so that any time you run into unfamiliar territory, you can summon help.

- *Tutorial Databases* — Not selected by default. If you are brand new to Notes, running the tutorial will give you an overview of the use of Notes. Because you're reading this book the tutorial may be a bit of overkill, so you may want to leave it unselected.

6. **After you make your selections, check the Total size of selected files to be sure that they will all fit in the disk you have selected**.

    If not, you need to make some tactical decisions about picking a different drive, deleting some files, deselecting some file groups, or installing on the network. If there is no potential disk space problem, select OK.

7. **Decide what icons to add and where.**

    Figure A-5 shows you the Adding Icons dialog box, in which you decide whether and where to add the Notes icon to a program group. You should leave the box next to Notes selected so that there will be an icon. Otherwise, every time you want to start Notes you would need to issue a bunch of commands, instead of just clicking an icon.

    Use the drop-down list next to Group Name to select the program group in which the icon will appear and then click OK.

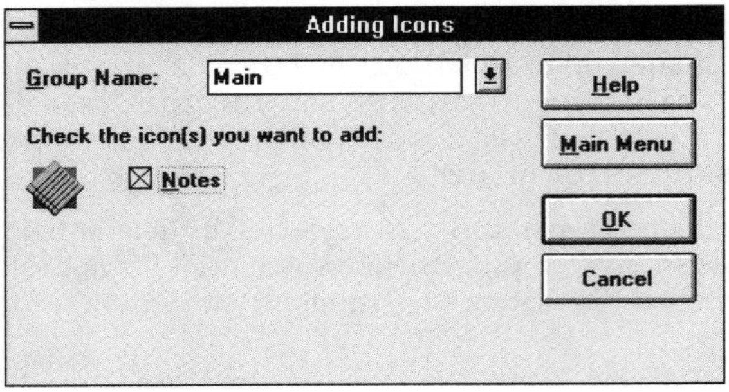

Figure A-5:
Use this
dialog box to
decide
where the
Notes icon
will appear.

```
┌─────────────────────────────────────────────────────────┐
│ ═     Adding Icons                                        │
│ Group Name:   [Main            ] [±]    ┌──────────┐      │
│                                          │  Help    │      │
│ Check the icon(s) you want to add:      └──────────┘      │
│                                          ┌──────────┐      │
│   ◇◇   ☒ Notes                          │ Main Menu│      │
│                                          └──────────┘      │
│                                          ┌──────────┐      │
│                                          │   OK     │      │
│                                          └──────────┘      │
│                                          ┌──────────┐      │
│                                          │ Cancel   │      │
│                                          └──────────┘      │
└─────────────────────────────────────────────────────────┘
```

Install will do most of the rest of the work, pausing occasionally to ask you to insert one or another of the disks. Pop the requested disk into the disk drive, press Enter, and sink back into a reverie until you get the next disk request. Helpful little screens appear that show you how the installation is progressing.

When the directories are all created, the files are transferred, and the icons are in place, a dialog box like the one in Figure A-6 appears, allowing you to choose whether to Launch Notes or simply Exit Install. Whichever you choose, you may take pride in the knowledge that you have successfully installed Notes on your computer.

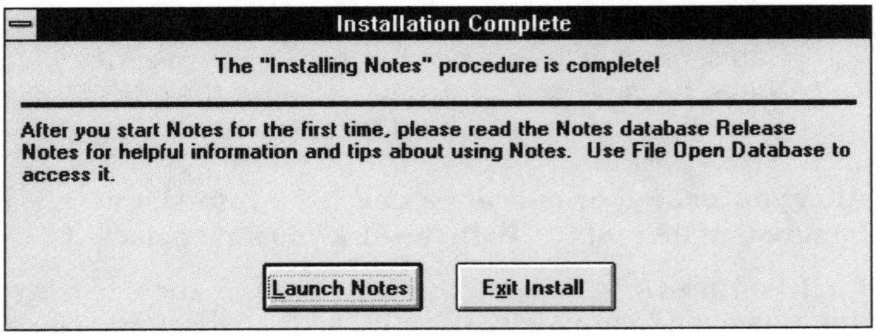

Figure A-6:
When you
see this
dialog box,
the install
process is
over. Nice
job.

```
┌─────────────────────────────────────────────────────────┐
│ ═     Installation Complete                               │
│        The "Installing Notes" procedure is complete!      │
│ ────────────────────────────────────────────────────     │
│ After you start Notes for the first time, please read the Notes database Release │
│ Notes for helpful information and tips about using Notes.  Use File Open Database to │
│ access it.                                                │
│                                                           │
│              ┌──────────────┐  ┌──────────────┐           │
│              │ Launch Notes │  │ Exit Install │           │
│              └──────────────┘  └──────────────┘           │
└─────────────────────────────────────────────────────────┘
```

Now that installation is complete, you are ready to set up your workstation. If your workstation will be connected to a LAN, this is a good time to read or reread Chapter 2. If this is a remote workstation, you should read Appendix E and then read or reread Chapter 2.

Appendix B

The Lotus Notes SmartIcons

• •

*W*hat follows is a kind of art gallery of the SmartIcons and a brief description of what each one does. Remember the following:

- These are the SmartIcons for Release 3 of Notes.
- This book does not cover the functions of all the SmartIcons.
- You can find out what a SmartIcon does by pointing to it and holding down the right mouse button (unless you use Macintosh).
- The SmartIcons are useful only if you have a mouse.
- The order of the SmartIcons in this appendix is not exactly the same as the order on your screen. Some of them appear in more than one palette, but they are described only once here.
- The order in which they are presented here is the order in which they appear in the palettes. There are extra icons not included in any palette but that you can add to palettes. These are described near the end of the SmartIcon list.

Saves a memo, file, database, view or whatever you are working on

Same as using File⇨Open Database

Same as File⇨Print

Undoes the last action you did. Same as Edit⇨Undo

Same as Edit⇨Cut

Same as Edit⇨Copy

Same as Edit⇨Paste

▤	Same as Edit⇨Clear
▤	Opens the next document in the view
▤	Opens the previous document in the view
▤	Opens the next unread document in the view
▤	Opens the previous unread document in the view
▤	Same as Edit⇨Insert⇨File Attachment
▤	Same as Edit⇨Find
▤	Same as View⇨Show Ruler (toggles between showing and hiding the ruler)
B	Same as Text⇨Bold (toggles between adding and removing boldface)
I	Same as Text⇨Italic (toggles between adding and removing italics)
U	Same as Text⇨Underline (toggles between adding and removing underlining)
▤	Same as Text⇨Alignment⇨Center
▤	Same as Text⇨Alignment⇨Right
▤	Same as Tools⇨Scan Unread
▤	Same as Tools⇨Spell Check
▤	Opens the Help database if you installed it
▤	Same as File⇨New Database
▤	Same as File⇨Database⇨Information

Same as File⇨Database⇨Access Control

Same as Edit⇨Insert⇨Button

Same as Edit⇨Insert⇨Object (an OLÉ object)

Same as Text⇨Paragraph

Same as Text⇨Font (for font style, size, color, and enhancements)

Same as Design⇨Icon

Same as Design⇨View Attributes

Same as Design⇨Selection Formula

Same as Design⇨Form Formula

Same as Design⇨New Column

Same as Design⇨Column Definition

Same as Design⇨Form Attributes

Same as Design⇨New Field

Same as Design⇨Field Definition

Same as Design⇨Use Shared Field

Same as Design⇨Synopsis

Same as Design⇨Document Info

Same as Edit⇨Insert⇨Page Break

Same as File⇨Import

Indent all lines in a paragraph

Indent first line of a paragraph

Same as Edit⇨Insert⇨Table

Same as Edit⇨Table⇨Insert Column or Row

Same as Edit⇨Table⇨Delete Column or Row

Same as Edit⇨Table⇨Format

Same as Mail⇨Open

Same as Mail⇨Compose⇨Memo

Same as Mail⇨Address

Same as Mail⇨Forward

Same as Mail⇨Send

Same as Mail⇨Scan Unread (mail database only)

Same as Tools⇨Categorize

Same as Tools⇨Unread Marks⇨Mark All Read

Same as Edit⇨Edit Document

Same as Tools⇨Call

Same as Tools⇨Hang Up

Same as Tools⇨Setup⇨Mail

Same as Tools⇨Setup⇨Location

Same as Tools⇨Setup⇨Ports

Same as Tools⇨Replicate

Same as File⇨Page Setup

Same as File⇨Print Setup

Navigates to next main document

Navigates to previous main document

Navigates to next document, whether main or response

Navigates to previous document, whether main or response

Navigates to next selected document

Navigates to previous selected document

Same as View⇨Expand

Same as View⇨Collapse

Same as View⇨Expand All

Same as View⇨Collapse All

Same as Tools⇨Unread Marks⇨Mark Selected Read

Same as View⇨Refresh Fields

Start 1-2-3 for Windows

Start Ami Pro

Start Freelance for Windows

Start cc:Mail for Windows

Start Organizer

Those are the icons that appear in the seven palettes by default. The following icons are additional icons that you can add to a palette by using Tools⇨SmartIcons.

The SmartIcons labeled Macro Button have no preassigned function. They are lonely SmartIcons waiting for some power user to write a macro (a mini program of recorded keystrokes that you can play back when needed) and assign that macro to one of the buttons. Later, when that icon is clicked, the assigned macro runs.

Repeat the last search

Same as Edit⇨Header/Footer

Same as Edit⇨Insert⇨Popup

Same as Edit⇨Links

Same as Edit⇨Make Doc Link

Same as Edit⇨Paste Special

Same as Edit⇨Select All

Same as File⇨Database⇨Copy

Same as File⇨Exit

Same as File⇨Export

Same as <u>F</u>ile⇨<u>F</u>ull Text Search⇨<u>C</u>reate Index

Same as <u>F</u>ile⇨<u>F</u>ull Text Search⇨Information

Same as <u>F</u>ile⇨<u>F</u>ull Text Search⇨<u>U</u>pdate Index

Same as <u>F</u>ile⇨New <u>R</u>eplica

SmartIcons Floating (allows you to determine where the icon palette will be displayed).

Moves to next set of SmartIcons

Same as <u>T</u>ext⇨<u>A</u>lignment⇨<u>F</u>ull

Same as <u>T</u>ext⇨<u>A</u>lign⇨<u>L</u>eft

Same as <u>T</u>ext⇨<u>E</u>nlarge (Fontsize)

Same as <u>T</u>ext⇨<u>N</u>ormal

Same as <u>T</u>ext⇨<u>R</u>educe (Fontsize)

Same as T<u>o</u>ols⇨Unread <u>M</u>arks⇨Mark A<u>l</u>l Unread

Same as T<u>o</u>ols⇨ Unread <u>M</u>arks⇨Mark Selected <u>U</u>nread

Same as T<u>o</u>ols⇨Scan <u>U</u>nread⇨<u>C</u>hoose Preferred

Same as T<u>o</u>ols⇨Smart<u>I</u>cons

Same as <u>V</u>iew⇨Show <u>S</u>erver Names

Same as <u>V</u>iew⇨Show <u>U</u>nread

Same as <u>W</u>indow⇨<u>C</u>ascade

Same as <u>W</u>indow⇨<u>T</u>ile

Same as <u>W</u>indow⇨<u>W</u>orkspace (shows the main Notes desktop)

Macro Button

Macro Button

Macro Button

Start Improv for Windows

Start Lotus Notes: Document Imaging (LN:DI)

Macro Button

Macro Button

Macro Button

Macro Button

Macro Button

Macro Button

Macro Button

Macro Button

Macro Button

Macro Button

Smart Text

Lotus SmartPics

Macro Button

Menus, Accelerator Keys, and Function Keys

. . . .

*T*his appendix gives you an overview of the main menu items and items available within each selection. It does not give the complete menu hierarchy, only the main levels. Note that depending on the context in which you are working (composing a memo, designing a database, looking at a view, weeding your garden), you may see additional menu items, and some menu items may be grayed out (inactive) for that context.

Also included in this appendix is a list of the function keys in Notes.

The Menu and Accelerator Keys

The following is the Lotus Notes Workstation Menu with keyboard Accelerators where appropriate.

File

New Database (Ctrl+N)

New Replica

Open Database (Ctrl+O)

Close Window (Ctrl+W)

Save (Ctrl+S)

Database

Information

Delete

Copy

Access Control

Compact

Use Different Server

Full Text Search

Information

Update Index

Create Index

Delete Index

Attach

Import

Export

Administration

Register User

Register from File

Register Server

Register Certifier

Certify ID

ID file

Remote Server Console

Print (Ctrl+P)

Print Setup

Page Setup

Exit (Alt+F4)

Edit

Undo (Ctrl+Z)

Cut (Ctrl+X)

Copy (Ctrl+C)

Paste (Ctrl+V)

Clear (Delete)

Edit Document (Ctrl+E)

Find (Ctrl+F)

Find Next (Ctrl+G)

Select All (Ctrl+A)

Deselect All

Select by Date

Make Doclink

Links

Insert

    Object

    File Attachment

    Table

    Button

    Popup

    Page Break (Ctrl+L)

Actions Button

Header/Footer

Security

Read Access

Encryption Keys

View

Refresh Unread (F9)

Edit Mode (Ctrl+E)

Arrange Icons

Show Unread

Show Server Names

Mail

Open

Scan Unread (Ctrl+M)

Compose

Address

Forward

Send

Send User ID

Compose

Menu depends on the database you are currently using.

Text

Font (Ctrl+K)

Alignment

> Left
>
> Right
>
> Center
>
> Full
>
> None

Paragraph (Ctrl+J)

Paragraph Styles

Normal (Ctrl+T)

Bold (Ctrl+B)

Italic (Ctrl+I)

Underline (Ctrl+U)

Enlarge (F2)

Reduce (Shift+F2)

Tools

Spell Check

Categorize

Run Macros

Run Background Macros

Refresh Fields

> Selected Documents
>
> All Documents

Unread Marks

   Mark Selected Read

   Mark All Read

   Mark Selected Unread

   Mark All Unread

   Exchange Read

Scan Unread

   Selected Databases

   Preferred Databases

   Choose Preferred

Call

Replicate

Hang Up

User Logoff (F5)

User ID

   Information

   Password

      Set

      Clear

   Encryption Keys

   Certificates

   Create Safe Copy

   Merge Copy

   Switch To

SmartIcons

Setup

>   User
>
>   Mail
>
>   Location
>
>   Ports

Design

Icon

Views

Forms

Shared Fields

Macros

Help Document

>   Using Database
>
>   About Database

Refresh Design

Replace Design

Synopsis

Document Info

Window

Tile

Cascade

Minimize All

Maximize All

The items listed in Table C-1 allow you to switch among open views, documents, and the current workspace.

Table C-1	Function Keys	
Key	**Windows and OS/2**	**Macintosh**
F1	Open context-sensitive help	Undo last action
F2	Enlarge text to next available point size	Cut current selection
Shift+F2	Reduce text to next available point size	
F3	Go to next selected document	Copy current selection
Shift+F3	Go to previous selected document	
F4	Go to next unread document	Paste current selection
Shift+F4	Go to previous unread document	
Alt+F4	Exit Notes	
F5	Cancel current user access to Notes	
Alt+F5	Use the window's zoom box	
Ctrl+F6	Cycle through open windows	Use the Window menu
F7	Indent paragraph's first line	
Shift+F7	Outdent paragraph's first line	
F8	Indent entire paragraph	
Shift+F8	Outdent entire paragraph	
F9	If the active window is . . . a document — update all fields a view — update the view the workspace — update all databases on the current workspace page	
Shift+F9	When the active window is . . . a document or view — rebuild all views in the current database the workspace — rebuild the view indexes for all databases on the entire workspace (can be time consuming!)	
Alt or F10	Activate main menu	Use the menu bar
Alt+F10	Use the window's zoom box	

The Lotus Notes Database Templates

Why reinvent the wheel? The time may come when you need to create a database for your own use, or (if you're a truly generous and helpful person) a database for lots of your co-workers to use. There are different types of databases. Most are one-of-a-kind, created at a particular organization for some purpose unique to its function. However, there are some databases that are put to use in many organizations.

The generous and helpful folks at Lotus determined the 11 most common databases and created templates for them. Now, rather than people at every Notes-using company in the world starting to build a database from the ground up, they can simply retrieve a template, tailor it to their own needs, and voilà — they're done.

You need to choose to install these templates. As you are performing install you will see a list of groups of files you may install with Notes. The Template Application Files group is selected by default, so all you have to do is not deselect it. In other words, leave the X in the box next to Template Application Files, and the templates will be installed. If you already installed Notes and chose not to install the templates, start the install program again and select only the Template Application Files. See Appendix A for more information about install.

Putting the Templates to Work

To create a database using these templates, choose File⇨New Database. In the New Database dialog box shown in Figure D-1, select the template for the database you are creating in the Template list box.

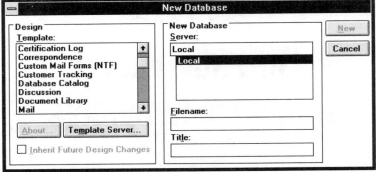

Figure D-1:
The
available
templates
are listed in
the New
Database
dialog box.

Here is a list and brief description of the database templates available in Notes. We included a list of the forms and views that are included with the template, but of course you can create as many new forms and views as you like.

Correspondence

Stores names and addresses and allows you to create letters, faxes, and mail merge documents. Forms include Person documents (name and address and other information), Letter, Fax, and Merge. Views include records by company, records by name, records by category, and correspondence by date.

Customer Tracking and Response

Helps you keep track of customers or clients. Forms that already exist in the database are Customer Profile, Contact Profile, Action Item, Call Report, Incoming Correspondence, Meeting Report, Miscellaneous Activity, and Outgoing Correspondence. Views include activity by company name, activity by account manager, activity by account status, action items by status, action items by person, contact list by contact name, and contact list by company name.

Discussion

A database in which users can discuss, argue, or express their views on predetermined topics. Users can also compose response documents to main documents that another user composed. Forms include Main Topic, Response, and Response to Response documents. Views include entries by author, entries by category, and a main view in which all documents and their responses are listed by date.

Document Library

A database of completed standard documents used by an organization, such as employee forms, schedules, or policies. Forms include Documents, Responses, and Responses to Responses. Views include documents by author, by category, and by title.

Mail

Not to be confused with a mail database stored on a server (which receives incoming mail), this mail database template can be stored on the user's local workstation and may be used for storage of extra mail memos or for archiving old memos so that they don't swell the size of the main mail database. Only documents specifically copied to this database appear here. (It is not a replica of the server-based mail database.) Views and forms are the same as those for the main mail database.

Meeting Tracking

As an army travels on its stomach (which would be very slow and painful), so a corporation travels on its meetings. Wouldn't it be disastrous if people lost track of the meetings that are held from day to day? Yes, it certainly would, so this database allows those interested (if any) to keep a strict account of the organization's meetings. Forms include Meeting Agenda, Meeting Minutes, Action Items, and Responses. Views include meetings by date, meetings by topic, meetings by keyword, action items by person, action items by status, and open action items by due date.

A meeting is a place where minutes are kept and hours are lost.

News and Custom View

Provides a means for disseminating newsworthy items to the organization. It can contain newsletters, news posted by individuals in the company, or feeds from newswire services (if you have the proper additional software to gather news into a Notes database). Forms include News Items, Newswire Articles, Newsletters, and Responses. Views include news by date, news by keyword, news by type, and news and responses by date.

Reservation Scheduler and Setup

Of course, you won't be having meetings unless you can get first dibs on the conference room. This database allows you to reserve rooms, pieces of equipment, or any other resource that needs to be requested in advance. Forms include Time Block and custom forms that you create. Views include available resources, reserved resources by date and time, reserved resources by event, and reserved resources by person.

Service Request Tracking

For keeping track of internal or external service or material requests. The database calculates the length of time each request is open and keeps a history of the progress of the request. Forms include Requests and Responses. Views include all requests by date received, all requests by assignments, open requests by date received, completion days by assignee, requests by department/requester, and request type.

Status Reports

Used by individuals or departments to report on the status of projects or the amount of work done (if any) over a given period of time. Forms include Objective, Status Reports, and Responses. Views include reports by person, reports by division/period, reports by period, and issues by period.

Things To Do

Guess what this is for. It may be belaboring the obvious, but individuals and groups use this database as a reminder of the things that need to be done. You can also get a summary of completed tasks and a list of overdue items (if any — we assume that you are a hard worker and always get everything done on time). Forms include Tasks and Comment/Response. Views include completed items by category, completed items date, completed items by project, open items by project, open items by project/priority, open items by due date, open items by priority, and all by status and project.

Appendix E

Remote Setup

● ●

*A*t the beginning of Chapter 2, we discussed the steps for starting Notes for the very first time — but we made one big assumption: namely, that the computer was connected to the network.

In this chapter we discuss what you do if the computer you use isn't connected to the network, either because you always use it away from the office (and dial in to the Notes server with your modem), or because it's a so-called *stand-alone* workstation that's never connected to a server.

Before You Start . . .

This chapter assumes that you have successfully installed the Notes program on your computer's hard disk and that you are ready to set it up for the first time. If that is not the case, stop right here and refer to Appendix A and don't come back until you have the program installed.

This chapter is divided into two sections: "Setting Up a Remote Workstation" and "Setting Up a Stand-Alone Workstation." Read the first section if you are installing Notes on a computer that's going to occasionally connect to a Notes server via a modem. (Maybe it's the computer you have at home that you'll be using to dial in to your company's servers.) Read the second section if you are installing Notes on a computer that will never connect to a server.

Setting Up a Remote Workstation

When you start Notes for the very first time, you need to have some information handy that only your administrator knows. Call your administrator and ask for the answers to the following questions:

The Question	*The Answer*
What is my password?	( )
What is my exact User Name?	( )
What is the name of my home server?	( )
What is my server's telephone number?	( )
What's my time zone?	( )
Do we follow Daylight Savings Time?	( ) Yes or ( ) No

When you start Notes for the first time ever, it's smart enough to figure out that it has to set itself up, so you'll see the dialog box shown in Figure E-1.

Because you are setting up remotely, choose Remote connection (via modem).

When you click OK in the Notes Workstation Setup dialog box, you'll be presented with another dialog box, shown in Figure E-2.

Using the worksheet full of answers that you got from your administrator, fill in all the appropriate fields: your name, the server's name, and the server's telephone number.

You will also have to tell Notes what kind of modem you have by choosing it from the Modem type: drop-down list.

If your modem's name is not in the list, choose the first one in the list (Auto Configure).

Use the Phone dialing prefix field if you have to dial 9 to get an outside line, or if you have to enter *70 (for push-button phones) or 1170 (for rotary phones) to disable Call Waiting. (The beep that Call Waiting uses to tell you that there's another call will wreak havoc if your computer's trying to call your server.)

Make sure that you have selected the correct Serial port — most likely it's COM1, but some computers have the modem plugged into COM2.

When you click OK, Notes will place a call to the server to get a copy of your mail database and to get your User ID. So don't be surprised to hear Notes make a phone call!

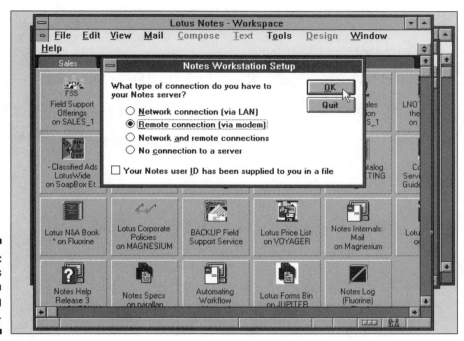

Figure E-1:
The Notes
Workstation
Setup dialog
box.

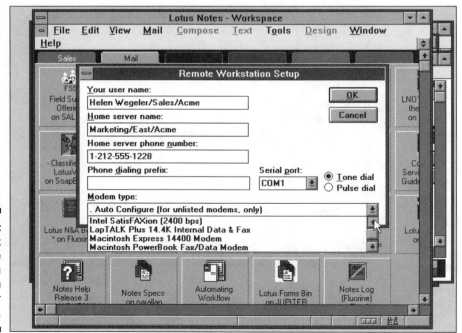

Figure E-2:
Fill in this box
with the
information
you got from
your
administrator.

The last dialog box that you'll have to deal with during setup asks you about your time zone. Pick the appropriate time zone, tell Notes know whether you observe EST, and click OK.

Once you have completed the call and answered the questions about time zones, the setup process is complete and you can begin to use the program. Congratulations and welcome to the wonderful world of Notes!

If you're new to Notes, refer to Chapter 2 to get more information about how to use the program in general. Refer to Chapter 14 for more information about using your new remote workstation.

Setting Up a Stand-Alone Workstation

When you start the program for the first time ever, it's smart enough to figure out that it has to set itself up, so you'll see the dialog box shown in Figure E-3.

Figure E-3:
This dialog box appears when you start the program for the first time.

Because you will not be connecting to a server, choose No connection to a server.

When you click OK in the Notes Workstation Setup dialog box, you'll be presented with another dialog box, shown in Figure E-4. Enter your name in the dialog box. When you click OK, Notes creates a User ID for you and then asks about your time zone.

Once you have answered the questions about your time zone, you're done! That wasn't so bad, was it? Refer to Chapter 2 to learn more about how to use the program.

Figure E-4:
Hey, good looking! What's your name?

Appendix F

Macintosh Tips

• •

*A*s they say at Lotus, "Notes is Notes is Notes," which is their (not-so-funny) way of saying that Notes is *cross-platform*. In other words, Notes works the same way regardless of your workstation's operating system. Using Notes on a Windows PC is no different from using Notes on Macintosh — the commands are the same, the menus are the same, the colors are the same — everything is the same.

Well, almost. In this appendix, we'll explore the relatively few (and relatively insignificant) differences for Mac users.

If you're not a Mac user, don't bother reading this appendix.

No Right Mouse Button

On a Windows PC, you use the right mouse button for two things: to see what a SmartIcon is going to do before you click it and to quickly close a document.

If you want to see the SmartIcon hints on a Mac, you have to turn on Show Balloons and then point to the SmartIcon that you want to check out.

And there's no way to quickly close a document with the mouse on a Mac. You have to either press Esc, choose File⇨Close Window, or press ⌘+W.

Command Instead of Ctrl

On a Windows PC, many of the menu commands have keyboard shortcuts — for example, to open a new database, you can choose File⇨Open Database or press Ctrl+O.

Because Macintosh keyboards don't have a Ctrl key, you use the Command (⌘) key instead.

Command Key Combinations

While we're on the subject of the Command key, it's worth mentioning that many of the menu shortcuts are different on a Mac. For example, to close a document on a Windows PC you press Ctrl+F4, but on a Macintosh you press ⌘+W.

Don't worry—all the keyboard shortcuts are listed right in the menus.

Dialog Boxes

If you sometimes use Notes on a PC and you sometimes use Notes on a Mac, you'll notice small cosmetic differences between the dialog boxes and menus. They work the same way; they just look a little different.

No Background Program

You cannot run the background program macros on your Macintosh—which may not be such a big deal, because you probably don't even know (or care) what a background program is in the first place! But it means no background macros and no background replication if you use Macintosh.

No Local Full Text Indexes

You cannot create a Full-text Indexes for a database that's stored locally on your Mac's hard disk. Bummer.

Notes Data Folder

On a Macintosh, all the modem command files, local databases, and so on are stored in a folder that's referred to as your Notes Data Folder. On a Windows PC, it's called your Local Data Directory. Same things, just different words.

NOTES.INI

Windows workstations have a file called NOTES.INI, stored in the Windows subdirectory. On a Mac, the analogous file is called Notes Preferences and is stored in your Preferences Folder.

No Underlined Menu Options

In Windows, you can choose an option from a menu by typing the underlined character — like the F in File or the O in Open database. Mac menus don't have underlined characters, so you always have to choose options from a Mac menu with the mouse.

Balloon Help

To see SmartIcon hints on a Macintosh, you have to choose Show Balloons.

Glossary

● ●

Accelerator Key A keystroke combination used to accomplish the same thing as choosing a menu item. Ctrl+Z is the accelerator key for Edit⇨Undo.

Access Control List The part of every Notes database that determines who can do what in that database. See also *No Access, Depositor, Reader, Author, Editor, Designer,* and *Manager.*

ACL An abbreviation for Access Control List.

Administrator The person who is in charge of running the Notes servers at your company and to whom you'll turn when you have questions or problems.

Application designer The person at your company who created the database(s) you use.

Application server A Notes server that is only used for application databases—in other words, it does not have anybody's e-mail databases on it.

Attachment A file (Lotus 1-2-3 worksheet, Microsoft Word document, and so on) that has been included in a Notes document. You can only put attachments in a rich text field.

Author (1) The person who composed a document and (usually) the only person who can edit it or delete it. (2) A level of access you can have to a database. As an author, you can read documents, compose new documents, edit your own documents, and delete your own documents. (3) The people who wrote this book.

Background program The program you run in conjunction with Notes to replicate databases so that you can still use Notes while replication is going on.

Background replication A way to replicate (by using the background program) without tying up Notes.

Balloon Help What you use on a Mac to see the SmartIcon hints.

Banyan The company that makes Vines.

Boston baked beans A gourmet delight from the "Land of the Bean and the Cod."

cc:Mail A (different) program from Lotus that's used for e-mail. At many companies, some people use Notes for e-mail and other people use cc:Mail.

Certificate A special "stamp" for your USER.ID that your administrator gives to you. You have to have a certificate specific to your company to use the servers at your company.

Common name The part of your Notes User Name that sounds like what your mother calls you. For example, if your User Name is Stephen Londergan/Lotus, your common name is just Stephen Londergan.

Compound document A document containing information from more than one program.

Connection document A document in your Personal N&A Book that tells your workstation when and how to call the server.

Custom form An e-mail form that you can use, even though it's not in your mail database. Access it by choosing Mail⇨Compose⇨Custom Forms.

Database A collection of Notes documents and views.

Database template A shell of a database that you use as a starting point to create your own database. Saves you lots of work.

DDE Dynamic Data Exchange. A copy of a document created in another application and placed in a Notes document. It retains a link to the original document so that changes to the original are reflected in the copy.

Delivery report A return message that tells you when a message you sent was delivered to the recipient's mail database.

Depositor A level of access that you can have to a database. As a Depositor, you can only add documents to a database. You cannot read, edit, or delete them.

Designer A level of access that you can have to a database. In addition to having all the rights that have Editors have, Designers can change the database's forms and views.

DESKTOP.DSK The file on your workstation that keeps track of what databases are on your workstation and which documents in them you have already read.

Doclink An icon in one document that you can double-click to quickly go to a different document.

Document (1) An individual item in a Notes database. In other database programs, a document would be called a record. (2) A piece of paper with stuff written on it.

Domain (1) All the Notes servers at your company. (2) What a king is in charge of.

Editor A level of access that you can have to a database. Editors can read documents, compose documents, and edit documents, even if they didn't compose the documents in the first place.

Electronic signature A special, numeric code added to a document that proves it really was written by the person who wrote it.

E-mail An electronic mail message.

Embedded object Information included in a Notes document that came from another program. You can double-click an object to edit it if you have the originating program on your computer.

Encryption A procedure in which a document or part of a document is scrambled, except when opened by a person who has the proper decryption key.

Encryption key The numeric code used to scramble and unscramble a document or part of a document.

Error message A dialog box that Notes shows when you make those all-too-frequent mistakes.

Export A way to turn Notes documents into files for use in other programs, like Lotus 1-2-3 or WordPerfect.

Fax A process of sending a picture of a document over a phone line. Didn't I hear the phone ringing? Just the fax, Ma'am.

Field A place in a database form for specific individual pieces of information. *First Name* might be a field in a personnel data form.

Footer Text that appears at the bottom of every printed page.

Form What you use to compose, edit, and read documents.

Full-text index A procedure that locates words and phrases in all documents in a database so that you can later search for text in those documents.

Full-Text Search Searching for text or phrases in documents in a database.

Gateway A special program that runs on a Notes server and converts Notes e-mail messages to different formats, like faxes.

Group A collection of users' names, defined in either the Public or your Personal N&A Book. Using group names saves having to type the individual names of people in a group when sending them e-mail.

Groupware Software that enables several people to work together on computers.

Header (1) Text that appears at the top of every printed page. (2) What you take when you fall over something.

Help document A special collection of tips about how to use a database.

Hierarchical name A User Name that includes not only your common name but also your organization and the level or department in that organization.

Home Server The one and only Notes server that has *your* e-mail database on it.

Import What you do when you want to turn a foreign file, like a Lotus 1-2-3 worksheet, into documents in a Notes database.

Input validation formula A formula included in a form that checks to be sure you entered data in a field and that it's the right data type.

Install A process or program used to place a usable copy of a program on a hard disk.

LAN An abbreviation for Local Area Network. Rhymes with "man." It's really just a bunch of wires that are used to connect your computer to other computers.

LAN workstation A computer that (1) has Notes installed on it and (2) is plugged into the network.

Lemming A small Arctic rodent with a short tail and fur-covered feet.

LMBCS Lotus Multi-Byte Character Set: a set of characters including standard keyboard characters and characters not found on keyboards.

LN:DI Abbreviation for a program called Lotus Notes Document Imaging. Pronounced "lindy," it's a special program that lets you include scanned images in a Notes document.

Location setup A process that you go through to switch from workstation-based mail to server-based mail.

Lotus Notes The program that this book is about.

Macro A mini-computer program of Notes commands.

Mail database The database that holds all your incoming and outgoing e-mail messages. No one but you can read the documents in your mail database.

Mail server A Notes server that has mail databases on it.

MAILBOX A special kind of Notes database that holds messages that are pending delivery.

Manager The highest level of access available for a database.

Mycophile A fungus fancier.

Mime A person who works without talking. If only they ran meetings!

Modem command file A special ASCII file that Notes needs to use a modem. Every brand of modem has its own modem command file.

Modem Hardware that lets you use your Notes workstation to place a phone call to your Notes server. Useful if you need to read your e-mail and other Notes databases when you're at home or on a business trip.

Mouse A device that rolls around your desktop and makes it easier to make selections on the screen. You expected us to make some dumb joke about rodents here, didn't you?

NetBIOS The most commonly-used protocol for Notes. Pronounced "net BYE-oce."

Network A collection of computers that are connected by a wire and that use a network operating system.

Network operating system A type of software used to connect computers. Some common network operating systems include Novell, Banyan, and Pathworks. Sometimes called NOS.

NLM An operating system that's used only on some Notes servers but never on workstations.

No Access A level of access to a database. If you have No Access to a database, you can't use that database. Period!

NOS Abbreviation for *network operating system*.

Notes data directory The directory on your PC's hard disk that has your local databases, DESKTOP.DSK, and modem command files in it.

Notes data folder The folder on your Macintosh that has your local databases, DESKTOP.DSK, and modem command files in it.

Notes log A special Notes database that keeps track of all the phone calls you've made from your remote workstation— if you've made any, that is.

NOTES.INI An ASCII file on every Notes workstation that holds configuration information for that workstation.

Novell The most popular network operating system.

Object See *Embedded object*.

OLÉ Abbreviation for *Object Linking and Embedding*; it's that part of the operating system that lets you include information from other programs in a Notes document. Pronounced "OLAY." See *Embedded object*.

OLÉ object See *Embedded object.*

Operating system The program that runs your computer. Notes runs with the DOS/Windows, OS/2, Unix, and Macintosh operating systems.

OS/2 An operating system that can be used on Notes workstations and servers.

Page break A code you insert in a long document that instructs Notes to print subsequent text on a new sheet of paper. Normally page breaks are not visible.

Password A secret code that you have to enter every time you use your USER.ID.

Person document One kind of document in an N&A Book. In the Public N&A Book, there's a Person document for each user at your company. You can also compose a Person document in your Personal N&A Book to give one of your friends an e-mail nickname.

Personal N&A Book A database on your computer's hard disk in which you can enter person, group, and connection documents.

Platform Another fancy computer word that means the same as operating system.

Policy document A document that describes the purpose of a database and the rules for its use.

Popup A part of a Notes document that has hidden text associated with it. You see this hidden text by clicking on the word.

Port The name for the part of your computer where your network or modem is plugged in. Some computers have more than one port; yours might have one port for the network and one port for the modem.

PowerBook A portable Macintosh computer.

Power tie A knot tied around the neck symbolizing extreme corporate fealty but mistaken for a symbol of corporate authority.

Preferences document The Macintosh equivalent of NOTES.INI.

Private key The part of your User ID that's used to decrypt your encrypted mail messages.

Private view A view that's only on your workstation.

Protocol Techie-term for the part of your network operating system that is used to connect your Notes workstation with your Notes servers. You might hear about protocols called NetBIOS, SPX, or TCP/IP. Then again, you may never hear protocols mentioned.

Public key The part of your USER.ID that other people use to encrypt mail messages for you.

Public N&A Book The database on the Notes server that defines all the Notes users, servers, groups, and connections at your company.

Query Builder A dialog box you fill out that makes it easy to define the criteria for a Full Text Search.

Query by Form A way to enter the criteria for a Full Text Search, using the same form that was used to enter the document in the first place.

Read Access List A way to control which people can read a document that you compose. You set a document's Read Access List by choosing Edit⇨Security⇨Read Access.

Reader A level of access that you can have to a database. As a Reader, you can only read the documents that other people have composed; you cannot compose your own.

Relational database A database program that allows the full sharing of data between databases and between forms within databases.

Remote workstation A Notes workstation that is not connected to a Notes server via a network. Instead, remote workstations often use a modem to talk to the Notes server.

Replica ID A special serial number that every database has that identifies it as the same database, even if there are copies of it on other servers.

Replication The process used to synchronize two copies of a database between two servers or between a server and a workstation.

ResEdit The program you use on a Macintosh to edit your Notes Preferences document.

Return receipt A special kind of e-mail message that tells you when a recipient read an e-mail that you sent.

Rich text A special field type that can include more than one font and formatting (like bold and italics), and can contain embedded objects and attachments.

Ruler The part of the Notes screen that you can use (if you choose to display it) to set margins and tabs in a rich text field.

Selecting (1) Designating text or data to be deleted, copied, or changed in some way. (2) Choosing documents in a view for such group treatment as categorizing, printing, or deletion.

Selection formula A Notes formula used to designate which documents will be replicated.

Search Bar The dialog box at the top of the screen (if you choose to display it) that allows you to specify the text to search for and rules for the search.

Server A shared computer that stores Notes databases.

Server-based mail A setting you use that causes Notes to send off your messages immediately; the opposite of workstation-based mail.

Signature Also called an *electronic signature*; a way for you to guarantee to the recipient of a message that it really, honestly, absolutely came from *you*.

SmartIcon A picture representing an action you can take. Click the SmartIcon to make the action take place.

SmartIcon palette A collection of SmartIcons.

SPX A protocol made by Novell.

Static text Text in a form that is not associated with a field. The title of a form is an example of static text.

Status Bar (1) A line of information at the bottom of the Notes window, part of which you can use to change parts of your document. (2) A drinking establishment on Main Street where they have cold beer and hot tunes. Closed Sundays; shoes and shirts required.

Tables (1) Small spreadsheets that you can insert into Notes documents. (2) A place to put your cold beer while you're listening to the hot tunes at the Status Bar. Closed Sundays; shoes and shirts required.

TCP/IP A protocol.

Template A special kind of Notes database used to create other Notes databases.

Unix An operating system that can be used on Notes workstations and servers.

Unread marks Stars or colored text used in views to show you which documents you haven't read yet.

View A summary of the documents in a database. Most databases have more than one view.

Vines (1) A network operating system. (2) Places where grapes grow.

WAN (1) Wide Area Network: a bunch of computers connected in some other way than by network cables. Most frequently used are phone lines, satellites, broadcast, and tin cans with string. (2) How you look when you don't take your vitamin pills.

Windows An operating environment that can be used on Notes workstations and servers.

Workspace The Notes screen.

Workstation The computer at your desk, or (if you have a laptop) the computer in your briefcase. It's the computer that each person uses to work with Notes.

Workstation-based e-mail A setting that you use when your computer is not connected to a LAN, which causes Notes to queue up your outgoing e-mail until you place a phone call to a Notes server.

WorldCom A company that lets you use their Notes servers for an hourly fee.

Index

• Symbols •

~ (tilde), for temporary files, 293
... (ellipses), in menus, 29
⌘ (Command) key on Macintosh, 155, 337
  key combinations, 338
➤ (triangle), in menus, 28-29

• A •

accelerator keys, 319-325, 341
Accent Sensitive option, for Find, 70, 183
Accept button (Tools Check Spelling dialog box), 185
Access Control List, 341
  database creator name on, 147
  groups in, 146
  for new database, 145-146
Add Icon (Open Database dialog box), 95
Adding Icons dialog box, 309-310
Additional Setup dialog box, for modem, 215-217
Address button (memo form), 49
addresses, 49-51
  groups and, 85
  and Name and Address Book, 58
  using personal document to insert, 86
administrator, 302, 341
  control of access to server, 94
  importance of, 20
  and information to begin using Notes, 19-20
  and setup information for remote workstation, 332
  user certification, 17
  and user name changes, 292
Agenda STF file, exporting view to, 247
alignment, 154, 165-166
All by Category view, 67
All by Size view, 42, 64
Alt key, to access menus, 27
analog telephone line, 299

appending to Clipboard, 154
application designer, 341
ASCII file, Stop Word file as, 265
Attachment SmartIcon, 270
attachments, 39, 74-76, 121-122, 341
  deleting, 78
  detaching, 67, 122
  information for recipient, 76
  launching, 122
  multiple files as, 76
  paper clip symbol for, 39, 103
  preventing replication, 236, 285
  rich text fields for, 116, 240
author, 341
Author access level, 146
Auto Configur, for modem, 216
automatic DDE link, 250
automatic reply, to incoming messages, 276-278

• B •

background color of forms, 138, 194
background program, 341
background replication, 230, 288, 341
  notifying Notes of, 289
Backspace key, and reading e-mail, 38
backup copy, of User ID, 17
Backwards search, 70
Balloon Help (Macintosh), 339, 341
  ⇨Show Balloons, 30
Banyan, 341
Basic Delivery Report, 52-53
baud, 213
bcc: field (blind courtesy copy), 51
  deleting, 196
beep
  as new e-mail indicator, 12, 26
  turning off, 279
  WAV files to replace, 275
Beeper Gateway, 296

beepers, sending messages to, 296
bits per second (BPS), 213
blank memo form, 48-54
  customizing, 192
blind courtesy copy (bcc: field), 51, 196
Body field, 52
bold text, 154
  in rich text fields, 115
borders, for table cells, 172, 175
bottom margin, 162, 182
box around word, as popup indicator, 119, 188
BPS (bits per second), 213
bugs, 293
busy signal, and scheduled call to server, 233
buttons
  Ctrl key for information about, 119
  in documents, 117-119

• C •

Call Server dialog box, 237
Call Waiting, 332
Carthage Today, 297
case sensitivity
  in Find, 70, 183
  in index creation, 265
  of passwords, 206
Categories (Design View Attributes dialog box), 199
categories for documents, 39, 54, 67-69, 104-105
  automatic for e-mail, 278-279
  creating, 68, 271
  expanding and collapsing, 105-106
Categorize dialog box, 67
Categorize SmartIcon, 271
categorized columns, vs. sorted column, 104-105
cc: field (courtesy copy), 51
  deleting, 196

cc:Mail, 341
cell borders, for tables, 172, 175
cell height, in tables, 173
center alignment, 166
    for header or footer text, 180
certificates, 17, 94, 201, 341
    expiration, 201
    name changes and, 291
    problems with, 300
    User ID and, 207
Change Link dialog box, 250
character formats
    changing, 151-160
    in rich text fields, 13, 152
check box field, 114
check mark
    for memos to delete, 65
    in view, 39
Choose User ID to Switch to
        dialog box, 83-84
clearing memos from screen, 38
client (DDE), 248
Clipboard, 240
    copying hidden text to, 165
    cutting or copying to, 154
    pasting contents of, 270
    to add data to Notes document,
        79
closing
    databases, 31
    document, 273
collapsed categories,
        105-106, 199
collation sequence, changing, 209
color
    background for forms, 138, 194
    customizing, 209
    of fields, 135-136
    of font, 154
    for unread documents, 199
column heading of spreadsheet,
        and field names in Notes
        database, 245
Column Width box (Edit Table
        Format dialog box), 174
columns in table
    adding, 176
    deleting, 177-178
    width of, 175
columns in view
    adding, 197-198
    changing definition, 142
    deleting, 198
    e-mail, 40

formula for, 143-144
inserting, 143-144
title for, 143
width of, 142-143
command files, for modem, 216
Command key (⌘ on Macintosh),
        155, 337
    key combinations, 338
common name, 341
companion products,
        295-297
Company Name and Address
        Book, 50
    copying names to group from,
        85
Compose menu, 46-48,
        123-124
    ⇨Connection⇨Remote, 218,
        288
    ⇨Group, 85, 293
    ⇨Memo, 192
    ⇨Memo to Manager, 54-55
    ⇨Person, 86, 284
    ⇨Phone Message, 55
    ⇨Reply, 56
    ⇨Reply to All, 56
compose sequence, for foreign-
        language characters, 160
composing documents
    databases for, 122
    from remote location, 228
    restrictions on, 123
compound documents, 15, 116,
        249, 341
compression of files, 76
CompuServe, 46
    address on, 284
    servers, 296
computed fields, 112-113, 139
computers
    preparing for replication,
        212-224
    reading e-mail on different,
        82-84
    using away from office, 224-232
        See also remote computing
Confirmed option, for Delivery
        report, 53
connection document, 342
        See also remote connection
        documents
@Contains formula, 278-279
context-sensitive help,
        97-98

converting documents, to
        different type, 243-244
copies of database,
        219-224. *See also* replication
copy and paste
    between other programs and
        Notes, 239-240
    for icons, 201
    to insert data in memo, 73-74
Copy SmartIcon, 270
copying
    attachments to hard disk, 122
    and hidden paragraphs, 165
    to clipboard, 154
    User ID to floppy disk, 83
Correct button (Tools Check
        Spelling dialog box), 185
Correspondence template, 328
Criteria Text box (Search box),
        255-256
cropping documents, 182
cross-platform, 337
Ctrl key, 155
    for information about buttons,
        119
    and selecting text, 153
    to switch views, 274
cursor, 152
custom form, 342
Customer Tracking and Re-
        sponse template, 328
customizing, 191-209
    blank memo form, 192
    color, 209
    forms, 82
    icons, 200-201
    new database, 133
    views, 196-198
Cut SmartIcon, 270
cutting to clipboard, 154

• *D* •

data entry
    automatic to fields, 195
    default values in fields, 113
    in keyword fields, 114
    restricting with section fields,
        117
    rules for database, 125-126
    in tables, 173
Database Access Control List
        dialog box, 221-222

database creation, 131-147
  form modification, 133-140
  icons, 144-145
  templates for, 131
  user access, 145-146
  views, 140-144
database icons, 28
  adding e-mail to other
    computer, 84
  changing appearance,
    41-42
  creating, 144-145
  on desktop, 24
  location on, 32
  moving and deleting,
    32-33
  pages of, 31
database lists, subdirectories on,
  92, 93
database templates, 131, 342, 347
  included with Notes,
    327-330
  replicating, 229
databases, 12-13, 89-100, 342
  See also e-mail database
  closing, 31
  for composing documents, 122
  customizing new, 133
  data entry rules, 125-126
  F9 to update, 274
  finding new, 90-91
  Full Text Search of multiple,
    260-261
  header or footer for document
    printed in, 180-181
  for help, 98, 100
  Help Document for, 98-99
  icon for personal mail,
    24-25
  making copy of, 219-224
  Notes documentation, 100
  number of unread documents
    in, 31-32
  opening, 31, 90, 94
  permission to create index for,
    264
  Policy Document for,
    96-97
  problems opening, 301
  replica stub as empty, 221
  replication to update, 18
  See also replication

restriction on composing
  messages for, 123
selecting for replication, 229
selecting to scan for unread
  documents, 208
size of, attachments and, 75
date, in header or footer, 180
date fields, 51, 116
@Date formula, 277
Days of week field, for scheduled
  calls, 233
dBASE, 247
DDE (Dynamic Data Exchange),
  248-250, 342
  creating link, 248-249
  updating links, 250
default settings, for tab stops,
  164
default values in fields, 113
Define button (Tools Check
  Spelling dialog box), 185
deleting
  attachments, 78
  cc: and bcc: fields, 196
  columns in view, 198
  database icons, 33
  documents, 109, 127
  e-mail database, 292
  messages, 63, 65-67
  page breaks, 170
  problem solving, 301
  row or column from table,
    177-178
  selected text, 270
  temporary files, 293
  text, 154
delivery confirmation report, 53,
  342
delivery failure report, 52
Delivery Priority field, 52
Delivery Report field, 52-53
Depositor, 146, 342
deselecting documents, 107
Design Column Definition dialog
  box, 142, 197
Design Form Attributes dialog
  box, 194
Design Keyword Format dialog
  box, 137
design limitations, 293
Design menu, 325
  ⇨Form Attributes, 138, 195

  ⇨Forms⇨Edit, 133
  ⇨Forms⇨Memo, 192
  ⇨Forms⇨Memo⇨New Copy,
    195-196
  ⇨Icon, 144, 200
  ⇨Macros⇨New, 276
  ⇨New Column, 143
  ⇨New Field, 139
  ⇨View Attributes, 144, 198-199
  ⇨Views, 141, 197
Design Views dialog box, 141
Designer, 146, 342
desktop, 27-34
  adding icon to, 94
  creating, 22
  database icons on, 24
desktop pages, 31, 33
  tabs for, 34
DESKTOP.DSK, 342
detaching attachments, 67, 77,
  122
dialog boxes, on Macintosh, 338
digital telephone line, 299
directories
  for installing Notes, 307-309
  on server, 92
disabling Notes access, time-out
  procedure for, 207
discussion database, 12
  template for, 328
disk space
  conserving on server, 67
  for database index, 262
  and returning messages, 63
disks, for installing Lotus Notes
  Client, 305
display. *See* screen display
Do Location Setup every time
  Notes is started box, 225
doclinks, 119-120, 186-187, 342
  problem solving, 300
"Document contains an unrecognized feature..." error
  message, 76
Document Library template, 329
Document Save dialog box, 60
Document Separation, when
  printing multiple docu-
  ments, 72
documentation, for Notes, 99, 294
documentation databases for
  Notes, 100
  installing, 309

documents, 12, 13, 89,
111-130, 342. *See also* rich
text fields; unread
documents
buttons, 117-119
compound, 15, 116, 249, 341
connections between, 119-120,
186-187
converting to different type,
243-244
cropping, 182
date fields in, 116
deleting, 109, 127
displaying number of new, 274
in e-mail database, 37
as e-mail message, 128
editing, 127
fields in, 112-117
hiding, 130
icons in, 121-122
importing files to, 241-242
moving around while
composing, 124
name fields in, 117
number fields, 116
objects, 120-121
person, 86, 284, 345
popups, 119
private, 274-275
problems deleting, 301
read and unread, 103-104
reading, 108
remote connection, 218.
See also remote connection
documents
saving, 124-125
searching contents, 70
section fields, 117
selecting in views,
106-107
static text in, 112
Tab key to check for new, 273
text fields in, 114
truncating during replication,
236, 285
domain, 342
Done button (Tools Check
Spelling dialog box), 185
double-clicking, right mouse
button, 273
draft quality box (File Print
dialog box), 126

Draft Quality print, 72
drives, for installing Notes, 308
Dynamic Data Exchange (DDE),
248-250, 342

• E •

e-mail, 10-12, 37-43, 342
automatic reply to,
276-278
fax delivery as, 295
status bar to check for, 281-282
views for incoming, 39-43
vs. other communication forms,
45-46
e-mail database, 14
adding icon to other computer,
84
deleting, 292
index for, 71
opening, 37
size of, 64
vs. mailbox, 226
e-mail server, name and using
other computers, 84
Edit Header/Footer dialog box,
179
Edit Links dialog box,
249-250
Edit menu, 321-322
⇨Attachment⇨Information, 76
⇨Copy, 270
⇨Find, 41, 69, 183-184
⇨Header/Footer, 179
⇨Insert⇨Object, 251
⇨Insert⇨Page Break, 170
⇨Insert⇨Popup, 188
⇨Insert⇨Table, 171
⇨Links, 249
⇨Make Doclink, 186
⇨Paste, 186, 270
⇨Paste Special, 248, 251
⇨Security⇨Encryption keys,
129
⇨Security⇨Encryption Keys,
Add, 203
⇨Security⇨Read Access List,
130, 274
⇨Select All, 161
⇨Table⇨Delete Row/Column,
177
⇨Table⇨Format, 174

⇨Table⇨Insert Row/Column,
176
edit mode, 60, 127
and doclink, 186
to change popup, 189
Edit Table Format dialog box, 175
Edit text box (Tools Check
Spelling dialog box), 185
editable fields, 112-113, 139
editing
documents, 127
and hidden paragraphs, 165
problems with fields, 300
restricted to document creator,
117
Editor, 146, 342
electronic signature, 81, 342, 346
ellipses (...), in menus, 29
embedded objects, 120, 342
files as, 251
in rich text fields, 13
empty database, 221
encryptable fields, red corner
markers for, 52
encryption, 80-81, 342
of fields, 128-129
key for, 128-129, 202-205, 342
restricting access to key, 205
sending key, 204
end markers, for memo fields, 49
Enter key, and reading
e-mail, 38
error messages, 342
"Document contains an
unrecognized feature...," 76
"Modem could not connect dial
tone," 299
"Network operation did not
complete in a reasonable
amount of time," 300
"Remote system is no longer
responding," 300
"Server *servername* is not
responding," 300
"Unable to interpret time or
date," 116
"You are not authorized to
access that database," 301
"Your ID has not been certified
to access the server," 94
Error Validating Field dialog box,
126

Esc key
  to clear memo, 38
  to close database, 31
example files, installing, 309
Excel, 247
Exchange document Read Marks
  box, 229
excluding words from index, 265
exiting, Lotus Notes, 26
expanded categories, 105, 199
expiration, of certificates, 201
Export dialog box, 243, 247
exporting, 342
  from view, 247-248
eyeglasses icon, 123

• F •

faxes, 46, 342
  database for, 14
  delivery as e-mail, 295
Field Definition dialog box, 136,
  139
field definitions, in memo forms,
  193
field markers, red for encryptable
  fields, 203
field names, and column
  headings of spreadsheet,
  245
field titles, changing in memo
  form, 193
fields, 13, 343. *See also* memo
  fields
  adding to form, 138-140
  automatic data entry to, 195
  color of, 135-136
  default values in, 113
  deleting from forms, 196
  encryption of, 128-129
  problems editing, 300
  selecting all text in, 153
  size of, 14
File Attachment Information
  dialog box, file compression
  statistics, 76
File Attachment SmartIcon, 75
File menu, 319-320
  ⇨Attach, 75, 80, 240
  ⇨Close Window, 31, 38
  ⇨Database⇨Access Control
    list, 145, 221
  ⇨Database⇨Copy, 147
  ⇨Database⇨Information, 64, 66

  ⇨Database⇨Information
    ⇨Replication, 285
  ⇨Database⇨Information
    ⇨Replication⇨Selective,
    234, 286-287
  ⇨Database⇨Information
    ⇨Replication⇨Truncate...,
    236
  ⇨Exit, 26
  ⇨Export, 243
  ⇨Full Text Search⇨Create
    Index, 263
  ⇨Full Text Search⇨Delete
    Index, 265
  ⇨Full Text
    Search⇨Information, 265
  ⇨Full Text Search⇨Update
    Index, 262, 265
  ⇨Import, 79-80,
    245-246
  ⇨New, 132
  ⇨New Database,
    327-328
  ⇨New Replica, 219
  ⇨Open Database, 33, 90
  ⇨Page Setup, 162, 180
  ⇨Print, 71, 108, 269
  ⇨Print Setup⇨Setup
    ⇨Landscape, 175
  ⇨Print Setup⇨Setup ⇨Paper
    Size, 162
  ⇨Save, 125
file name, for new database, 133
File Print dialog box, 71-72, 126
file types
  for exporting document, 244
  for importing, 242
files.
    See also documents;
    encryption
  as attachments, 75
  importing, 78-80, 241-242
Find and Replace dialog box,
  183-184
finding
  messages, 69-71
  new database, 90-91
first line indent, 162
first page, suppressing header or
  footer on, 181
Fit to Window button (Table
  Width box), 171, 172
floppy disk, for backup of User
  ID, 82-83

Font dialog box, 135-136, 154
fonts
  changing, 154
  changing size, 154
  for field titles, 193
  lists of, 155
footers, 343
  page numbers in, 178
foreign language characters, 160
Format menu, 115
formatting
  paragraphs, 154, 160-168
  static text, 135
forms, 90, 343
  adding new field, 138-140
  adding static text to, 135
  background color of, 138, 194
  blank for composing memo,
    48-54
  custom, 82, 192
  keyword field option, 136-137
  modifying for new database,
    133-140
  saving, 140
  using for Full Text Search, 259
Formula field, for view column,
  143-144, 198
formulas
  for column, 142
  for macros, 278
  for selective replication, 235,
    286
Forward SmartIcon, 271
From: field, in memo, 51
full alignment, 166
Full Text Create Index dialog box,
  263
Full Text Search, 253-266, 343
  index creation, 262-265
  index for, 254, 343
    See also index
  of multiple databases, 260-261
  performing, 254-261
  problem solving, 301
  query builder for,
    257-259, 345
  Query by form, 259-260, 345
  reading documents from, 257
  results listing by weight,
    256-257
  view for, 256
Full Text Search bar, 255-256
  Search button, 71
function keys, 326

• G •

gateways, 18, 343
  and memo address, 51
graphics, preventing replication, 285
graphs, in compound document, 15
grayed-out menu options, 28
green box around word, as popup indicator, 119, 188
groups, 85, 282-284, 343
  in Access Control List, 146
  creating, 283
  nested levels, 284
  of Notes servers, 91
groupware, 9-18, 343
  uses of, 10
Guess button (Tools Check Spelling dialog box), 185

• H •

Hang up when Done box (Tools Replicate dialog box), 230
hanging indent, 162
hard disk, User ID copied to, 23
Hayes modems, 216
headers, 178-181, 343
  page numbers in, 178
Headers and Footers dialog box, 181
Help, 97-100
  context-sensitive, 97-98
  database for, 98
  installing, 309
  for installing Notes, 306
Help Document, 98-99, 343
Help menu,⇨About..., for Policy Document, 97
hiding
  documents, 130
  paragraphs, 164-165
hierarchical name, 343
high priority messages, 52
home server, 23, 343
  phone number of, 217

• I •

I-beam, 152
IBM-style keyboard, foreign language characters on, 160

icons. *See also* SmartIcons
  adding to desktop, 94
  creating, 144-145
  customizing, 200-201
  in documents, 121-122
  installing, 309-310
  used in book, 5
Ignore button (Tools Check Spelling dialog box), 185
imperial measurement units, 162, 209
Import dialog box, 241
importing files, 78-80, 241-242, 343
  file types for, 242
  multiple documents, 244-246
incoming messages, automatic reply to, 276-278
indents
  first line, 162
  paragraphs, 154
index, 254, 343
  creation, 262-265
  for e-mail database, 71
  on Macintosh, 338
  maintenance of, 262-263, 264-265
  permission to create, 264
  problems creating, 301
  and Search bar, 255
Index Breaks field, 265
InFax, 295
information
  about SmartIcons, 30
  about User ID, 208
  required to begin using Notes, 19-20
  sharing, 10
Inheritance feature, 124
input validation formula, 343
Insert Attachment(s) dialog box, 75
Insert Popup dialog box, 189
Insert Row/Column dialog box, 176
Insert Table dialog box, 171
inserting
  attachments, 270
  Clipboard data to memo, 73-74
  columns in views, 143-144
  rows in table, 176
insertion point, 152

installing, 343
  Notes as workstation, 305-310
International button, for customizing, 162, 209
Internet addresses, 284
italics text, 154
  in rich text fields, 115

• K •

key, to access encrypted fields, 128-129, 202-205, 342
keyword fields, 114, 140
  adding options to, 136-137

• L •

landscape orientation, 175
LANs (local area networks), 16, 18, 343
  workstations, 343
laptop computers, 213
  problem connecting to servers, 299
laser printers, 126
Launch button, for attachments, 77
launching
  attachments, 122
  problem solving, 302
left alignment, 165
  for header or footer text, 180
left margin, for tables, 171
line spacing, 166
linked objects, in rich text fields, 13
lists. *See also* views
LMBCS (Lotus MultiByte Character Set), 160, 343
LN:DI, 343
Location setup, 343
  for remote computing, 225-226
lock out, from computer, 293
logging off computer, 84
Lotus 1-2-3, sending memo from, 48
Lotus 1-2-3 worksheet
  exporting view to, 247-248
  importing as multiple documents, 244-246

Lotus MultiByte Character Set (LMBCS), 160
Lotus Notes
 benefits of, 1
 companion products, 295-297
 directory for, 307-309
 disabling access to, 81
 documentation, 99
 documentation databases, 100
 exiting, 26
 information required to begin using, 19-20
 installing as workstation, 305-310
 Release 3 or Release 2, 76
 running from personal computer or public copy, 307
 setting up, 22-25
 starting, 21
 what it is, 14
 what it isn't, 13
 working with other programs, 239
low priority messages, 52

• *M* •

Macintosh, 12, 18, 26, 230, 239
 Command key (⌘) on, 155, 337
 foreign language characters on, 160
 and Full Text indexes, 301
 function keys, 326
 index for database, 263
 installing Notes in, 306
 page settings dialog box for, 182
 port for modem, 215
 SmartIcons hints on, 30
 switching programs, 27
 tips, 337-339
Macro SmartIcon button, 316
macros, 49, 343
 on Macintosh, 338
 to automate categorizing mail, 278-279
 to send form letter, 276
mail. *See* e-mail
Mail Address SmartIcon, 271
Mail Certificate Request dialog box, 202

mail database, 344
Mail Gateway, 297
Mail menu, 50, 322
 ⇨Accept Encryption Key, 205
 ⇨Address, 50, 226
 ⇨Compose⇨Custom Forms, 82
 ⇨Compose⇨Custom Forms, Reply with History, 287
 ⇨Compose⇨Memo, 47, 192
 ⇨Forward, 56, 128, 198, 271
 ⇨Send, 61
 ⇨Send User ID⇨Encryption Key, 204
 ⇨Send User ID⇨Request Certificate, 202
 ⇨Send User ID⇨Request New Name, 208, 292
mail server, 344
Mail template, 329
MAIL.BOX database, 344
 for workstation-based e-mail, 226
Manager, 146, 344
 listing server as, 221-222
manual DDE link, 250
manuals, for Lotus Notes, 99, 294
margins, 182
 for paragraphs, 162
MDM file extension, 216
measurement units, imperial or metric, 162, 209
Meeting Tracking template, 329
memo fields
 bcc: field, 51
 Body field, 52
 cc: field, 51
 Date: field, 51
 Delivery Priority field, 52
 Delivery Report field, 52-53
 end markers for, 49
 From: field, 51
 Receipt Report field, 53, 54
 Subject: field, 51
 To:, 49-50
memo form
 customizing blank, 192
 for recipients' displays, 195
Memo to Manager (Compose menu), 47
memory, 297

memos, 37
 background color for, 194
 blank form for composing, 48-54
 clearing from screen, 38
 composing, 46-48
 importing files to, 78-80
 including original in reply, 287
 inserting Clipboard data, 73-74
 marking for deletion, 65
 unfinished, 43
menus, 319-325
 grayed-out options on, 28
 making selection on Macintosh, 339
 on Notes desktop, 27-29
merging, new certification into User ID, 202
message management, 63-72
messages, 37. *See also* error messages; sending messages
 assigning to multiple categories, 68
 automatic reply to incoming, 276-278
 categories for, 54, 67-69
 finding, 69-71
 "New mail has been delivered to you," 281
 Notes documents as, 128
 preventing replication of long, 285
 reading on other computer, 82-84
 sending to beepers, 296
 signing, 81
metric measurement units, 162, 209
modem, 16, 213-217, 344
 configuring, 215
 enabling serial port for, 214
 selecting brand in setup, 216
 setup for remote workstation, 332
 speaker volume for, 216
 speed and dialing server, 236
modem command files, 216, 344
"Modem could not connect dial tone" error message, 299

mouse, 344
  for designing icon, 144
  to change column width, 142-143
  for using SmartIcons, 311
moving, database icons, 32-33
multi-task, 26-27

• N •

Name and Address Books
  at remote location, 226
  Company, 50
  Company, copying names to group from, 85
  icon for, 25
  information pages in, 59-60
  Personal, 22, 85, 288
  Public, 57-60, 283
name fields, 117
names
  for attachments when saving, 77
  changing for User ID, 208
  for desktop pages, 33, 34
  for memo form, 196
  for views, 144
NetBIOS, 344
network connection, informing Notes of, 225-226
network operating system, 344
"Network operation did not complete in a reasonable amount of time" message, 300
networks, 16, 23, 344
  install directly from, 305
New Database dialog box, 132, 327-328
new documents, Tab key to check for, 273
"New mail has been delivered to you" message, 281
New Replica dialog box, 220
New Style Name text box, 168
News and Custom View template, 329
NLM, 344
No Access, 344
"No help is available for this database" dialog box, 99

non-English characters, 160
normal style text, 154
NOS, 344
Notes. *See* Lotus Notes
Notes data directory, 344
  temporary files in, 293
Notes Data Folder (Macintosh), 338, 344
Notes Express, 1
Notes icon, locating, 21
Notes log, 344
Notes Preferences file, in Macintosh, 339
Notes server, database location on, 90
Notes Workstation Setup dialog box, 22, 23, 333
NOTES.INI file, 275, 339, 344
notifications of e-mail, turning off, 279
Novell, 344
number fields, 116

• O •

object linking and embedding (OLÉ), 115-116, 120, 251, 344
objects, 120-121
  in compound documents, 116
OLÉ (object linking and embedding), 115-116, 120, 251, 344
Only Replicate Documents Saved in the Last 90 days button, 220
Open button (Open Database dialog box), 94
Open Database dialog box, 91-96
  server names on, 92
opening
  databases, 31, 90, 94
  document for reading, 108
  e-mail database, 37
  memos, 37
  multiple databases, 260
operating systems, 12, 18, 345
  and Fit to Window for table, 172
opinions, in database, 12
OS/2, 12, 18, 26, 239, 345
  background replication in, 230-231
  function keys, 326
  installing Notes in, 305

scheduling calls, 232-234
switching programs, 27
outdents, for paragraphs, 154
OutFax, 295-296

• P •

Page Break SmartIcon, 170
page breaks, 170, 345
  deleting, 170
  preventing within paragraphs, 162-163
  when printing multiple documents, 72
page numbers, in headers or footers, 178
pages in desktop, 31, 33
  names for, 33, 34
palette selector, 28
palettes of SmartIcons, 30
paper clip symbol, for attached files, 39, 103
paper copies, vs. e-mail, 11-12
Paradox, 247
paragraphs
  alignment, 165-166
  formatting, 154, 160-168
  hiding, 164-165
  preventing page breaks in, 162-163
  spacing above and below, 166
  styles for, 167-168
  tabs in, 164
parent directory, returning to, on server, 92, 93
password, 23-24, 292-293, 345
  for accessing Notes, 81
  removing from User ID, 207
  for User ID, 83, 205-208
Paste SmartIcon, 270
Paste Special dialog box, 248-249
pasting, 154
  after copying, 73-74
pending e-mail, 226
person documents, 86, 284, 345
personal data files, installing, 308
personal mail database, icon for, 24-25
Personal Name and Address Book, 22, 85, 288, 345
  icon for, 25
  setup for remote use, 217

phone bills, replication and, 234-236
phone call
 "live" to server, 236-237
 for sending mail, 226
Phone dialing prefix field, 332
phone lines, digital or analog, 299
Phone Message (Compose menu), 47
phone messages, 55
phone numbers, for servers, 217
PhoneNotes, 297
pictures, in columns of view, 102-103
pipe symbol, in memo name, 196
platforms, 18, 345
Policy Document
 for database, 96-97, 345
 for template, 132
popups, 119, 187-189, 345
port, 345
 enabling for modem, 214-215
Port Setup dialog box, 214
PowerBook, 345
Preferences document, 345
Print Selected Document (File Print dialog box), 108
Print SmartIcon, 71, 269
Print View (File Print dialog box), 108
printing, 71-72, 126
 crop marks, 182
 fonts for, 155
 and hidden paragraphs, 164
 from view, 108
private documents, 274-275
private key, 345
private view, 345
problem solving, 299-302
 for certificates, 300
 deleting documents, 301
 doclinks, 300
 field editing, 300
 Full Text Search, 301
 laptop connection to server, 299
 launching objects, 302
 opening databases, 301
 removing borders, 175
 servers, 300
 user name changes, 291-292

program files, installing, 308
protocols, 18, 345
public key, 345
Public Name and Address Book, 57-60, 283, 345
 icon for, 25

• **Q** •

Query Builder, 257-259, 345
 for multiple databases, 261
Query Builder dialog box, 184
Query by form, 259-260, 345
 for multiple databases, 261

• **R** •

radio button field, 114
Read Access list, 130, 274, 346
Reader, 146, 346
Reader access only, for database, 123-124
reading documents, 108
 from Full Text Search, 257
 from remote location, 227
 and hiding paragraphs, 164
reading e-mail, on other computer, 82-84
Receipt Report field, 53, 54, 197
Receive documents from server box (Tools Replicate dialog box), 223, 229
recipients
 inserting in memo, 49-50
 sender control of memo form appearance for, 195
red field markers, for encryptable fields, 52, 203
references, database for, 14
Refresh (View menu), 109
relational databases, 13, 346
Remember icon, 5
remote computing, 224-232
 and composing documents, 228
 location setup, 225-226
 modem for, 16, 213-217
 and reading documents, 227
 and reading e-mail, 227
 scheduling calls in, 232-234
 setup, 331-335
remote connection documents, 218

editing to schedule automatic calls, 232-234
 reviewing, 218-219
 for scheduling replication, 288
"Remote system is no longer responding" message, 300
remote workstations, 16, 346
 setup, 332-333
 truncating messages to, 285
replacing text, with Find and replace, 184
replica ID, 346
replica stub copy, 221
Replicate Access Control List button, 219
Replicate database templates box, 229
replication, 18, 212, 285, 346
 background, 230, 288
 of database templates, 229
 and phone bills, 234-236
 preparing computer for, 212-224
 scheduling, 288-290
 selecting databases for, 229
 selecting documents for, 286-287
 selective, 234-236
 statistics on, 232
 time for first, 221, 222-224
Replication Settings dialog box, 285
Replication Statistics dialog box, 224
replies, 56
 automatic to incoming messages, 276-278
Reply button, in document, 118
Reply (Compose menu), 48
Reply to All (Compose menu), 48
ResEdit, 346
Reservation Scheduler and Setup template, 330
Return receipt, 346
reverse video, for selected text, 152
rich text fields, 13, 115-116, 346
 for attaching files, 75, 240
 formatted text in, 115, 152
 paragraph formats in, 161
 potential contents, 14
 tables in, 170

right alignment, 165
  of header or footer text, 180
right margin, 162
right mouse button, 30
  absent in Macintosh, 337
  double-clicking, 273
  for SmartIcon description, 279
rows in table
  deleting, 177-178
  inserting, 176
ruler, 346
  to set margins and tabs, 164
Run in Background (Tools
    Replicate dialog box), 223
running Notes, from personal
    computer or public copy,
    307

• S •

Save Attachment dialog box, 78
saving, 294
  attachments, 77
  before deleting row or column,
    178
  documents, 124-125
  form modifications, 140
  memos, 60
  views, 144
scheduled calls
  in remote computing, 232-234
  for replications, 288-290
  to multiple servers, 233-234
screen display, 49
  clearing memo from, 38
  fonts for, 155
  ruler on, 164
search bar, 346
  for multiple databases, 261
Search button (Search Bar),
    255-256
search and replace,
    183-184
Search selected Documents
    option, 70
Search within View, 70
section fields, 117
security, 201. *See also* password
  for unattended Notes worksta-
    tion, 293
  and User ID, 17, 83
Selected database(s) check box
    (Tools Replicate dialog
    box), 223

selected text, deleting, 270
selecting, 346
  databases to scan for unread
    documents, 208
  documents for replication,
    286-287
  documents in views, 106-107
  text for formatting, 152-153
selection bar, 107
selection formula, 346
selective replication, 234-236
Selective Replication dialog box,
    235, 286-287
Send button (memo form), 49, 61
Send documents to server check
    box (Tools Replicate dialog
    box), 223, 229
sending encryption key, 204
sending messages, 45-61, 60
  composition, 46-48
  memo writing etiquette, 45-46
  telephone call for, 226
serial port, enabling for modem,
    214-215
server, (DDE), 248
Server-based mail, 225, 346
server disk space, conserving, 67
Server drop-down box (Tools
    Replicate dialog box), 228
server names, for Notes
    databases, 91
"Server *servername* is not
    responding" error message,
    300
servers, 346
  busy signal from, 233
  checking for templates, 132
  in CompuServe, 296
  dialing "live," 236-237
  disk space for index, 262
  home, 23
  new database on, 147
  for Notes, 16
  problem connecting laptop to,
    299
  problems with, 300
  selecting for new database, 132
  telephone numbers in Personal
    Name and Address Book,
    217
  in WorldCom, 296
Service Request Tracking
    template, 330

setup
  for remote workstation, 332-333
  for stand-alone workstation,
    334-335
SHARE.EXE, 289
Shift+click, to select large text
    block, 153
signature, electronic, 81, 342, 346
signing messages, 81
size of font, changing, 154, 157
size of memos, sorting view by,
    42
SkyTel alpha-numeric beeper,
    296
SmartIcon palette, 346
SmartIcon Palette Selector, 30
SmartIcons, 28, 29-30, 154, 155,
    269-271, 311-318, 346
  Attachment, 270
  Categorize, 271
  Copy, 270
  Cut, 270
  File Attachment, 75
  Forward, 271
  information about, 30
  Mail Address, 271
  Page Break, 170
  Paste, 270
  Print, 71, 269
  right mouse button for
    description, 279
  Spell Check, 184, 269
  Table Format, 174
  for text formatting, 159
software. *See also* groupware
  embedded data from other, 120
  running multiple, 26
sorted columns, vs. categorized
    column, 104-105
sorting, 104
  keyword list, 140
  memos by date, 41
  view by memo size, 42
Space between columns (Insert
    Table dialog box), 172
Space between rows (Insert
    Table dialog box), 172
spacebar, to select documents,
    107
speaker volume, for modem, 216
Specifying Directories for the
    Notes Files dialog box,
    307-309

speed of modem, 213-214
and dialing server, 236
Spell Check SmartIcon, 184, 269
spell checker, 184-185, 292
splash screen, 21
spreadsheets. *See also* Lotus
1-2-3 worksheet
in compound document, 15
SPX, 346
stand-alone computer, 331
setup for, 334-335
standard keyword field, 114
Start page numbers at: option,
for database headers, 181
starting Lotus Notes, 21
static text, 346
adding to forms, 135
in documents, 112
for field description, 139
statistics, for replication, 232
status bar, 28, 33, 347
for font changes, 156-157
to check for e-mail, 281-282
Status Reports template, 330
Stop Word file, for index, 265
strikethrough text, 154
structured text file, exporting
view to, 247
styles, for paragraphs,
167-168
subdirectories, on server, 92
Subject: field, 51
subscript text, 154
Sun computers, Unix, 18
superscript text, 154
switching programs, 27
switching views, Ctrl key for, 274

• T •

Tab key
and reading e-mail, 38
to check for new documents,
273
tab stops, for paragraphs, 164
Table Format SmartIcon, 174
tables, 170-178, 347
changing, 174
data entry in, 173
inserting rows in, 176
tabs, for desktop pages, 28, 34,
227
tabular text file, exporting view
to, 247

Tasks field, for scheduled calls,
233
TCP/IP, 347
Technical Stuff icon, 5
telephone. *See* phone
TEMP directory, 293
template application files,
installing, 308
templates. *See* database
templates
temporary files, deleting, 293
text, adding to memo form, 193
text color, and background
memo color, 194
text enhancements, 158, 159
in e-mail, 11
text fields, 114
Text menu, 323
⇨Font, 135
⇨Paragraph, 161
⇨Paragraph ⇨Pagination,
162-163
⇨Paragraph ⇨Paragraph
⇨Spacing, 166
⇨Paragraph Styles, 168
Text Paragraph dialog box, 161,
163, 166
Things to Do template, 330
tilde (~), for temporary files, 293
time, in header or footer, 179
time-out procedure, for disabling
Notes access, 207
time savers, 281-290
time zone, in Notes setup, 24, 334
Tip icon, 5
title bar, [Deleted] on, 65
titles
of new columns, 143
for new database, 132-133
TMP file extension, 293
To: field, in memo, 49-50
Tools menu, 205, 323-325
⇨Call, 236
⇨Categorize, 67
⇨Replicate, 223, 228
⇨Replicate ⇨Run in Back-
ground, 288
⇨Scan Unread ⇨Choose
Preferred, 208
⇨Scan Unread ⇨Preferred
Databases, 273
⇨Setup ⇨Location, 225
⇨Setup ⇨Mail, 279

⇨Setup ⇨Ports, 214
⇨Setup ⇨Setup ⇨User menu,
208
⇨Setup ⇨User ⇨Background
Program, 289
⇨Setup ⇨User ⇨International,
162
⇨SmartIcons, 30
⇨Spell Check, 184, 269, 292
⇨User ID ⇨Certificates, 201, 207
⇨User ID ⇨Encryption Keys
⇨New, 203
⇨User ID ⇨Information, 208
⇨User ID ⇨Information
⇨Change User Name, 291
⇨User ID ⇨Merge Copy, 202
⇨User ID ⇨Password ⇨Clear,
207
⇨User ID ⇨Password ⇨Set, 83,
205-206, 207, 293
⇨User ID ⇨Switch to, 83
⇨User Logoff, 207
Tools Replicate dialog box, 223,
228
top margin, 162, 182
transaction-based systems, 13
Transfer outgoing mail (Tools
Replicate dialog box), 229
trash can, in view, 39, 66, 109
triangle (➤), in menus, 28-29
truncating documents, during
replication, 236, 285
tutorial databases, installing, 309

• U •

"Unable to interpret time or
date" error message, 116
underlined text, 154
undo operation, 155
unfinished memos, 43
Unix, 12, 18, 26, 239, 347
unread documents, 103-104
going to next, 270
indicator in incoming e-mail
view, 39, 199
marking after remote reading,
229
number in database,
31-32
selecting databases to scan for,
208

unread marks, 347
updating databases, 274
updating links, 250
user access, to database, 145-146
User ID, 17, 201, 293
  and certification, 207
  changing name, 208,
    291-292
  encrypted field key in, 128
  as file, 22
  filename and location, 23
  on floppy disk, 82-83
  information about, 208
  merging new certification into,
    202
  password for, 205-208
  and reading encrypted
    message, 80
  removing password from, 207
User Name, 24
User Setup dialog box, 208

• V •

video clips, in rich text fields, 13
View menu, 104, 322
  ▷All by Category, 67
  ▷All by Date, 41
  ▷All by Person, 41
  ▷All by Size, 42, 64
  ▷Arrange Icons, 33
  ▷Collapse, 105
  ▷Connections, 218-219, 232
  ▷Drafts by Category, 43
  e-mail database views for, 40
  ▷Edit Mode, 127
  ▷Expand, 105
  ▷Groups, 283
  ▷Refresh, 31-32, 109

▷Show Page Breaks, 164, 169
▷Show Ruler, 164
▷Show Search Bar, 71, 255
▷Show Server Names, 32, 227
views, 13, 90, 101-104, 347.
  See also columns in view
  adding column, 197-198
  after opening database, 95-97
  attachments, 42
  and categorizing messages, 68
  changing, 104
  creating for new database,
    140-144
  Ctrl key to switch, 274
  customizing, 196-198
  deleting documents in, 109
  displaying while creating, 144
  exporting from, 247-248
  for Full Text Search, 256
  for incoming e-mail, 39-43
  inserting columns, 143-144
  marking memos for deletion, 65
  pictures in columns, 102-103
  printing from, 108
  saving, 144
  selecting documents in, 106-107
  unreaded documents indicated
    on, 39
Vines, 347

• W •

WANs (wide area networks), 18,
  347
Warning icon, 5
WAV files, to replace beep, 275
white space, 166
Whole Word search, for Find, 70,
  183

width of columns
  in tables, 175
  in view, 142-143
Window menu, 325
Windows (Microsoft), 12, 18, 26,
  239, 347
  background replication in,
    230-231
  function keys, 326
  installing Notes in, 305
  scheduling calls, 232-234
  SHARE.EXE, 289
  switching programs in, 27
  temporary files, 293
  WAV files, 275
word
  green box around, 119
  selecting, 153
word wrap, preventing, 166
workflow, database for, 14
workpage tabs, 28, 34
  for local databases, 227
Worksheet Import Settings dialog
  box, 246
workspace, 347
Workstation-based mail, 225, 347
workstations, 16, 347
  installing Notes as, 305-310
  running Notes from, 307
WorldCom, 296, 347

• Y •

"You are not authorized to
  access that database"
  message, 301
"Your ID has not been certified to
  access the server" error
  message, 94

☐ **YES!**

Please keep me informed about IDG's World of Computer Knowledge.
Send me the latest IDG Books catalog.

COMPUTER
BOOK SERIES
FROM IDG

NO POSTAGE
NECESSARY
IF MAILED
IN THE
UNITED STATES

BUSINESS REPLY MAIL
FIRST CLASS MAIL   PERMIT NO. 2605   SAN MATEO, CALIFORNIA

IDG Books Worldwide
155 Bovet Road
San Mateo, CA 94402-9833